KU-237-113

# Customer Service in Ireland

Deirdre Kilkenny - Tutor.

Reception skills class.

# CUSTOMER SERVICE IN IRELAND

## THIRD EDITION

**Suzanne Twomey**

*Gill & Macmillan*

Gill & Macmillan
Hume Avenue, Park West
Dublin 12
with associated companies throughout the world
www.gillmacmillan.ie

© Suzanne Twomey 2002, 2007, 2012
978 07171 5260 5

Print origination in Ireland by O'K Graphic Design, Dublin

Printed by GraphyCems, Spain

*The paper used in this book is made from the wood pulp of managed forests. For every tree felled, at least one tree is planted, thereby renewing natural resources.*

All rights reserved.
No part of this publication may be copied, reproduced or transmitted, in any form or by any means, without permission of the publishers or else under the terms of any licence permitting limited copying issued by the Irish Copyright Licensing Agency.

A CIP catalogue record for this book is available from the British Library.

# CONTENTS

# ACKNOWLEDGMENTS

I would like to offer thanks to the following, all of whom made valuable contributions to this book:

Niamh Connolly at the National Council for the Blind of Ireland; Michael Quinlan and Colm Good at Henry Ford & Co Ltd; Gerry Murphy, Deputy Ombudsman, Banking Division of the Financial Services Ombudsman; and Kevin Galligan, Managing Director, and Louise Lawler, Customer Services Officer, DX Network Services Ltd Ireland.

*For Christopher and Margaret Twomey*

'*We cannot always oblige; but we can always speak obligingly.*'

VOLTAIRE

# THE CUSTOMER IS YOUR BUSINESS

**Topics covered in this chapter:**

- **What is customer service?**
- **What is good customer practice?**
- **What are internal customers?**
- **What are external customers?**
- **Listening skills**
- **The value of good customer contact staff**
- **How to satisfy complaints**
- **How to respond to compliments**
- **How to complain**
- **The organisation chart**

*No matter what goods you make or service you provide, you are in the same business as everyone else – the customer business.*

In the past, most people tended to think more about the job that they were doing than the people they were doing the job for. For example, a man might make clothes or furniture of the finest quality without ever considering the specific needs of his customers. Thus, customers who had any specific requirements were not very well catered for. Pregnant women had to resign themselves to wearing tents and people with disabilities had to pay for expensive alterations to clothes and furniture. People who were outside the limited bands of what was considered normal height, weight or shoe size found it impossible to shop in the ordinary manner. Likewise, banks closed at 1 p.m. like everyone else because they, like everyone else, worked hard and needed to eat too. It didn't seem to occur to them that lunchtime was often the only time that many people had any opportunity to do their banking. It wasn't until the 1980s in Ireland that many organisations began to rethink their attitudes. They began to realise that there was no such thing as a 'normal' customer. They discovered that customers were individuals rather than a homogenous mass and that the exception was the rule. To limit your product or service to those within a certain common standard was to exclude you from a very large and lucrative market. Maybe the average family now has 2.5 children, but there are still many families that are much larger and continue to require cars and houses to accommodate them. The average woman may hover around a size 12 or 14, yet most women are not that size and fewer still claim that that size fits them perfectly.

In addition to learning that each customer was different, organisations began to realise that the customer was the most important part of their establishment and not an unappreciative and irritating inconvenience. From managing director to dishwasher, everyone's job depended on customers coming in, buying products or hiring services and coming back for more. It was no good saying that a customer didn't appreciate what you were trying to achieve if they complained that the chair you made was uncomfortable or that they were greedy because the sliver of ham you served as a main course was too small. The bottom line was that money talks. The customer provides the money and if you lose your customers, you lose your business. With this in mind, the action suddenly changed from the boardroom to the shop floor. Customer service became an important selling point and competition grew between businesses to see who could offer the best customer care. In this chapter we will be looking at the customer. We will look at what a customer is and how the way in which we treat them can affect their perception of the product or service we are offering. We will also evaluate the knock-on effects of good and bad customer perceptions.

## What is customer service?

> **Customer service can be defined as the provision of a product or service of a sufficient quality and in a sufficient manner that reaches or exceeds the customer's expectations.**

For example, if a furniture company agrees to deliver a sofa to your house by 4 p.m. on Monday and does so, that is good customer service. If they arrive three days late and dump it in the rain, outside your door, because you are out and didn't expect them, that's bad customer service. If they arrive on time, take it into the house for you, arrange it and the other furniture in your sitting room to your liking and take away your old sofa for free disposal, then that's excellent customer service. Now ask yourself – if you had a choice between good customer service, i.e. the company that reaches your expectations, and excellent customer service, i.e. the company that exceeds your expectations, which one would you pick?

### Why should I care about customer service?

Whether you are the employer or the employee of any company or organisation, if you wish to continue earning a salary, then you need to care about customer service.

Starkly put, a company that neglects its customers or treats them with disdain will lose them.

**Why should I worry about new developments in customer service if the customers seem happy enough?**

The fact is that the competition between companies in some markets can be so fierce that customer care can be used as a means to distinguish you from the competition. To that end, the standard of customer care is always rising, so what was considered excellent customer care two years ago has long since been superseded. Businesses have to continually come up with new forms of customer service in order to gain a temporary edge over the competition. As soon as the other companies quickly follow suit, that temporary edge is lost. In the 1960s, a car with a radio was a rare luxury; nowadays, a CD player with interchanger would not impress that much. Many of the things we now take for granted in our cars began their lives as luxurious customer incentives, even such things as being able to choose the colour of your car, safety belts, headrests and back window wipers.

> Customer service is about going the extra mile. Or as far as is necessary to achieve the stellar standards of customer service for which Brown Thomas is famous. All our customer-service team have excellent people skills, are great communicators and are gracious under fire. They like to exceed, not just fulfil customer expectations.
>
> (Quoted from the Brown Thomas manual, *Career Paths*)

## What is good customer practice?

Good customer practice is anything that helps add to the customer's belief that he has received good customer service.

## What are the elements of good customer practice?

Good customer practice can be divided into tangible and intangible elements.
    The tangible elements of good customer practice are:
* performance
* quality
* reliability
* cost.

The intangible elements of good customer practice are:
* courtesy
* genuine concern for the customer
* a genuine desire to help them coupled with the ability to do so.

For example, a television that was competitively priced, lasted for over 12 years, never broke down and had excellent sound quality and picture definition could be said to display all the tangible elements of good customer practice employed by the manufacturer.

If the television did malfunction at 12 years of age and it was quickly mended at a reasonable price, and if, at the same time, no pressure was put on you to replace it despite the need to locate an obsolete part, then the after-sales service of that company could be said to display many of the intangible elements of good customer practice.

## What is an organisation?

An organisation is when a group of people come together and organise themselves in order to achieve certain goals. This is a very general definition for a very general concept. The goals of an organisation may be to generate profit, as with most companies. They may also be to look after the needy, to spread information about hygiene or the prevention of dangerous diseases. There are also religious organisations that seek to diffuse their faith throughout the world or organisations that seek to increase awareness of a certain language, skill, sport or culture.

## What is business?

A business is when one or more people come together to provide a service or sell a product in return for money or some other benefit. There are as many different types and sizes of businesses as there are businesses. The vast majority of businesses are attempting to make a profit and to expand. Some businesses have been set up to provide funds for various charities, for example Oxfam shops. (For more on types of businesses, see the business glossary in Appendix One.)

Whatever business, service or company you are, it pays to be a customer-oriented one.

## The underlying principles of customer-oriented organisations

A customer-oriented organisation is committed to providing the best possible service for its customers. It does this by:
- Listening to customers.
- Assessing the needs and wants of customers and then meeting those needs.
- Maintaining good communication between the organisation, its customers and its employees.
- Constantly monitoring and offering feedback.

For examples of customer-oriented organisations, see pages 132–4.

## What is a customer?

A customer is a person or organisation that requires goods or services from another.

## Customer terminology

- Existing customer.
- Former customer.
- Potential customer.
- External customer.
- Internal customer.
- Non-paying customer.
- Corporate customer.
- Individual customer.

## What is an existing customer?

An existing customer is a customer who is currently availing of your product or service. This may be long term, as in buying a car from your dealership every three years for the last 20 years, medium term, as in a gym membership, or very short term, as in currently using the shampoo you sell.

## What is a former customer?

A former customer is a customer who once used your service or a customer who once regularly used your service but no longer does so.

They may have stopped using your services for reasons beyond your control, such as death, relocation or, for example, because you run a crèche and their children are now too old to need it. On the other hand, they may have stopped using your services for reasons you can control and there may be a possibility that you can win them back if you try hard enough. Price and customer service might be typical factors that could be improved upon.

## What is a potential customer?

A potential customer is someone who may become a customer in the future if the correct inducements are offered. They could be first-time customers. For example, an 18-year-old with a newly acquired full driving licence is a potential car dealership customer. If you give them a good deal and treat them well, you may end up with a loyal customer who will return to you regularly in the future. Potential customers can also be seduced away from competitors if you can offer them a better deal and standard of service.

## What is an external and internal customer?

An external customer is a person unconnected with the company, who walks in off the street and pays for a product or service.

The internal customer is an employee within the chain of service in your company who will have to be satisfied with the product or service offered before it reaches the external customer.

Here are some examples to illustrate the difference between the external and internal customer.

### First example

A customer in a shoe shop is interested in seeing one of the shoes on display, but in a different size. The salesman phones the stockroom upstairs to ask them to bring down the appropriate shoe. No one answers the phone, the salesman cannot leave the shop floor and the customer leaves with a bad impression of the shop.

The customer who wished to try on the shoe in a different size is the external customer.

The salesman who needs his colleagues to serve him with the correct shoe is the internal customer.

The salesman did his job, but as in most work situations, he needed his work colleagues to do their jobs too. They needed to serve him so that he in turn could serve the external customer.

### Second example

The external customer is the person who walks up to the counter of a fast food restaurant and orders a burger.

The internal customer is the person who serves that external customer when they are asking the chef to fulfil the order.

The chef, in turn, becomes the internal customer when he asks his assistant to get him some ingredients.

The administration staff themselves are internal customers when they ask a cleaner to vacuum their office. The cleaner, in turn, becomes an internal customer when he collects his paycheques from the administration staff.

### Third example

The external customer enters a furniture store and buys a bed. The salesman fills in the delivery form. The person in the stockroom misreads the form and gives the wrong bed to the deliveryman. The deliveryman arrives on time and at the correct address but with the wrong bed.

The salesman and the deliveryman both did their job but were let down by the stockperson. The external customer has been disappointed and his attitude towards the company may change, not because of the staff he met, but because of the one in the background who failed to do their job.

The salesman who passes the delivery form on to the stockperson is his internal customer. The stockperson cannot do his job unless he receives these forms.

The stockperson passes on the incorrect bed to his internal customer, the deliveryman. The deliveryman cannot deliver stock unless it is given to him by the stockperson.

Who is the internal customer in this scenario? Just ask yourself who is dependent on someone else within the organisation doing their job first before they can do their part of the job.

The stockperson cannot get stock out for delivery unless the salesman has told him what stock to retrieve.

The deliveryman cannot deliver goods unless the stockperson has given him stock and the salesperson has given him the correct customer address.

The salesperson cannot register a satisfactory sale until the correct stock is delivered to the correct address.

Essentially, everyone is dependent on everyone else to do their job competently. Each is, in turn, the other's internal customer.

### Fourth example

Imagine there is a house on fire and the owner is screaming for help. The owner is the external customer who needs his house fire put out.

There is a water pump a short distance away. The local volunteer fire service forms a bucket brigade from the pump to the house. One person pumps the water into a bucket. The bucket is then passed along from person to person who form the line of the bucket brigade stretching from the pump to the house. The person nearest the house then throws the water on the fire. They then pass the empty bucket back down the line to the pump for refilling. All these people are serving the external customer, the homeowner. However, they all depend on each other to do their part. If any one of them fails to do their part, then the entire system breaks down and the external customer is let down. So if anyone in the line fails to pass back the empty bucket, then the person at the pump cannot fill it. Likewise, if the person at the pump fails to refill the bucket, then the bucket brigade cannot pass the water up towards the house. In this way, everyone on this bucket brigade is an internal customer. The person at the house is waiting to be served with a bucket of water so that they can douse the flames. Each person in turn on the bucket brigade must wait to be served the empty bucket so they can then serve the person next in line with the empty bucket. The person at the pump must be served the empty bucket in order to fill it and in turn serve the bucket brigade with a refilled bucket.

## What is a non-paying customer?

A non-paying customer is someone who walks in off the street to avail of a service without paying.

Most examples of this are in the public sector, for example the primary school student attending class, the person making enquiries at the tax office, the person collecting their unemployment benefit or a foreign tourist visiting the local information centre.

Though these customers do not pay directly, or possibly do not pay at all, they are still crucial to the organisation that they have supported. It is obvious that a primary school that has no pupils ceases to exist, just like any company without customers. Likewise, if government offices and other ostensibly free services are not used, they will be discontinued.

## What is a corporate customer?

Corporate clients are customers that represent a large business or organisation. They are buying goods or using services on behalf of the corporation that they work for.

An example would be someone who buys clothes for the children's department of a large retail chain. They're not thinking of what would look nice on their own children, but are shopping with a view to what will sell and garner their chain of stores the biggest profit.

## What is an individual customer?

An individual client works independently of a large organisation. They buy goods or supply services for themselves.

It is possible for one person to be both a corporate and individual client. For example, a person staying at a hotel for a conference might be a corporate client. The same person might take her family on holiday to that same hotel. In that instance, the customer would be an individual client.

## How can you identify the needs of internal, external, individual and corporate clients?

Individual clients can be divided into internal and external customers.

* *The internal custome*r needs to be supplied with all the equipment and materials that he needs to do his job. He needs a good work environment that conforms to recognised health and safety standards. He needs to be adequately and regularly remunerated for his service. On a personal level, he needs to feel that his work is recognised, appreciated and, where appropriate, rewarded.
* *The external customer* needs to feel that her custom is appreciated. She wants good, friendly, efficient service and value for money. She wants to have confidence in the product or service that she is buying. She also wants to feel confident that the retailer or service provider will look after and honour any guarantees or after-sales service agreements that have been made.
* *The corporate customer* needs to be impressed by the product or service that is being provided. He wants to feel that he is getting the absolute best value for money for his company. He may need to feel that the retailer or service provider has an image compatible with that of his own company. He will want an organisation that is flexible and is willing to co-operate with his own corporation.

By identifying and satisfying the needs of the internal and external customer, there are many knock-on benefits for the organisation. By satisfying the internal customer, they will improve staff morale. This in turn will improve productivity, as staff will take a greater interest and pride in their work. By encouraging employee participation, the organisation will benefit by hearing suggestions that will improve efficiency from those who are directly involved in manufacturing goods or supplying the service. This will improve waste within the company and help minimise mistakes. As a result, there will be some reduction in costs and a corresponding increase in profits. The company will also develop a more positive and mutually beneficial relationship with customers and their suppliers.

In satisfying the external customer, you will be pleasing the customer and improving your image in their eyes. In that way you will have acquired another positive advocate for your company and will benefit from the free publicity that that will generate. This will enhance your company's reputation and will help distinguish your company from its competitors. Customers who are extremely pleased with a good service are less likely to be price sensitive. For example, a supermarket with a free car park can charge a little more than a supermarket without a car park and not lose its volume of custom. Improved customer service will lead to improved customer loyalty and a more understanding attitude from them when things do occasionally go wrong. A company that is seen as caring for their customers will have the same customers returning again and again, bringing more customers with them.

Customers are essential to business and our treatment of them should reinforce this. All organisations need as many customers as possible and that includes repeat business. If a customer is unhappy with us for any reason, we risk losing their continued custom and, what's worse, a dissatisfied customer is very likely to tell others about our shortcomings. Therefore, one unresolved problem can lose you existing and potential customers. Some customers can be difficult, even unreasonable, but, regardless of how troublesome they are, they must be treated carefully because they have the potential to do great damage to your reputation or business, no matter how blameless you and your staff might be. This is why *the customer is always right*. This doesn't mean they *are* right all the time, but to win a point may be to lose a customer, and that means you are still the loser. It is therefore extremely important that any staff member dealing directly with customers has well-developed contact skills, starting with a positive mental attitude.

## Welcome complaints

As an employee you must learn to welcome complaints. An old Chinese proverb tells us 'every problem is an opportunity'. If a customer complains and you deal with that complaint pleasantly and helpfully, that customer will feel happier doing business with you than with another similar company that doesn't deal with complaints as positively as you do. As we saw above, businesses that fail to satisfy customer expectations not only run the risk of losing that particular customer but also of losing the custom of other potential customers as a result. It has been estimated that a dissatisfied customer will tell on average ten people about their experience and the ten may in turn mention it to others. That can mean a lot of lost business! See every complaint as an opportunity to gain further business.

Not only should you welcome complaints, but you should make it easy for customers to complain. If you do not hear any complaints it doesn't mean that people aren't complaining. It may mean that they are complaining to future potential customers or they may be moving their custom to your rivals and telling them what a terrible service you are offering. If a customer has a genuine grievance but chooses not to complain, they may pay up and shut up the first time, but the next time, they will certainly take their business elsewhere. By welcoming and even encouraging complaints, you can rectify a problem before more customers experience it and also retain the custom of the person who complained. That individual customer who complained has done you a favour, because many customers that followed might have been of the 'say nothing, but never return' kind. And you may even win back customers who had already left you because of the same problem but who had never complained about it. The customer who complained and was listened to is very likely to switch their allegiance to you. Strangely, they may also prove more loyal than a customer who never experienced a problem in the first place. *And* they may recommend you to others.

Therefore, by satisfying one customer you may in fact be gaining or retaining many more.

Your customers may also feel encouraged to complain more often to you and to make suggestions. This could give you a good indication of how customers perceive you and might also provide some useful ideas as to how you could improve your customer service. When solving one problem where a customer's needs were not being met, you may in fact be creating a new trend that will bring you increased customers. By listening to your customers you are coming closer to becoming a customer-driven organisation, which will help increase your business.

Complaints are therefore to be welcomed as valuable insights into how your company can develop and remain competitive in the future.

Expect customers to sometimes be unhappy and to switch from you. Expect some of your services to fail. Expect some of your more successful and enduring services to lose their popularity over time. You can't win them all. However, you *can* learn from them all. Try to find out why certain things have gone wrong and store that information so that you avoid making a similar mistake in the future.

If, despite your best efforts, you do get rejected by a customer, don't take it personally. And don't take it out on the departing customer – think of the potential customers you could lose. It's even possible the customer might come back if you resist giving them a piece of your mind. If a particular company does not engage the services of your organisation or switches to another company regardless of the lengths you went to to keep them, try to learn from it. See what went wrong or what could have been handled better and make sure that you improve. If a customer is very hostile, be as pleasant and sympathetic as possible. Don't let them get you down. Stay positive. Remind yourself of occasions in the past when you were successful in dealing with difficult customers. Above all, don't let a bad experience with one customer make you unhelpful or hostile to the next customer. Finally, remember to smile. It will make a big difference to the way you feel and your customer's response.

## Listen actively

The *Collins English Dictionary* defines the verb 'to hear' as: to perceive (a sound) by ear; the same dictionary defines the verb 'to listen' as: 1. to concentrate on hearing something; 2. to heed or pay attention to.

Hearing is easy, but listening is not. We hear our alarm clock but unless we are already awake, we do not listen to it. The radio is playing in the background. We hear the discussion but can't recall a word spoken. We were not listening to it. Listening differs from hearing in that it requires a conscious effort. We filter out all the other sounds around us and concentrate on the important ones. Active listening requires even more concentration. We listen to our favourite records over and over again but we often do not know what most of the words are. We listen to a recipe on the television but can't recall it an hour later. Active listening requires concentration and an effort to memorise.

- An active listener should prepare to listen. Research any background information that will be helpful to your understanding of what you are about to hear.
- An active listener will have a pen and paper and any relevant notes on standby.
- An active listener will listen with an open mind, whatever their own personal feelings.
- An active listener will not interrupt or distract the speaker; they wait their turn.
- An active listener can have a positive effect on the performance of the speaker. They can offer the speaker encouragement by showing that they are paying attention. This can be done by displaying positive body language. Make eye contact with the speaker, nod, lean towards them, and if useful, take occasional notes.
- An active listener will have a positive attitude towards the speaker. They will listen with the intention of learning as much as possible.
- If an active listener is unsure about something, they will take the opportunity at the end to ask questions and to seek clarification.
- A good listener will honour any confidences that are entrusted to them.

There are three different levels of listening.
- *Factual listening.* Here the listener is simply listening to acquire straightforward information; for example, listening to the shipping forecast or the soccer results on the radio.
- *Interpretative listening.* Here the listener not only learns from the factual information but may also learn the speaker's emotional response to it. It might be clear from the speaker's tone of voice that they are unhappy about a particular football result. The tone of a speaker may convey their dislike for the person that they are talking to.
- *Contextual listening.* This form of listening requires background information. For example, if the speaker tells you that when Michael walked into the room Mary fainted and Tom crushed the glass in his hand, you cannot fully understand the significance of what has occured without knowing what happened before this event. To fully understand what the speaker has said, we need to know the context. So if we knew that this information was taken from a detective novel and that Mary had thought that Michael was dead and that Tom had thought that he had successfully murdered him, it would greatly add to our understanding of what the speaker is saying.

There also three listening methods.

- *Passive listening.* This is the most common form of listening. We could be driving along while also listening to music or a play on the radio. Passive listening requires little or no effort on our part. We are not trying hard to remember information, nor do we expect to respond to what we are hearing. A lot of passive listening is for pleasure.
- *Active listening.* This is where the listener makes a strong effort to understand and retain what they have heard. This would involve possibly taking notes. The listener might seek clarification on certain points from the speaker. An example of active listening would be a lecture or presentation.
- *Interactive listening.* This is where the listener interacts with the speaker. There may be no distinction between speaker and listener. This might be in a tutorial situation, in a brainstorming session or in a conversation.

## The benefits of listening to customers

In evaluating the benefits of listening to customers we need to take both internal and external customers into account.

The benefits of listening to internal customers are manifold. Employees who feel that they are listened to perform better. They begin to feel that they are valued for their opinion and thus as members of staff. This improves staff morale, which leads to greater productivity. It also helps reduce staff turnover, which is a great drain on the resources of any organisation. Recruitment and training both take time and money. If you can retain the staff you already have you are spared that expense. Employees are also the people dealing directly with customers, products and services. They are therefore best placed to come up with practical solutions to current problems. So by listening to internal customers and applying their suggestions, companies can save money through greater efficiency and increased production.

The external customer is the most important person involved with your organisation. Companies spend millions every year trying to win new customers. Even when companies are doing badly the last thing they are advised to cut back on is advertising. However, it is much cheaper to keep an existing customer than to try and attract a new one. A company that spends a lot of money getting customers and then loses them through poor customer practice is simply throwing its money away. We have seen already how potential customers can be lost through customers' unhappy experiences. Advertising will not win over the friends and colleagues of these customers, as they will tend to trust those they know have no specific agenda.

Listening to customers will make them feel appreciated. Customers who have a complaint that is dealt with well are likely to remain loyal and will pass on their positive experiences to others. They will also help the company hold on to many more customers who were not willing to complain.

Listening to customers isn't just about listening to complaints. By surveying, interviewing and forming focus groups with your customers you can learn what they like or dislike about your organisation. They will also come up with ideas about what they would like to see in the future. Listening to customers therefore provides you with an excellent innovation tool.

## The role of customer service in organisational effectiveness

The role of most companies and organisations is to create revenue. Good customer service is a means of doing that. It will improve profitability by increasing customer satisfaction and by enhancing the organisation's reputation.

Good customer service will also make the organisation more effective by encouraging employee participation, improving staff morale and increasing productivity. This in turn reduces costs and generates greater profit. Remember, staff are the internal customers of an organisation and their well-being can greatly affect the productivity and the general service provided by that organisation.

## The role of customer contact staff in an organisation

Customer contact staff are those who deal directly with the customer. They play a crucial role because they represent the organisation in the eyes of the company and any complaints that customers make are normally directed at this level. The good or bad treatment that customers receive from the contact staff is critical to their overall positive or negative perception of the organisation.

## Remember how important you are to the customer's perception of your company

The customer contact person is the company's ambassador. Often they may be the only visible human face of the organisation. Therefore the customer will judge the company based on that person's performance. A customer contact person with a negative attitude will allow the customer to think that the front-line staff are unpleasant, incompetent or unhelpful. As a result, the whole organisation will be seen that way and, even if untrue, it will make no difference because the customer is being forced to deal with an unsatisfactory customer contact person. In such circumstances, the customer might take their business elsewhere while reporting a negative business experience to friends.

A customer contact person with a positive attitude is invaluable to an organisation. Not only do they give a positive image which reflects on the whole company, but if there is a problem and they solve it, they will greatly impress the customer. In turn, the customer will have a higher regard for the company and will be even more likely to remain loyal than if the problem had never occurred. They will also pass on their positive experience of the company to their friends.

## Identify the skills, qualities and attitudes required to perform effectively when dealing with customers in an organisation

The skills required to perform effectively when dealing with customers are:

- communication skills
- good listening skills
- diplomacy skills
- a thorough knowledge of the product or service being provided
- an ability to view the problem from the customer's perspective
- problem-solving skills
- an ability to anticipate the future needs and wants of customers.

The customer contact staff need a strong positive attitude in dealing with customers. They also need a sincere desire to help the customer and a positive and enthusiastic attitude towards the goods and services that their organisation is providing.

The qualities required to perform effectively when dealing with customers are:

- sincerity
- patience
- confidence
- interest
- empathy
- enthusiasm
- diligence
- efficiency
- a sense of humour
- tact.

## Explain the importance of good presentation (written, face to face, telephone, etc.) in relation to communication with customers

Good presentation in relation to communication with customers is vital in building trust. A business that takes care with the presentation of its written communication and in the appearance of its premises and employees is telling its customers that it will take similar care of them. An impressive office suite exudes financial security and long-term stability. However, not every customer may get to see inside the building, so a letter or fax from such an organisation has to reflect the same qualities.

Speaking to an employee either in person or on the phone is the human contact with the organisation. A badly dressed employee is telling the customer that the company tolerates this kind of sloppiness, and such an attitude may extend beyond just clothing. Similarly, a badly handled telephone conversation could be the customer's only experience of the organisation. As a result they could justifiably infer that a company that has rude or incompetent telephone staff will have the same lack of care in other areas of customer service too.

## Complaints

Complaints are an opportunity to impress customers with your commitment to good service. Complaints should be handled quickly and efficiently. If you are in contact with a customer and you are in a position to help them, do so even if it is not strictly your problem. The more quickly a complaint is dealt with, the better. If someone is injured and they receive medical attention within the first hour it greatly increases their chances of survival and a full recovery. The hour after an injury is often referred to as the golden hour and is the time when medical assistance has the most positive effect. There should be a golden hour in dealing with complaints as well. If a customer has a problem, the quicker it is resolved, the less damage the problem will have done to the customer's impression of the company. The longer they wait, the more annoyed they become and when the problem is finally resolved you will have nonetheless lost the customer's goodwill.

Here are some general guidelines for handling complaints.

1.  Listen actively to the complaint. In other words, listen with an open mind and pay attention to what they are saying. If necessary, take notes. Do not interrupt. It is important for the complainant to be allowed an opportunity to vent their frustration. Stay quiet, except for sympathetic nods and active listening sounds.

2.  Respond. Consider your response carefully. Do not reply with excuses or point out curtly that all this is the customer's fault. Do not react with hostility. All these responses will make the customer more irate. Instead, repeat the main points of the complaint back to the customer and get confirmation that you have got the facts straight.

3.  Express regret at what has happened. You are not admitting liability, you are simply saying that you are sorry that the customer has had an unhappy experience.

4.  Empathise. Show the customer that you have some understanding of how they feel. For example: 'I can see why you are upset, that would upset me too'; 'I agree, there's nothing worse than when that happens'; 'I know how annoying that can be'. However, do not overplay the empathy; you may inadvertently just encourage the customer to become even more emotional as they concentrate on their grievance.

5.  Advise. Advise the customer on what their options are. These will vary depending on the situation and on the culpability of the organisation. For example, you could inform the customer how to lodge a formal complaint with the manufacturer or you could advise them on errors they have made in selecting or installing a piece of equipment which they have assumed was defective.

6.  Describe. Tell them what steps you are going to take to help them with their grievance.

7.  Thank them. Always thank the customer for bringing the problem to your attention. By complaining, they have helped ensure that another customer doesn't have the same unfortunate experience.

8. Report. Keep the customer updated on how you are dealing with their complaint. There is no point dealing well with the customer if you do not follow it up and keep them informed. Even if you fail to resolve the problem in the way in which you promised, let them know. Then they will know that you sincerely did your best to help them.

### Sample situation 1 – customer care desk of a supermarket

A customer approaches the desk. She is very annoyed. She had bought a baby gym for her granddaughter's first Christmas but on opening it to check it, she discovered that four of the attachments depicted on the box were missing.

A dialogue between a member of the customer care staff and the customer might go something like this:

*Customer approaches the customer care desk.*
*Staff:* Can I help you, madam?
*Customer:* I would like to complain about this toy that I bought here last week. I bought it thinking that it was the same as it was on the box but it wasn't.
*Staff:* Can I see the box please?
*Customer:* Here it is. It's supposed to be a baby gym but some parts are missing.
*Staff (examining the box):* What parts are missing?
*Customer:* Well, the duck and the mirror. You can see them clearly on the box cover but when you take out the actual gym, they're not there. Oh, and the bell is missing as well. I'm very annoyed. I meant to wrap it up and give it to my granddaughter. It's lucky I checked it. Otherwise, what would she have thought of me? Oh, the clock was missing too.
*Staff:* So the bell, the clock, the mirror and the duck were missing? *Repeating the key points of the complaint.*
*Customer:* Yes.
*Staff:* I am very sorry that parts were missing from the gym, madam. *Expressing regret for the inconvenience caused to the customer.* I can certainly understand your annoyance. It must have been very annoying and it was a good job that you checked the box before you wrapped it. *Empathising with the customer.* What I will do is this. I will take back the original baby gym that you bought and replace it with another one that we have in stock. Before I give it to you, I will open it up to see if it has all its bits and pieces. *Describing to the customer what you are going to do.* Would that be acceptable?
*Customer:* Yes, thanks, that would be fine.
*Staff:* Right, I will do that right now. *Doing what you said you would do.* Here you are.
*Customer:* Thank you for dealing with my complaint so promptly.
*Staff:* And thank you for bringing this to my attention. It is quite possible that there are parts missing from other boxes. Now that you have told us about it, we will

check all the other boxes and send any incomplete baby gyms back to the manufacturer. We don't want any other little child disappointed. *Thanking the customer for bringing the complaint to your attention.*

### Sample situation 2 – in a restaurant

*Customer:* Waiter, can I speak to the manager, please?

*Waiter:* Certainly. One moment, please.

*Manager:* Good evening, sir. I'm Mary Browne, the manager. What seems to be the problem?

*Customer:* I would like to complain about my meal.

*Manager:* What was the matter?

*Customer:* The dessert was too cold, and not the freshest.

*Manager:* What dessert did you have?

*Customer:* The lemon cheesecake.

*Manager:* I am sorry to hear that our dessert was not up to our usual standard. I would like to assure you that this is not a usual occurrence. Tell me, was the rest of the meal satisfactory?

*Customer:* Yes, it was.

*Manager:* Did the other members of your party enjoy their desserts?

*Customer:* Yes, they did.

*Manager:* Well, what I will do is this. I will strike the cheesecake from your bill and I will let you pick another dessert free of charge from our dessert trolley. Would that be acceptable?

*Customer:* I don't really feel like a dessert now.

*Manager:* How about a free coffee?

*Customer:* Yes. Thank you.

*Manager:* No problem, and thank you for telling me about the cheesecake, I will take it off the menu immediately.

Remember that the complainant may be frustrated, anxious and hostile. They may expect you to be hostile and so might be on the defensive and might even have rehearsed what they are going to say. The customer's objective will be to get some satisfaction from your organisation, possibly compensation. Be courteous and understanding. Do not keep the customer waiting. Give an explanation, an apology if required, and explain what action you intend to take.

## Handling awkward or undesirable customers

This depends on the individual situation, but a lot of the time the same rules apply as for handling complaints. However, you need to be even more patient and diplomatic. Do not take the customer's behaviour personally. Remember that if a customer is being very awkward or unreasonable, other customers could be watching how you deal with the situation. If you deal with it well, then you will win their sympathy and support. Therefore, even if an awkward customer is still angry when they leave, you may still benefit from the attitudes of the other customers in terms of increased custom.

If the customer becomes extremely hostile or is drunk, you may need to call on the assistance of your fellow workers or a security guard.

In the United States a recently developed concept has taken a small hold in customer care. This is called 'fire the customer'. This theory argues that businesses are there first and foremost to make money. Businesses provide customer care in order to maintain that business. This means that if a customer is being unreasonable and trying to placate that customer is going to cost more than that customer will ever return to the company, then the company should refuse to continue trying to satisfy that customer.

If your customer is very irate, here are some additional skills you can employ:

- Get in early. If a customer has been waiting a long time to be served, rather than waiting and possibly hoping that they won't complain, say, 'I apologise for the delay, I'll try not to keep you longer than is necessary.' This shows that you have sympathy for your customers.

- Recognise the customer's needs. If a customer is annoyed, acknowledge the reason behind it. 'I understand that you expected your cooker to be delivered yesterday and that you had to take the day off to wait for our deliveryman. I can appreciate how angry you were when the cooker never arrived.'

- Acknowledge the customer's situation. 'I see that you are in a rush and I will try and settle this as quickly as possible.' Or, 'I understand that this delay is costing you time and money.'

- Be honest; admit it if you or your company made a mistake. Even if you did make a mistake, remember that customers appreciate honesty and that no one is perfect. However, use your discretion and be aware of litigious situations. Do not say you agree with a customer if you do not. Instead, give a neutral response. If a customer says that the brand of car you are selling is rubbish and that's why he is unhappy with his one, say something like, 'Well I think you have just been unfortunate.'

- Timing your response. Sometimes a customer just wants a solution. If you solve their problem immediately they are totally happy. For instance, a customer returns a faulty DVD and is handed a new one immediately; that generally works fine for small problems. However, with bigger issues a customer may be so angry that they want to vent their anger and will not listen to your solution. If the customer is returning a defective cooker after Christmas, getting a new cooker may not be enough. They may want to tell you how much your defective product ruined their Christmas. So let them express their annoyance to you, give them the time to calm down and then present your solution.

- If they are very angry you might throw in a little sweetener. For example, when giving them a replacement cooker after the original defective model ruined their Christmas, you could throw in a toaster or some extra accessories. A small gesture like that can work wonders.

- Watch your body language. Don't stand there with your arms folded or your hands on your hips with a surly expression on your face. This will only further antagonise the customer. Let your body language be open and non-aggressive. Also it should show that you are paying attention to the customer. Every customer gets angrier when they know their grievance has not been listened to. Make sure your body language is appropriate, and that includes your facial expression.

- Explain the situation to the customer. Do not assume that a customer is as familiar with your business as you are and never make them feel foolish if they are not. Customers cannot know everything. So explain the what, where and why of the problem to them. The more a customer knows about your procedures, the more in control they will feel in future. This often makes them much more loyal customers.

- If they need advice, give it; if you work in a business, you should know as much about your product as possible. Then your advice will reassure customers and will help solve problems more easily. It also allows you to offer the customer choices.

- Customers often feel angry because they feel powerless when a problem occurs. If you can offer them a choice, then you are giving them back power; this can calm the customer considerably. It also shows that you value their opinion and that you respect their powers of judgment.

- Bond with the customer. Try to find common ground on any topic, not just the problem at hand. Talk about the weather, sport, etc. If you can agree on the problem, all the better. 'Yes I do think the older models were more user friendly. Like you, I have had problems adapting to the new ones, but now I actually prefer these ones because they are more reliable.'

- Reassure the customer that you are making every effort to help them. Reinforce this by making tangible efforts in front of them. It can be very effective if you can make a relevant phone call in front of them, rather than putting it off until after they have gone. Beware, while it is good to promise that you will do everything in your power to help the customer, it is counterproductive to guarantee results when you may not be able to deliver, or worse, you know even when you are talking to the customer that you cannot deliver. It may placate the customer temporarily, but ultimately they will be angrier.

- Redirect the customer's attention from their anger. Let's say the customer is very angry because they have had a bad holiday experience. You could redirect the customer's anger from yourself towards a customer complaints form. The customer will recognise that you are not the final arbitrator in this case and will concentrate on filling in the form carefully.

- Ask the customer to step into a private area in your business. This is a very useful thing to do if you feel the customer is showboating for other customers in the store. It never looks good when a customer is complaining in front of other customers. However, you will have to use your judgment here. Many customers realise that you don't want a scene and will feel that if they leave the public area of your business they will have lost a crucial edge. Therefore, it is important to make sure that if you invite a customer into an office, you give them a valid reason why it's in their interest to acquiesce. For example, 'If you could come into the office with me, we can phone our main office/fill in a complaints form.'

- Avoid the imperative. Do not order your customers about. Instead of saying, 'Show me the product,' say 'Could you show me the shoes, please?' By softening your language you are less likely to irritate the complainant who might otherwise feel that they are on trial.

- If a customer comes into your business all guns blazing, extremely irate, and then you point out their error, it can be very hard for them to admit they are wrong. An example would be a customer who comes in claiming that their camcorder doesn't work and after listening to a tirade, you discover that they didn't switch it from mains to battery power when they tried to use it. In a situation like that, the best thing is to offer them a way out. Say something like, 'These models differ from a lot of camcorders, I should have pointed that out to you.' The important thing is not to humiliate the customer, though you may be tempted, but to offer them a way to save face. That way they are more likely to return.

*Time wasters.* A time waster is someone who walks into a place of business expecting to be treated like a customer, with no intention of ever becoming one. Time wasters are not to be mistaken for customers who are shopping around or who come into premises looking for a product or service but do not see what they want. It can be hard to spot the difference, so err on the side of caution. But if you are certain that someone is a time waster, you don't want them to waste time that you could more productively put towards dealing with genuine customers. Cut down your sales talk to a minimum and politely but firmly bring them to the point of sale. When they refuse to buy, you can politely bid them goodbye and detach yourself from them and turn your attention to your other customers.

## Respond to compliments

Irish people in general find it hard to accept compliments. We tend to be self-deprecating: 'All I did was make a phone call,' 'It was nothing,' and so on. If you do get a compliment from a customer, then you doubtless earned it; there have probably been many times when you received no acknowledgement for your efforts. So accept the compliment graciously. Tell the customer that it was your pleasure. Tell them that you are delighted that they are so happy with your company and that you hope you will be able to continue to assist them in the future. Urge them to get in contact with you if they have any problems in the future.

It is good customer care practice to monitor spontaneous compliments in the same way as you would analyse a comment card or the results of a customer satisfaction survey. Analyse spontaneous compliments with the following questions.

1. How often are certain areas complimented?

2. What gets the most compliments and why?

3. What age group compliments the most and where are those compliments targeted?

4. What income group, if known, compliments the most and where are those compliments targeted?

5. Are compliments increasing or declining in certain areas?

6. Are these increases or decreases reflected in the commercial success of those areas?

7. Is there any area conspicuous by the lack of praise that it receives? If so, why?

It is also important to bear in mind that what satisfies today may not do so tomorrow. For example, an interesting and exciting menu is not so appealing if it has not been altered in six months. A new waiting room will not seem so charming if it is left to become tatty and dirty. So never use compliments as an excuse to relax and leave things as they are. Customer care is an ongoing process. Today your innovation may win you praise, but if you stagnate, your customers will switch from you to the next big thing. So take the compliment, congratulate yourself on your success and then quickly move on to the next big challenge.

## Do not think of the sale more than the customer. If you do, you may lose their repeat business

A woman goes into a lingerie department to buy a bra. The sales assistant is very helpful. She is very happy with what she decided to purchase but she feels that they are a bit expensive. The saleswoman then tries to sell her matching underwear. The customer feels under pressure but the saleswoman is so intent on her sale that she does not see the warning signals and pushes on. The customer buys the bra and leaves the underwear. She is happy about the bra and would have gone back except that she feels that the saleswoman is too aggressive.

## Always try and see things from the customer's perspective

Mary colours her own hair because it is cheaper, she hates going to the hairdresser and likes to have control over the amount of colour she puts in it. She used to go to Hair Today to get her hair cut. They always gave her an excellent cut but she hated the lecture they gave her on the perils of dying your own hair. Mary feels that it is her hair to do with as she likes. She feels that she is not endangering her own or anyone else's health and suspects that the hairdressers only see an opportunity to dye her hair and charge her for it.

Now Mary goes elsewhere. Here we have a service provider offering an excellent service but losing custom because they fail to see the customer's perspective.

## How to complain

We are all customers sometimes, even when we are internal customers acting on behalf of external customers. So it is an important skill to be able to complain effectively.

### Be clear about your objective

Do you want:

*   to express your dissatisfaction
*   a product or service to be improved/repaired
*   an apology
*   compensation
*   legal redress?

You cannot complain effectively if you haven't decided what outcome you want.

### Know your rights

It is futile to go storming into a premises demanding a full refund when you are not legally entitled to it. Knowledge is power and if you are making any serious complaint, you should know exactly what you are entitled to. There are many regulatory bodies that pertain to various services and industries. There is also the Citizens Advice Bureau. Be sure to consult the relevant sources.

### Follow the rules

If you follow the rules you may lose your case, no matter how worthy it is. For example, there is often a time limit to complaining. If you exceed that limit, no matter how much you were wronged there is nothing that can be done.

### Have proof

Get photographs, witnesses, receipts and doctors' reports. Bring in the defective product. Keep a diary of long-standing problems or a record of any transactions.

### Put it in writing, get it in writing

While meeting a person face to face and complaining might be effective, later on, the other side can claim it never happened. So make sure you complain in writing. If necessary register the letter so that you can prove that it was sent and received on given dates. Keep copies of everything you send and receive. Keep copies of all emails but remember that they are not recognised in a court of law in the same way a written document is. Make a note of all texts and phone calls, but again they are essentially your word against theirs.

### Quit when you're ahead

Don't always accept the first offer. Sometimes businesses are hoping you don't realise your full entitlement and if you accept a small settlement you may be losing out on much more. Conversely, don't be greedy. Some companies might offer you quite a generous settlement relative to your complaint and it would be foolish to reject it in the hopes of getting more. The key is to be informed and to consider any offer made as carefully as possible.

### Control your anger

Once you lose your temper, you have lost the fight. You have moved from reason to emotion and this will only detract from your case.

## The organisation chart

The purpose of an organisation chart is to visually express the chain of authority and responsibility within a company. This chain can be disrupted if there is poor communication up and down this chart. It should not be seen merely as a means of recognising who is in charge of another, but rather, who is an internal customer of another.

### Sample organisation chart

The higher the organisation chart, the more layers of authority there are. This can make communication more difficult and can prevent those furthest removed from each other on the chart from empathising with each other's situations.

It is more desirable to have a flatter organisational structure. This means that there is less of a pecking order and everyone has access to people in authority; those with authority are more familiar with all their staff and the workings of their organisation and can therefore make more informed decisions. A flatter structure is also closer to the idea that all staff, especially management, are internal service providers and internal customers to each other. This develops the notion of the organisation as a team. Obviously, a flat organisation structure is easier to achieve with a small staff.

The disadvantage of a flat structure and with a smaller company generally is that the burden of responsibility rests on a small number of people. This can be very stressful where people struggle to be 'a jack of all trades' rather than the more specialised areas of responsibility and expertise that a larger, more hierarchically structured company might offer. If a person who is juggling many responsibilities in a smaller company takes ill, their illness has more impact and they can be harder to replace than when a more specialised person in a larger company cannot work. I would liken it to the difference between losing a finger or losing an arm. Neither is pleasant but one is infinitely more inconvenient.

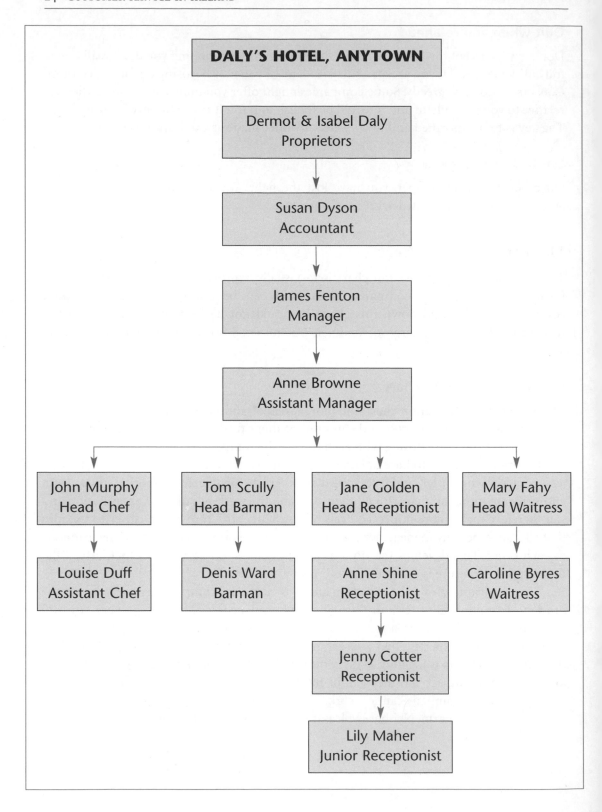

**DALY'S HOTEL, ANYTOWN**

Dermot & Isabel Daly
Proprietors

Susan Dyson
Accountant

James Fenton
Manager

Anne Browne
Assistant Manager

John Murphy
Head Chef

Tom Scully
Head Barman

Jane Golden
Head Receptionist

Mary Fahy
Head Waitress

Louise Duff
Assistant Chef

Denis Ward
Barman

Anne Shine
Receptionist

Caroline Byres
Waitress

Jenny Cotter
Receptionist

Lily Maher
Junior Receptionist

## Exercises

1. What is an external customer?
2. What is a corporate customer?
3. What is meant by 'customers are your business'?
4. 'Presentation is everything.' Would you agree? Justify your answer.
5. Write a speech where you advise your customer contact staff on how to deal with complaints.
6. How would you deal with complaints from internal customers?
7. Outline the steps customer care staff should take when dealing with a complaint.
8. How would you keep a positive attitude when dealing with awkward customers?
9. How can complaints be good for you?
10. What is active listening?
11. Outline what can be done to improve listening skills.
12. Are customer contact staff important to a company?
13. What skills should staff have to make them suitable for dealing with customers?
14. How should you respond to compliments from customers?

## Role-play practice

Using the guidelines given in this chapter, role-play the following situations.

*At the cinema* – John pre-booked four tickets on his credit card and now his party cannot go to the cinema. You are working at the ticket booth when he approaches you.

*At the supermarket* – Mr Thornton is returning some cod that he bought at your supermarket three days ago because it has gone off. The 'best before' date has not yet expired.

*In the bank* – Louise Goggin has just slipped on the marble floor. She is very annoyed.

*At the telephone company* – Mrs Smith is very annoyed because her telephone bill is extremely high. She does not know that her teenage son has been ringing up chatlines.

*At the restaurant* – A couple have arrived and are very annoyed to discover that their booking had been accidentally written in for last Friday night and not this Friday. The restaurant is extremely busy.

*At the car dealers* – Lorcan Foley has just won a small car as a result of a promotion campaign. However, he wants the money instead. The car dealer is under no obligation to accommodate him.

*At the boutique* – It is the week before Christmas and the shop is crammed with customers. A middle-aged woman comes in to complain loudly about a stained silk shirt that she is waving about.

*At the jewellers* – A man wishes to return a watch that has become waterlogged even though the manufacturer claims that it is water-resistant. He had been diving with it on. Water-resistant, however, does not mean waterproof to a depth of 30 metres.

*At the shoeshop* – An irate woman is returning a pair of sandals that broke the first time she wore them. This is not a brand that you stock, however.

*At the airport* – Vivienne Philips's luggage has been lost. She is hungry, tired and angry.

*At the hotel* – The Brosnans had booked a large suite in your hotel for the weekend three months ago. They never confirmed this and now have arrived at 1am expecting to book in. The hotel has a policy of keeping rooms until 10pm only. The Brosnans' rooms have been reassigned.

*At the travel agency* – A customer has returned from his skiing holiday very annoyed. He booked two weeks in December but due to exceptionally mild winter conditions, no snow has fallen yet.

# 2

# COMMUNICATIONS

---

**Topics covered in this chapter:**

- **What is communication?**
- **Verbal and non-verbal communication**
- **Body language**
- **Barriers to communication**
- **Perception**
- **How to inspire trust in your customers**
- **How to be a better customer**
- **Things you should never say to a customer**
- **Written communication**
- **Other forms of communication**

*For the purposes of this book we will take communication to be defined as the process by which a message is transmitted from one person to another.*

Though animals also communicate, we will concentrate on human communication. The person who sends the communication is referred to as the sender while the person who receives the communication is called the receiver. The means by which the sender sends the message is called the medium. For example, if one person writes a note to another, the medium of communication would be paper. When we talk, our voice is the medium we use. When the receiver receives the message, they may choose to respond. They might write a note back. The response is referred to as feedback. By responding, the receiver becomes the sender and the cycle begins again.

The sender is not someone the receiver necessarily knows or even knows of. When you visit an ATM machine you respond to commands typed in by a computer programmer. You read signs and advertisements without ever having considered that they had writers. You can also read the works of dead authors.

Similarly, the sender will not always know the receiver. When Shakespeare wrote his plays he aimed them at his contemporaries and not at us, which is why we might find parts of them difficult to understand. A sender may not have even intended the receiver to receive the message. An example of this occurred during the 2000 US presidential campaign when George W. Bush, standing on a stage, waved smilingly to someone in the crowd while telling the person next to him what he really thought. What he had forgotten was that he was wearing a microphone. He had intended his message for one person but inadvertently acquired millions of receivers around the world.

Verbal communication is any communication that uses words as its medium, so this includes not only all forms of spoken language but written language as well. Therefore, most forms of mass media and electronic communication using words in their messages are also using verbal communication.

Messages are not always verbal. In fact, non-verbal communication is extremely important. A wave or a smile can clearly communicate friendliness to another person. When we are trying to hide our nerves during a job interview our nervous actions betray us. The way we say things can communicate a lot more than what we actually say. 'That's it,' depending on how you say it, can be a statement of fact, a question and an expression of anger or joy. Non-verbal communication is any communication that does not need to use words to convey a message. If everyone, regardless of the language they speak, can understand it, then it is non-verbal communication.

Examples of aural non-verbal communication are music, alarms, knocking, crying, laughing, bells, clapping, sighing, etc.

Examples of visual non-verbal communication are body language (kinesics and proximics), photographs, signs, symbols, traffic lights, flags, uniforms and so on.

## Body language

*Kinesics* is how we move our bodies to convey a message, such as waving, smiling or folding our arms.

*Proximics* is how we position ourselves in relation to other people. For example, we sit closer to people that we know than to strangers. The space between ourselves and the next person is separated into three main zones: the public zone, the private zone and the intimate zone. For example, if a stranger stands close to you, you feel uncomfortable because they have left the public zone and entered your private zone. If a friend was standing as close to you, you would feel comfortable. If an acquaintance came even closer they would be moving into the intimate zone. This might also make you feel uncomfortable, for though you might be happy to have this person in your private zone, you may not wish them to be closer than that.

These zones do not have fixed distances, however. The zones expand and contract in relation to the amount of space available. For example, if you are sitting alone on an empty bus and a stranger sits next to you, you feel uncomfortable because your private zone in an empty bus is much wider. If the bus was full and the seat next to you was one of the last empty ones, then you would not feel uncomfortable about a stranger taking that seat. At a concert or on a subway people are more accepting of other people being crushed up against them because public and private zones cannot be distinguished in such crowded spaces.

Body language can also be broadly divided into two categories: positive and negative.

*Positive body language* expresses positive emotions. It can indicate happiness, pleasure, approval, encouragement and satisfaction. When dealing with customers, positive body language can create an atmosphere of efficiency and sincerity and can be invaluable in dealing with situations where the customer is dissatisfied, angry or even afraid.

*Negative body language* expresses negative emotions. They can indicate fear, anger, aggression, insincerity and dishonesty. When dealing with customers, negative body language is best avoided. However, it is important to be able to recognise negative body language and in demonstrating positive body language, you may hope to placate the customer.

The categories of positive and negative body language can be further subdivided into voluntary and involuntary body language.

*Voluntary body language* is what we choose to show or what other people choose to show us. For example, I may choose to show my approval of a musician's skill and choice of music at a concert by applauding. Sometimes, however, what we choose to show is far from what we really feel. For example, I may also applaud at the end of a concert I disliked because I may feel that it would be rude not to do so. I may therefore successfully conceal my true feelings. However, we very rarely manage to cover up what we really think entirely. We give ourselves away through involuntary gestures. I might seem to be clapping in approval at the end of a concert but my face might have a grim or bored expression. I might have yawned or looked at my watch throughout the performance. It is possible that nobody fully noticed this, but for any onlooker with a basic grasp of body language the cues are there to see.

*Involuntary body language* is defined as the messages we transmit unconsciously or sometimes (as in the case of lying or displaying nervousness at a job interview) unwillingly. They can often be a truer measure of our feelings than voluntary body language.

As humans, our brains are programmed to come up with the right answer. When we try to repress our honest emotions our body feels stress. Our heart rate increases and we sweat more. A lie-detector machine or polygraph, beloved of a thousand detective shows, does not detect lies, it detects pulse rate and perspiration. First, you are asked to answer a simple question honestly, and then to answer with a lie. The variations between these two answers can be used to see if you are stressed or not when you answer questions. If you are stressed, then you are probably lying. When we lie we need to relieve the stress our body feels. We usually do this by what are called displacement activities. We may scratch our head or shuffle our feet. Look at young children when you know they are lying. They will lie and then put their hands over their mouths to conceal where the lie came from. When we are older we do the same thing but we are less obvious about it. Thus, when we lie, the displacement activities that we perform are often designed to distract others away from our mouths, for example by scratching our nose, pulling at our ear or rubbing our head. Also, when we lie, we try to avoid eye contact. It is said that the eyes are the windows of the soul, so the liar likes to keep the shutters down.

The study of all forms of body language is very important for the customer care student. This way, we can learn if a customer is genuinely pleased with a service or is dissatisfied and simply does not wish to complain. Such customers are unlikely to return and are just as likely as any other customer to complain to friends. So if you can perceive that this customer is upset and help them resolve their problems, then you have saved the organisation from all the potential damage that one reticent customer could cause. In addition, you will probably retain the customer's loyalty, now that they know they can have problems solved without the stress of complaining.

## Some features of body language

It is important to note that gestures in body language can vary greatly in their meaning. For example, though folding one's arms can indicate a defensive attitude, sometimes it just means that the person wanted to relax and simply folded their arms. Therefore, it is important not to read a gesture out of context. The best way to read gestures is in clusters. One gesture on its own may mean nothing. A series of gestures expressing similar emotions is more indicative. If facial expression and stance also suggest a defensive attitude, then in that context, folding the arms can also seem defensive. Likewise, gestures can often be both voluntary and involuntary. Sometimes, we deliberately smile and sometimes it comes naturally. Whether it is deliberate or involuntary, sincere or feigned, only practice and observation will help you decide. To help you, here are some examples of positive and negative body language.

### Positive body language

1. When a person nods their head up and down it can indicate agreement and/or approval.

2. Bowing of the head alone or with the upper body can indicate a very formal greeting.

3. The use of regular or prolonged eye contact can show interest and attention, or even attraction.

4. A smile can be simply an indication of recognition or can demonstrate interest or pleasure.

5. Sticking out your tongue while writing or working is a sign of concentration. The part of the brain that deals with dexterity also controls the tongue, therefore many people do this unconsciously.

6. A person who pinches or strokes the chin is indicating deep thought.

7. Clapping is a sign of approval.

8. A person who waves their hands about is either trying to attract someone's attention or is expressing great delight or exultation.

9. When we raise an arm or hand it is either done at the time of our own choosing, as when we wish to attract someone's attention (as in calling for the bill in a restaurant or trying to get the chairperson's attention so that we may speak at a meeting), or as a direct response to a prompt, as in confirming one's presence at a roll call or voting.

10. When we place both index fingers on our lips we are showing pleasure or appreciation.

11. When a person raises their fist above the shoulder with the palm facing outwards they are making a gesture of victory, triumph or celebration. Generally when the fist or hand is turned outwards it is a positive sign. When it is turned inwards it tends to be negative.

12. Making a V shape with the index and middle finger, again with the palm of the hand turned outwards, indicates victory or peace.

13. Forming a circle by touching the top of your thumb with your index finger means that everything is okay.

14. When we tilt our head to one side we indicate interest or puzzlement.

15. If we raise and lower our eyebrows quickly we are acknowledging someone. It can be used in situations where a normal greeting might be disruptive, as in a concert or during an examination.

16. When our arms lie relaxed by our sides, we show that we are relaxed and open and perceive no immediate threat.

17. Folding your arms can indicate many things, but it depends on the context, the cluster of other signals of body language that you are giving and the manner in which the arms are folded. For example, when arms are folded loosely at the front it can indicate ease, confidence and authority.

18. Making the tips of our fingers of both hands meet, creating an impression of a church steeple, is called steepling and was a favourite gesture of Sir Arthur Conan Doyle when describing Sherlock Holmes's reaction to a new case or clue. It often indicates superiority or authority, but it can also indicate evaluation or a positive response.

19. Sometimes we lean our chin heavily on our hand with our elbow supporting us, sometimes with our fingers pushing into our cheek. This usually indicates feelings of deep interest.

20. When our palms are turned out we are showing that we have nothing to hide. This indicates openness and honesty.

21. When a person stands with their legs very slightly apart, they show readiness, for example before a race or sporting event, but it can also indicate confidence and relaxation.

22. When a person stands with their legs and heels very close together, a stance that comes from the military tradition, the gesture indicates deference and respect.

23. When we stand with the feet pointed towards another person it can show politeness, interest or feelings of attraction towards that person.

## Negative body language

1.   When we shake our head from side to side we show negation. We are disagreeing, refusing or denying something.

2.   When we scratch our head we show puzzlement or confusion.

3.   Slapping the side of our head quickly is a gesture of irritation or mild self-disgust. We may be trying to remember something and we have so far failed or we have just remembered something that we should or should not have done.

4.   When we quickly toss our heads we are making an angry or defiant gesture.

5.   We run our fingers through our hair for different reasons. Sometimes it can be in frustration and anger.

6.   We furrow our brow when we are angry, worried or afraid.

7.   Covering our eyes can mean many things. It could be an attempt not to see or be seen by someone. It could also suggest shame, anger or disappointment or it could be an attempt to remember something by blocking out external visual stimuli that might otherwise prove distracting.

8.   When someone winks, whether in fun or otherwise, there is always a conspiratorial aspect to it. A secret link is made between the person sending and the person receiving the wink. A wink can suggest secrecy, slyness or it can be taken as a flirtatious gesture.

9.   When we raise one eyebrow we register inquiry, surprise or disbelief but all with an underlying message of disapproval.

10.   Raising both eyebrows indicates more dramatically the same emotions that raising one eyebrow indicates. The difference is the intensity of the emotion expressed.

11.   When we lower both eyebrows over our eyes we are giving a menacing or warning look that indicates strong disapproval or deep anger. It is a warning to the intended receiver of this message to back down.

12.   If we put our fingers in our ears we are trying to block out an unpleasant sound or trying to avoid listening to someone. This is a gesture that you will see among young children or very immature adults.

13.   If we put our hands over our ears we could be attempting to avoid hearing something unpleasant and in that way it is a similar but marginally less irritating gesture than sticking your fingers in your ears. On a practical level it can be used to protect our ears from very loud sounds.

14.   When a person holds or wrinkles their nose they may be reacting to an unpleasant smell. It can also suggest that a person is disgusted by other unpleasant things such as food or even people.

15.   Yawning is a sign of boredom or tiredness.

16. When someone shrugs their shoulders they are generally abdicating responsibility of some sort. This gesture can mean, 'I don't know,' 'Don't ask me,' 'Don't blame me,' 'It's not my problem,' or 'So what?'

17. We tend to fold our arms tightly as a defence against criticism. It can suggest that we find that criticism unwelcome.

18. When we hold our arms out in a wide expansive gesture we are indicating our innocence by inviting the other person to scrutinise us. We are showing that we have nothing to hide. This gesture can mean, 'I don't know,' 'I haven't got it,' or 'Don't ask me, I had nothing to do with it.'

19. When we raise our fist with our palm clenched inwards we are making a threatening gesture, suggesting anger or intimidation. Gestures with the palm turned inwards tend to be negative.

20. Making a V shape with our index and middle fingers and palm turned inwards is an aggressive, offensive and deliberately provoking gesture.

21. The 'thumbs down' gesture comes from the Romans, when two slaves or gladiators would fight in an amphitheatre for the citizens' amusement. It is said that when one slave had the upper hand and was in a position to kill the other, the spectators would vote as to whether the loser should die or be spared. If the loser had fought bravely, he would be given the 'thumbs up' and would be allowed to live. If he got the 'thumbs down' then the other slave would kill him. There is, however, some dispute as to whether this was the true meaning of the 'thumbs down' gesture or not. Nevertheless this interpretation has been used in countless books of history, historical fiction and adventure. Nowadays – fortunately – it just means disapproval rather than death.

22. When we tap our feet on the ground, we show that we are bored, restless or frustrated.

23. Whereas tapping feet is often a gesture performed by an individual, stamping our feet is usually a group activity. Small children, however, are the exception and will stamp their feet alone when they are in a temper or defiant mood. Foot stamping is a much stronger and more aggressive display of anger and impatience than foot tapping. In a crowd, it can be a very menacing and sinister gesture, particularly as people behave in a far less logical and restrained manner once they have come to identify with the crowd that they are in.

24. When we rest our head on our hands, we are signifying tiredness or boredom.

25. When we put our head in our hands, we are showing that we are very tired or frustrated. It could also signify despair or depression.

26. When we put our hand to our forehead, we are showing stress, anxiety, frustration or pain. We could also be trying to remember something.

27. If we suddenly open up our eyes wide we are registering shock. It could be due to surprise, horror or sudden realisation.

28.   We rub our eyes when we are tired.

29.   Half-closed eyes may mean tiredness, intoxication, concentration or anger.

30.   When we avoid looking into other people's eyes it is because we are afraid of what they may see in ours. We could be lying or masking some other form of dishonesty. We could also be nervous, ashamed or just shy.

31.   Pulling, rubbing or touching the ear are all displacement activities. We are hiding scepticism or dishonesty.

32.   Rubbing, scratching or touching the nose is a displacement activity that indicates that a person is lying, perplexed or nervous.

33.   We cover our mouth out of trained politeness when we yawn but people sometimes do it to conceal a yawn.

34.   We clench our teeth in an attempt to control our anger. Sometimes we fail so it can often precede exploding in rage.

35.   We bite our nails, often out of habit, but people generally do it for comfort during occasions of insecurity and nervousness.

36.   We touch our chin when we are doubtful about something. We also do it when we are nervous or when we are lying.

37.   People jut out their jaws when they are being stubborn. It signifies determination and/or hostility.

38.   People who hold their chins low are displaying feelings of insecurity, inferiority and shyness.

39.   We touch our necks when we are insecure, doubtful or lying.

40.   We clasp the back of our neck with one hand mainly as a gesture of stress. However, it can also suggest anger or frustration.

41.   When we slowly scratch our neck, under our ear, we are reluctantly expressing doubt. The act is slow either because of our reluctance to offend or because we are still considering the situation.

42.   A person who folds their arms with their fists clenched generally means business. This is a highly hostile, though defensive, gesture.

43.   When we fold our arms with our thumbs turned upwards we are making a defensive but arrogant stand. We are very confident of the outcome. It's as if we are saying, 'Yeah, you and whose army?'

44.   When we stretch our arms behind our head with our fingers interlocked we are indicating confidence. If we combine this, however, with our body stretched out and ankles crossed while sitting, we are more than confident, we are arrogant and smug. When we are on the defensive we tend to try to unconsciously protect and cover our body. Therefore defensive body language often involves arm folding. When we feel

safe and confident our body language reflects this in open gestures that expose the body. The above gesture leaves the body totally exposed and vulnerable because the person does not expect to be attacked or is confident that he is protected.

45.  When we clasp or wring our fingers we are showing anxiety.

46.  If we interlock our fingers but hold them low on the body we are making a gesture of doubt or appraisal.

47.  When we examine our hand or fingernails carefully we are performing a displacement activity. It may be used to simply alleviate boredom, but it could also be an excuse to avert our eyes out of nervousness, embarrassment or indifference. As with all gestures, this has to be interpreted within the context of the situation.

To sum up, gestures that leave the body exposed indicate confidence and security. Gestures that attempt to cover the body, for example arm folding and leg crossing, tend to suggest a defensive attitude. Many gestures that are made around the mouth are attempts to distract from the fact that the sender of the message is lying. As we get older these gestures tend to become more subtle, but they fail to disappear completely. Body language gestures should be interpreted in clusters and in context. One individual gesture is not a conclusive indication of how someone feels. It should also be noted that we all have gestures that we perform a lot and others that we never use. Some families tend to pass on certain gestures or mannerisms. Body language is a good guide but not an exact science. When attempting to understand body language, the interpreter must use discretion.

## Communication and the customer

The customer is the most important person we come into contact with. However, they don't always feel that way. That is because staff don't always treat them as well as they should. Here are some guidelines you should follow when dealing with customers.

### Demonstrate positive body language and behaviour

1.  Look at the list of positive body language gestures and try to incorporate some of them into your customer care behaviour.

2.  Look people in the eye. This shows that you are really listening to them and can calm them down and/or please them.

3.  If someone is shouting at you, keep your own voice down. This will lead them to unconsciously lower their own voice in order to hear you.

4.  Smile. It can have a positive effect on customers.

5.  Be polite. Manners have been described as the oil on which society runs. Politeness can also create a good impression of a business.

6.  Have a good firm handshake.

7.  Make sure that you are always clean and neatly presented. Your appearance and even your smell are all part of body language. It will affect the customer's perception of you. All the smiling in the world will not counteract bad breath, soiled clothes or body odour.

8.  Know the details. The more detailed you can be about your business, the sooner the customer will understand it. They won't have to ask questions. They will gain confidence in you as a person who knows what they are talking about.

9.  Be honest. Customers are intelligent people and know when they are getting the hard sell. They will become cynical and closed to you if they think that you will always only give them advice that leads to them buying your product and/or buying your most expensive version. For example: Female customer with size 11 sports shoe in her hand, 'Do you have this runner in a size 12, that's his normal size?' Salesperson returns, 'I'm sorry we don't have it in a 12, but this is a very big size 11.' When talking to your customers give them an honest account of all products, listing pros and cons. The customer will trust you, make an informed choice and is far more likely to come back again. You may fool a customer into buying something expensive and unsuitable but if they realise what you have done, you have lost them (and the people they warn) forever. So be honest, be sincere.

## Be a good listener

Good listening skills are an important part of communication. By listening carefully you are getting a clear understanding of the situation.

When listening actively, being able to correctly interpret body language is a very important skill as it allows you to understand the emotional state of the other person. An aggressive posture might warn you in advance that extra care will be needed in handling this person and will help you avoid an unpleasant situation.

It is also a useful skill to be able to use your own body language in a positive way as other people will pick up on any negativity that your body language may be displaying. In tense situations try to adopt a relaxed, open posture and breathe deeply. You will also encourage people to continue talking if your body language reflects interest. For further details on listening, see Chapter 1.

> **Good language skills are important if you want to get your point across as effectively as possible. You can build up your vocabulary and practise your language skills in debates and public speaking.**

## Barriers to effective communication

You should also look out for barriers to effective customer communication and develop practical measures to remove them. The three main barriers to effective communication are physical, psychological and environmental.

*Physical barriers.* It can be hard for staff and customers to communicate if they are a good distance apart from one another or talking through a window, for example the sneezeguard at a delicatessen counter or the bullet-proof glass at the post office.

To prevent these necessary health and safety measures from impeding customer communication it might be possible to have at least one member of staff in a more accessible position. For example, there could be a break between the sneezeguards of the display units where a customer can see and talk to a staff member or, in the post office, lower windows with adequate speaking grilles and metal shields that drop down in immediate response to danger are sometimes installed.

Many other physical barriers to communication are accidental and should be identified and removed. The simplest way to do this is to enter the premises as a customer and identify them for yourself.

*Psychological barriers.* This is when the communication process is impeded because either the customer or the contact staff are emotionally distracted. For example, a teleservice operator may be blunt and off-hand with a customer, knowing that their rate of calls taken per hour is being monitored and if they spend too long with any one client they may be censured. Contact staff may be tired or hungry because they are working a long shift. They may be overstretched and resentful about having to apologise for factors outside their control.

To avoid these barriers ensure that staff are properly rostered for work and that they get adequate food and rest breaks. In teleservice less emphasis should be placed on the quantity of calls and more on the quality. Provide adequate equipment and facilities to allow employees to do their job properly.

*Environmental barriers.* If the premises are too noisy, customers will find it difficult to talk. If the premises are in a location that is difficult to reach, customers are less likely to call in to discuss their situation. In addition, premises that are uncomfortably hot or cold will discourage customers from visiting or staying as long as necessary. The premises might not have a suitable place for a private conversation.

Make sure that your premises are customer friendly if you want to encourage customer communication. Make sure you have a comfortable interview room where customers can talk in confidence.

## Perception

Perception is the process by which we obtain information through the stimulation of our senses. For example, we perceive light, shade, colour, texture and shape through our eyes and we also perceive texture and shape through touch. Our perception of the world around us is unique. No two people perceive it in the same way. Perception can be affected by thousands of variables. A short flight of steps might seem extremely long and dangerous to someone with chronic arthritis. Our assessment of whether something is expensive or not may depend on how much money we have, how badly we think we need the object, what it costs elsewhere and what we are used to paying for it. Think of people watching a soccer match in a stadium. While everyone is watching the same match they are all seeing it from a slightly different angle. Their perception of how good the match or the referee is depends on how well their team is doing. While most are caught up in the excitement of the game others are just waiting for it to end as their perception of soccer is that it's boring.

Similarly, every customer is different and, as a result, the individual's perception of what makes a good product or service can vary widely. One customer may value friendly staff and a wide choice. Another may see value for money and a convenient location as being of the utmost importance. A wealthy person may value quality, comfort and exclusivity over price, while a mother of five might consider value for money and nearby parking facilities as being essential. Therefore, where one customer may be very satisfied with an organisation, another may be very disappointed.

So we can define customer perceptions as the biased reactions of individual customers to the particular product or service they are obtaining, based on their own personal needs, wants and expectations. Customer perceptions can be influenced by many different factors. The surroundings, advertising and the presentation of the product or service all play a part. Naturally, the actual product or service itself is crucial, as is the customer's experience in acquiring that product or service, from initial inquiry to final delivery. The long-term experience of the customer with the product or service is also very important.

In looking at customer behaviour, it is possible to outline the potential consequences of good and bad first impressions.

Good first impressions can mean that:

- The customer is impressed by their initial perceptions and develops an agreeable attitude towards the company even before they have experienced the goods or service.
- The customer develops confidence in the company and is more sympathetic when things go wrong.
- Customer loyalty is increased.
- The customer recommends the company to others, thus generating free and positive publicity for the company.

Bad first impressions can mean that:

- The customer comes into contact with the company, is repelled by their impression of it and immediately withdraws to find another company to meet their expectations.
- The customer is dissatisfied and cancels an order.
- The customer disparages the company, generating unwelcome, negative publicity.
- The negative publicity affects the business and orders decrease.
- The customer may feel the need to seek recompense; they may involve the media or industry watchdogs and possibly take their grievance to court.
- The customer will be unsympathetic if problems arise in the future, tending to blame the problems on the company even if the company is not directly to blame, for example untimely or failed deliveries. This will then add to the unfavourable opinion already formed.

Where do our perceptions of other people come from?

- *Appearance.* First we form an impression from a person's appearance, size, shape, accent and the clothes they wear. Unfortunately, we often make the mistake of categorising or stereotyping people on a very superficial level.
- *Role.* Our perceptions of others are also affected by their role. A role is a regular pattern of behaviour which we expect the person-in-role to exhibit. For example, we expect a policeman to behave in a certain way and feel ashamed or shocked when they do not. Roles are useful in many ways. They help us know what to say and how to behave in certain situations.
- *Attributes.* Our dealings with others and what we hear about them will also contribute to our dealings with them.

## Customer perception – some examples

Surroundings can deeply affect customer perceptions. Imagine your feelings on walking into a restaurant where the wallpaper was peeling off the walls and a mousetrap was sitting in the corner. And would you leave a child in a crèche if you saw that two of its windows were broken?

Look also at how advertising and presentation affect our perceptions of expensive fragrances. They suggest luxury and sophistication. Advertising campaigns in the media concentrate on the sense of style inherent in the products. They use beautiful models and we are encouraged to buy the product so we can emulate them. As a result we are willing to pay high prices for the feeling of glamour and exclusivity these products offer. The fragrance itself is often irrelevant, except that other people might smell it and realise that you have paid a great deal of money for it.

Sports cars are another example of how our perceptions can be influenced by presentation. On a practical level, sports cars are very expensive and have high petrol consumption. They generally only seat two and have limited boot space. They often have very few of the creature comforts that we have come to expect in smaller, cheaper cars. They may not have heated rear windows, electric windows, CD players or even power steering. They often have a pull-down soft-top roof which, though attractive, is hardly practical in Ireland or the UK. They have enormous engines capable of massive acceleration and great speed, but as the national maximum speed limit is 120 kph, and that's on a motorway, where are you going to have a chance to enjoy it? The customer is aware of all this but doesn't mind. This is because the customer is influenced by countless films, advertisements, car races and car chases where sports cars are presented as desirable objects which project an image of wealth, prestige and attractiveness.

## How to inspire trust in your customers

It is only common sense to say that a customer who trusts you will stay with you, but how do you inspire that trust?

### First of all, ask yourself, what is trust?

*David Niven once said of his one-time housemate, the matinee idol Errol Flynn, 'You always knew precisely where you stood with him because he always let you down.'*

Trust is knowing what to expect from someone or something.

For example, if you book a holiday by the beach for two weeks in June in Ireland and it rains, you may be irritated but you don't feel deceived. You accept rain as a possibility. If, however, the same thing happens on the French Riviera, your trust in sunny holidays is diminished because you did not expect it to rain.

If you have a friend who is constantly late, you factor that into your arrangements. You might even say 'trust Mary to miss the flight' to mutual friends and see them all nod in agreement.

In business, you want your customer service to cause your existing customers to say 'trust that company to deliver on time' or even 'if you get it wrong, they will sort it out for you'.

### Secondly, know how to inspire that trust

#### Word of mouth

Trust is built up over time, but potential customers can be swayed by hearing the testimonials of your existing customers.

#### Offer a taster

Offer potential customers a special rate or bite-sized contract. This allows them to experience your excellent service first hand without being scared off by having to make a big commitment. It allows them to dip their toe in the water and if the water is fine, they can then dive in.

#### Be transparent

The more upfront you are, the more potential and existing customers will trust you. Customers are not stupid. Sometimes they pretend to know less than they do to test you. If they catch you out on a bluff, they won't trust you and will take their business elsewhere.

#### Be competent

Naturally, incompetence will lose you customers faster than anything. Who is going to buy bread from a baker who always burns the loaves?

#### Be consistent

Consistency is the backbone of trust because it delivers on expectations. For example, if your deliveryman is always a day late, clients will always expect him to be a day late and will start planning around that. If he then turns up on time and gets angry because they are not ready for him, then the customer will again have to adapt their routine to suit your company and may leave you for someone they can trust to come on a specific day rather than having to guess which day that might be.

As a client deals more and more with you and experiences a consistently good service, they will trust you more and more. Then, if there is a glitch in the future, they will be more understanding and supportive, as they will trust that this is a once-off.

### Be flexible

If a client needs to change a date or a specific requirement and you can easily accommodate them, then do. If this accommodation cost you nothing, then don't charge them up to the hilt for it either. Your client will then feel that they can trust you to act reasonably if future similar situations arise. If you are inflexible because you are within your rights to be so, you may win this battle but may lose a client that might have brought you in a lot of money in the future.

### Be courteous

People tend to trust people who treat them with respect. Good manners is the first indication of that. That means being on time, shaking hands and giving the customer time. The customer should feel by your posture, eye contact and general behaviour that they are valued by you. If you are willing to invest time and effort into talking to them, they will feel that you are taking them seriously.

### Get to know your customer

The more of an effort you make to get to know your customer, the better. The personal details can add a friendly touch, but more importantly, get to know what the customer needs and wants from you. This can work to your advantage. For example, you might ring up a customer to alert them to the fact that a new product that they might like has just arrived. As long as this is not overdone, the customer will be impressed by your knowledge of their business and will feel that they are being looked after.

Remember, this applies to both internal and external customers. Internal customers may have poor morale if they cannot trust their employers or colleagues. A deliveryman does not want to work for a company that cannot give him the correct address to deliver to. He does not want his time wasted waiting for stock that should have been ready to be loaded on his lorry when he arrived at the depot. A person who has chipped in time and again and helped the company out in a crisis may not be impressed if the company fails to return the favour when they are having difficulty. They will wonder why they are putting in the extra effort when they are treated as coldly as those who do the bare minimum or less.

### Be sincere

You can use every technique going, but if you don't mean it, most customers will see right through you. They may play along to your face but you may never see them again. Most of us have been the cringing subject of some fawning waiter's oleaginous attentions. He thinks he is charming a fat tip out of you but he has actually ruined your meal. Likewise, you may have been annoyed by a salesperson in a clothing store who indiscriminately praises everything you try on. How much more loyal would you be if you knew that a certain salesperson would always give you their honest opinion? Would you go back to a barbershop where the barber pulled a 'oh no not another customer' face every time someone walked in the door and then told you to 'come back soon' as you departed?

## Things that you should never say in front of a customer

### 'I have one at home and it works perfectly.'

Isn't it amazing that every time you bring in a defective product the employee who deals with you has the same one at home and it works fine? Even if it's true, don't say it. It adds nothing to the argument and is such a cliché at this stage that it only irritates customers.

### 'We have never had any complaints about that product/service before.'

Like the above, it's a cliché that really irritates the customer. Does it matter to the customer if everyone else who ever bought this product is in a heightened state of bliss because of it? The point is that theirs doesn't work and the fact that everyone else's is working perfectly doesn't restore their confidence in the product. Do you think that a customer will walk out satisfied because everyone else has had a good experience with the product? So what's the point in saying it?

### 'What are you doing that for?'

A person buys a new battery for their watch at the jewellers. The assistant offers to put it into the watch for the customer. The manager comes out and asks the above question. Here we have an example of a manager criticising an employee in front of a customer. This never creates a good impression. The fact that the employee was doing a little bit extra for the customer when they were checked only shows that though the employee may value the business's customers, management does not. This creates a very bad impression.

### 'Can you afford that?'

This can be a very offensive question. It implies that the employee has made a series of judgments about you, so never say it. If you suspect that a customer doesn't realise the price of something, subtly mention it in conversation.

'It's lovely, isn't it? I wish I could afford it but if I told my husband I spent X amount on one dress, he would strangle me.'

Better still, put price tags on things. Businesses lose custom every day because people are afraid to embarrass themselves by asking the price of a product and service.

### 'You are too old/fat for that.'

Not only is this insulting but it can be deemed discriminatory. If you do feel that a customer is making a bad choice and you don't want it on your conscience that they have left your premises looking like a perfect fright, be subtle. Try and direct the customer elsewhere. 'Look at this, I think this would really suit you, it is really your colour. Would you like to try this?' After that, all you can do is let them make up their own mind.

### 'You sure eat a lot of chocolate.'

Do not pass remarks on a customer's purchases. It is extremely rude. If you make a customer self-conscious about their purchases, they are unlikely to return. This advice doesn't limit itself to supermarkets. Who wants to visit a hairdresser or dentist who constantly gives them the third degree about how they look after themselves? What about a car salesman who derides your skill as a driver or your taste in cars?

### 'I only work here.'

Ah yes, the ultimate cop-out. It may help staff to disassociate themselves from a situation, but who wants to return to a business where if there's a problem that's the only response they can expect?

### 'We don't have/I wouldn't know.'

If this is trotted out, immediately it can give a very bad impression. It is important for the customer to feel that they are valued and that you are making an effort. If you just say either of the above and move on to the next customer, you look like you are too lazy to help or you just don't care. A better alternative would be, 'I'm pretty sure we don't have any of those left but I can check for you.' Or, 'I can check our other stores for you and order it.'

### 'Mr Bond . . . first name James I presume? Heh heh.'

Some people have names or addresses that other people find amusing. If you find a customer's name unusual or comical, keep it to yourself. Chances are you are not the first person that day even to make the same smart comment. Instead make sure you get the spellings and pronunciations right.

### 'J.K. Rowling, he's one of our most popular writers.'

Try as much as possible to be familiar with the products and services your company offers. If you don't know something, don't try and fake it; you will inevitably be caught out and what customer will trust you then?

### 'That man comes in here every week, spends an hour here wasting my time, has no idea what he's talking about and then spends a euro. Give me strength, now what is it you wanted?'

Never criticise a customer or fellow employee to another customer. It is petty and very unprofessional. It gives a very bad impression of your business. Customers will think your company is unstable and will wonder what you say about them to other customers.

*'It will be in next week, love.'*

When I was in college I would go to the local second-hand bookshop with my booklist. Sometimes they had what I wanted but whatever was missing, they promised it would be in the following week. Obviously I stopped believing them very quickly and demonstrated this behaviour to a fellow student by going in, in their company, and asking for a non-existent book. As usual they promised that it would be in next week.

Now if someone promises me a product will be in next week, I am very dubious.

*'So you are taking the bog-standard model?'*

This doesn't say very much about the vendor's tact or faith in their product. It makes the customer feel like the vendor is implying that they are a cheapskate. If it is unintentional, then it is just poor customer service training, but if it is part of a more manipulative attempt to sell more, then it can backfire.

1. A customer may get offended and walk out.
2. A customer may buy this time but never return.
3. A customer may upgrade out of embarrassment but never return because they really cannot afford upgrading purchases.
4. A customer may actually buy the more expensive version so as not to be embarrassed.

The question is this – is it worth losing some customers in order to embarrass a few into spending more?

Can you think of anything that has been said to you as a customer that could be added to this list? Have you been guilty of a few customer service gaffes yourself?

## Things that really annoy customers: a quick survey

*Supermarket baggers*

Before, they would whip out a plastic bag and chuck two tins of beans in on top of your fragile eggs and next to the raw fish and washing powder. This led to broken eggs and soapy cod. Now they wait for you to hand them your recyclable bags before they damage your shopping. Increasingly shops have people bagging for charity. Occasionally this is acceptable. If it happens too often it can put customers off.

Lots of customers like to bag their own shopping systematically and do not want someone else breaking their eggs and then charging them for the privilege. If it happens every week, it begins to feel like a tax.

*Shops or restaurants that do everything they can to make you feel unwelcome so they can shut down early*

*Queue jumpers*

*Over-attentive or pushy salespeople who won't let you browse in peace*

*Indifferent salespeople who ignore you despite the fact that you clearly need their attention*

## Obvious store walkers

You bend down to look at a book on the bottom shelf and then you feel the presence beside you. You have never stolen a thing in your life, yet instantly you feel guilty. As you move about the store, they follow you. Now all you want to do is leave the store, never to return.

> ### Outline the potential impact of organisational presentation on customer perceptions, for example as a result of the physical environment, written communications, personal appearance of staff
>
> How your business looks reflects your values and the quality of what you are selling. Clean and efficient premises will tell customers that they can expect a clean and efficient service. Likewise, substandard premises will send a negative message. Premises that provide a comfortable waiting area with magazines, water, coffee and a rest room will make customers feel welcome. They will also not be so annoyed at having to wait. This attention to detail will make the customer feel appreciated. Such an organisation, they may reason, will be more helpful in providing a good after-sales service and will be less likely to be dismissive of customer difficulties after they have got the customer's money.
>
> In addition, purchasing goods or a service, particularly an expensive one or a one-off, will be an occasion in the mind of the customer. If you are going to buy your dream home or car, you want it to be a special experience. You have probably saved long and hard for this moment. The business that treats all its customers as special by creating an attractive purchasing environment will benefit from repeat business.
>
> Large commercial institutions often have imposing offices in impressive premises that exude solidity and permanence, two qualities greatly desired by their customers. However, some customers may not often get a chance to see inside these buildings. Therefore, financial institutions and other large companies try to give a positive sense of their company through their correspondence. High-quality headed notepaper is used, sometimes embossed with an impressively designed letterhead. All correspondence is neatly and accurately typed and corresponds to a particular house style. All reference numbers are accurately displayed. Any company that does not take great care over its correspondence will put off many customers who will see only their inaccurate letters and poorly designed publicity material and judge the entire company on it.
>
> As with premises, personal appearance will strongly influence customer perception. A sloppy appearance will make people think that they can only expect a sloppy service. It will also show the customer that the company hasn't much respect for its customers. But on the other hand, clean, even minimalist, premises will drive some customers away, for example the kind of women's clothes shop that has about four items of clothes on strategic display on deluxe maple shelving. The shop has three glamorous assistants staring at you, or worse, discussing their night out with each other while

ignoring all the customers. This can be quite intimidating for some customers who may feel that they will not be catered for here. For other customers, the shop's air of exclusivity is a very strong attraction. It would appear that the less stock these shops have, the more each individual item costs.

The general rule of personal presentation for customer contact staff is that it is better to err on the side of conservatism. Unless you are selling trendy clothing, then dress conservatively, in a manner which will not offend anybody. Where appropriate, wear uniforms. They can create an efficient, business-like impression.

## If I was a better customer, would I get better service?

Once upon a time, a man bought a PC in a small computer shop. As soon as he bought that computer, he thought he owned them and felt he was entitled to their expert advice whenever he wanted. He rang them up and called them out to do the simplest of tasks and fix the simplest of errors. On one occasion they drove the 30-mile journey to his house to discover that he hadn't attached the printer to the computer. Whatever profit that had been made selling him the computer had long ago been eaten up by his constant demands. When next he went to buy a laptop, they did not seem to have any laptop to suit his needs. Funnily enough, no other shop in the town could help him either. In general, he had found over the years that none of the shops in the town were very good. They never seemed to have the things he wanted and never seemed to try very hard to get them.

Mary treated the staff of every coffeeshop or restaurant she entered like they were paid slaves. It came across in her tone but also in the way that she got extremely annoyed if there was any delay serving her or if the milk jug needed filling. Recently she was finding it more difficult to find people to go for coffee with her to the local coffeeshop and was amazed when her friend got a free latte from a member of staff for her birthday. They never did that for her, which only proved to her what an awful coffeeshop it was.

Brian thought it was incredibly bad form when the hotel he intended to book for his mate's bachelor party turned him down flat. Why any hotel would refuse the opportunity to rent out seven double rooms in this economic climate was beyond him.

Elizabeth worked as a clerk in a bank that had to be bailed out by the Irish taxpayer as a result of decisions made by people in the bank way above her modest payscale. Every day for months during the height of the crisis, members of the public would come in and scream at herself and her colleagues and call them crooks and thieves. She was now ashamed to tell people where she worked because even when they thought that they were being funny, all the same old jibes came out.

There is an old adage, 'the customer is always right'. Those of us who have ever dealt with customers on an ongoing basis know that cannot be taken literally and was never meant to be. It means that you should not immediately assume that the customer is wrong – very often they are right – but that you should presume that they are in the right until proven otherwise, and even then it may just be a misunderstanding based on poor communication on the business's part. In all cases you should treat the customer with courtesy. However, some customers do take it very literally and presume that they can be as obnoxious as they like and still be valued. Any belief system that constantly puts one group in the right and the other in the wrong is both unreasonable and dangerous. Should a customer be allowed to bully a staff member because the customer is always right? Most of us serve customers, be they external or internal, in our jobs but spend the rest of the time being customers ourselves. We may complain about bad treatment from customers in our own jobs, but are we just as guilty when we become customers ourselves? Have you ever heard a colleague exclaim that something/someone will just have to wait because they are too busy and then give out when someone else makes them wait?

As we have have all experienced, some people are terrible at customer service and indeed this book is a small attempt to address that. However, many people are also terrible customers. They are rude, impatient, lack understanding and complain unreasonably. These are the people who wear down frontline staff, sometimes so demoralising them that previously very pleasant receptionists become defensive and suspicious. In my experience, it is often the people who are bad at customer service themselves who make the worst customers, as they carry with them a bad attitude and an overblown sense of entitlement. So ask yourself what kind of customer you are. Could you show more empathy to frontline staff? Do you think that if customers showed more courtesy as well then it would also improve the customer experience?

## How to be a better customer

In order to be a better customer, you can apply the same techniques that we would use in dealing with customers.

- Be courteous. Good manners impress everyone. Certainly the customer who behaves courteously will receive the same in return.
- Make a good first impression. Try not to be arrogant or aggressive. If you subject a stranger to a string of verbal abuse, you immediately put them on the defensive, and if you are the one who is in error, you are going to feel fairly foolish afterwards. Even if you are in the right and everything gets settled, then it is still going to be awkward. It's better to begin with a smile and a calm voice, which can set up a more positive relationship. You can get firmer later if you need to.
- Be organised. If you are complaining about a broken part on your television set, the first thing they will want to know is the make and model. If you don't know, they can't help you and you might get frustrated at having made a long journey for nothing. If you are organised and bring all the details with you, they might be able to sort you out in minutes.
- Use the employee's name, but use it respectfully and not too often. If you use it too much it can be perceived as patronising or intimidating.
- Have a good attitude. Don't go on the attack. People who have a bad attitude bring out the worst in others, thus justifying and self-perpetuating their negative view of the world. All employees are entitled to be treated with dignity.
- Be informed. For example, if you are travelling abroad, try to be as aware and as

sensitive as possible to cultural differences in your relationships with staff.

- Be careful about asking to see the manager. You are here for 10 minutes. The supervisor will be working with the employee for years. Don't assume that a supervisor is always going to take your side.
- Be thankful. Sure, they were paid to do the job, but everyone likes to be appreciated. It helps to establish a relationship between the customer and the business and may ensure that they will go the extra mile for you next time.
- Be reasonable. There is a story, probably apocryphal, about a certain American singing diva that complained bitterly and demanded a personal supply of electricity to be given to her during the 14 August 2003 power blackout that saw electricity supply cut off from approximately 45 million people in the north-eastern United States and south-eastern Canada for several hours. Asking for the impossible won't get it for you, but it will annoy a lot of staff.

## Written communication

### Business letters

When preparing a business letter:
- keep it short
- make it clear
- be polite
- ensure that your facts are correct
- check all spelling and grammar.

The business letter is an extremely important aspect of customer contact. The person who writes the letter, like the person who answers the phone, is an ambassador for the company they represent. How well a business letter is written, organised and presented influences the customer's perceptions of that company. It may be the only experience that customer has of the organisation and so their entire impression may be formed by that business letter. This is a very important consideration when composing business letters.

In business correspondence, the rule is 'keep it short'. Get straight to the point and avoid wasting your customer's time. Also make sure you have expressed yourself clearly. If your letter is vague or ambiguous you will waste time and money clearing up any problems it may cause. It will also annoy the customer and give them a bad impression of the efficiency of your company. Be careful, however, of making a letter so short that it sounds curt. Always use the polite formalities and include an opening and closing salutation.

Make sure that you have the correct name and address of the recipient and that you have included your own name, business address and contact number. Include any reference numbers that you are using for records plus the recipient's reference numbers. All this will save time and confusion later. For example:

Your ref: TGH/78L
Our ref: IRT/ZXC

It is a good idea to have a subject heading above the body of the letter. It should state clearly and concisely what the purpose of this business letter is. This will ensure that your letter is quickly channelled to the right recipient and will help with filing and record retrieval. Use any of the following styles:

RE: Project 23478X completion date
Re: Death duties
Subject: Account number 456732 OP

Use an appropriate opening and closing salutation, for example:

Dear Mr Browne
Dear Sir
Dear Sirs
Dear Miss Bledsoe

If you know and use the name of the person you are writing to, then use the closing salutation 'Yours sincerely':

Dear Mrs Fitzgerald
Yours sincerely

If you do not know or use the name of the person to whom you are writing in the opening salutation, use 'Yours faithfully' in the complimentary close/closing salutation:

Dear Sir
Yours faithfully

## Standard format for a fully blocked letter on letterheaded paper

When you are writing a business letter, check the list below to make sure you have the details in standardised form and that you have not omitted any important elements:

Your ref:
Our ref:
Private/Urgent/Confidential, as applicable
Date
For the attention of . . ., where applicable
Addressee
Opening salutation
Subject heading
Body of letter
Complimentary close
Company name
Name of correspondent
Enclosures, if applicable

If a letter is typed then it is often signed beneath the closing salutation by the person sending the letter. This means there is a typed version of the name so that it can be read easily and there is also a handwritten signature which gives the letter authority and the personal touch.

Examples of business letters are shown on pages 55–58.

## Memoranda

Memoranda are more commonly referred to as memos. They are a means of correspondence used for internal communications within a company.

A memo can vary in length and in the degree of formality. It could be a simple memo about lunch arrangements or a longer confidential document, such as an employee profile. Whatever the memo is about, remember that it is a business document. It should be signed and dated. If the memo is being sent to more than one person, list all their names on the memo so that each person knows who else has received it. If the memo is intended to be confidential, that should also be stated.

Here is an example of a memo form. These are generally used for short handwritten notes.

> **Sample memo layout**
>
> [Name of organisation]
>
> To: ...............................    Dept: ...........................
>
> From: ...........................    Dept: ...........................
>
> Subject: .........................    Date: ...........................
>
> .........................................................................
>
> .........................................................................
>
> .........................................................................
>
> .........................................................................

## Reports

### The brief

Before you begin to do any work on a report make sure that you know exactly what is being asked of you. Find out who wants the report and why. If you have any queries, ask before you begin or you risk your report being completely off the point. Make sure that you are aware of any limitations placed on your report. For example, if you are asked to report on the current health and safety standards in your office and to suggest ways in which standards might be improved, you might be told that improvements should not cost the company more than €10,000. Your recommendations must then observe that budget limitation. Find out the deadline. It is pointless submitting a wonderful report after the deadline. In business your report may be crucial before a certain date and obsolete afterwards so it is important to make sure that you meet deadlines. If you are given two months to do a report it is in the belief that it will take you two months to compile it, so begin as soon as possible.

## Research

The variety and style of your research will depend on the nature of your report. However, you will be using all or some of the following methods.

*Observation.* For example, if you were asked to report on the number of cars that used the company car park, when they used it and how long they stayed, you could simply sit in the car park with a watch and notepad and observe them.

*Interview.* You could ask the car park attendant how many cars parked there every day. You could ask him when the peak times occurred and how long people remained in the car park over the course of the day.

*Survey.* You could compile a questionnaire on the use of the car park and hand it out to drivers as they enter the car park.

*Experiment.* If you were examining the fire safety standards of a company, you could set off the fire alarm and measure response times. Or you could place an obstacle in front of the fire exit and log the time it took for someone to notice and remove it. You could light some papers to see if the fire alarms and sprinkler systems were working.

*Consultation.* This is when you get some expert advice to help you compile your report. You might ask a fire officer to point out the potential fire hazards that exist in your office.

*Background reading.* To help compile your report you might consult relevant books, magazines, newspapers and documents. You could also surf the Internet.

Before you begin your research, compile a list of relevant questions that you need answered. These will be the objectives of your research. Record the information that you have gathered on separate loose-leaf pages, carefully acknowledging your sources. In this way you can shuffle your information into whatever order you want. Leave plenty of space on every sheet to add more information.

## The format

As all reports differ, not every report will have an identical format, but your report will have some, if not all, of the following elements.

*Summary.* This is written last but is placed at the front of the report. Sometimes it is referred to as an executive summary. In business, people do not always have the time to read each report thoroughly. The summary enables them to get the gist of the report without reading the whole thing. Then if they find something in the summary they want to examine further they can go into the body of the report. Summaries are mainly included in longer reports.

*Terms of reference.* This is where the compiler of the report states the brief they have been given. For example: 'On 10th June 2011, the Managing Director, Mr O'Brien, asked me to compile a report on the manner in which the company car park is currently used and to suggest ways in which the car parking problems could be solved. The report was to be submitted by 9th September 2011.'

*Procedure/introduction.* In this section, the person who compiled the report outlines the methods used to obtain the information that forms the basis of their report. This is an important section as it adds credence to the rest of the report. People in business will not accept criticism or recommendations for change from groundless arguments.

*Findings.* Now the report writer gets to the body of the report and gives the results of their research.

*Conclusions/recommendations.* This section outlines the report writer's conclusions and recommendations. (Depending on the size of this section, it might be divided into two subsections for conclusions and recommendations.) A simple example of a conclusion and a recommendation would be if water was coming through a ceiling. You might conclude that the roof was leaking and the recommendation resulting from that conclusion would be that the roof should be prepared. When describing your conclusions and recommendations, it is best to be diplomatic rather than upset any colleagues unduly.

*Appendices (singular = appendix).* At the end of the report any further relevant information can be attached that is too cumbersome to include in the body of the report. You might attach maps, diagrams or some tabular information. These could then be referred to in the body of the report.

*Bibliography.* Here you list the books, papers and Internet sites that you consulted for research purposes. For example:

> Smith, John M. [*Book title*]. [Place of publication]: [Name of publisher], [Year of publication].

## Other forms of communication commonly used in business

Here are the relative advantages and disadvantages of various means of transmitting information.

### Facsimile transmission (fax)

*Advantages.* Transmission is fast. Quality of reproduction is excellent. Graphics can easily be sent anywhere. Feedback can be rapid and the cost is competitive. Documents do not have to be specially retyped for transmission, as with telex. Once the original document is correct, the reproduction made by the fax will also be correct. A fax will give you a printout confirming that your document has been received at the other end. As well as buying a fax machine, it is possible to rent one from a telephone company. However, now many computers have in-built fax facilities.

*Disadvantages.* Transmission is dependent on both sender and receiver having fax facilities. A fax can be engaged over long periods of time in the same way as a telephone can be. Sometimes the transmission gets disrupted. Faxes are at present mainly limited to the business environment. Faxes sent at busy times or when the office is empty can be overlooked, depending on where the fax machine is. Paper and ink must be replaced regularly. A fax cannot be used as evidence in a court of law.

## Telex

*Advantages.* There is no charge for telex connection. A broadcast telex allows you to send the same message simultaneously to up to ten different telex numbers. Modern telex terminals will set up the call, send and clear the message automatically. You can also have a VDU on your terminal with full word-processing facilities and high-speed printer and you can carry on using your word-processing facilities while your terminal is receiving messages. You can also use an easicall facility that sends routine messages at off-peak times and keeps retrying busy numbers. The great advantage of a telex is that a document sent by telex can be used in a court of law as it can be proved that it was sent at a specific time on a specific date.

*Disadvantages.* At present telex is more expensive to use than fax. You must pay a rental charge for the line each quarter and for the telex itself. There are charges for international calls, national calls and operator-assisted calls. The cost of the actual telex message is based on the transmitting time, duration and distance. Therefore, information must be expressed as concisely as possible. A document has to be retyped in order to be sent by telex. Graphics cannot be sent by telex.

## Electronic mail (e-mail)

*Advantages.* E-mail is fast and reliable. Replies can be sent quickly. Messages can be sent at times that are convenient to everyone. A receiver does not have to be at their computer at the time the message arrives in order to receive it. Special codes can be inserted so that messages can be read by authorised personnel only. Messages can be sent from anywhere once a computer and telephone are available. Messages can be sent to many people at once. If necessary, a printed copy of the e-mail can be obtained. Other documents and computer files such as graphics and spreadsheets can be sent along with or attached to the message. Information that is in electronic form can easily be edited or reused.

*Disadvantages.* E-mail printouts are less tidy than letters. E-mail is fast and convenient and may be used without thought. Security is poor unless encryption software is used. Many large companies and institutions are wary of it. Downloading information may allow viruses to infect your system. It can be expensive to use. You may be the target of unwanted advertising or other e-mail. E-mail has its own codes and jargon, which can be confusing. What you say in an e-mail message is never fully private and may come back to haunt you even after you thought that you had safely deleted it. It therefore can never be treated as confidential.

## Mobile phones

*Advantages.* These are very convenient. You can travel and work away from your office and still receive important calls. You can ring for assistance at the scene of an accident, if you get lost or if your house is being robbed. You can take your telephone around the world with you. People can ring you from home without the hassle of arranging times and locations. You can ring from anywhere without having to deal with local telephone systems. Several people travelling independently of one another can maintain contact easily. Nowadays, sending bulk SMS messages to clients is used more and more as a marketing and customer service tool. Salons will tell you by SMS when they are having a promotion and schools will SMS parents and students about exams. Stena Line Ferries will SMS your mobile to let you know if your sailing is due to depart on time.

*Disadvantages.* They can be expensive. It costs more to make and receive calls from mobiles. They can be stolen and used by others if they are turned on when taken. Most have a four-digit code which can be broken in a few hours. Their batteries have to be recharged regularly and have a tendency to run down at the least convenient times. Despite recharging, the batteries themselves need to be replaced after a while. They can have anti-social effects and may annoy others. Finally, with a mobile phone in your pocket, there is no escaping the office.

Turley's TV and Hi-Fi Store
4 Lester Square
Long Road
Ballyharrison
Co. Anywhere
Tel: 054-678 923
Fax: 054-789 764

Our ref: PFD/QW

15 October 2011

Mr Tom O'Brien
45 Main Street
Kinvara
Co. Anywhere

Re: Defective Mitsunami 6780 22" colour television

Dear Mr O'Brien

It was with a great deal of regret that I received your letter yesterday. I was surprised that a Mitsunami television set could be so troublesome. I assure you that this is one of our most tried and trusted brands. However, I have read the service records and can fully understand your anger and I am eager to rectify the situation as quickly as possible.

We have dealt with Mitsunami products for over 15 years and their products have always been of the highest standards. As you are well within your three-year warranty there will be no problem in replacing your television with another Mitsunami 6780. I would urge you to give Mitsunami another chance and if this set fails to satisfy your expectations, I will be happy to provide an equivalent replacement of the brand name of your choice.

If this solution is amenable to you, give me a call as soon as you can and I will make arrangements to replace your current set free of charge. Once again, I would like to apologise for the inconvenience caused to you.


Yours sincerely


Rosemary Turley
General Manager

Murphy & Clarke
Carpet Merchants
32 Main Street
Anytown
Tel: 055-556 655
Fax: 055-665 566

Your ref: abc/123
Our ref: def/456

12 February 2012

Mrs Vivienne Lockwood
Lockwood's Interior Design Services
4 The Square
Pemberly
Anothertown

Re: Outstanding balance on account no. 890

Dear Mrs Lockwood

It has come to our attention that the above account of 12 December 2011 has yet to be settled. The outstanding balance is currently €734.

We would be grateful if you would rectify this situation as soon as possible. For further information, please see the statement enclosed.

Yours sincerely

Lucinda Clarke
Accounts Dept

Enc

Murphy & Clarke
Carpet Merchants
32 Main Street
Anytown
Tel: 055-556 655
Fax: 055-665 566


Your ref: abc/123
Our ref: def/456

23 May 2012

Mrs Vivienne Lockwood
Lockwood's Interior Design Services
4 The Square
Pemberly
Anothertown

Re: Outstanding balance on account no. 890

Dear Mrs Lockwood

We have written to you three times since 12 February requesting that you settle your account of 12 December 2011. The outstanding balance is €734.

As we stated in our third letter, dated 2 April, if payment was not received by 30 April, then we would be forced to take legal action. As you have failed to respond to any of our letters, I am now informing you that legal action is being taken.


Yours sincerely


Phillippa Joyce
General Manager

**O'BRIEN & SMITH (TAX CONSULTANTS)**
26 High Street, Galway
Telephone: 0806-213 4672
Fax: 0806-213 5545

Our ref: TR/QOC

10th April 2012

Mr Michael Brennan
14 Castle Street
Listowel
Co. Kerry

Dear Mr Brennan

Tax

Thank you for your letter of 5th April in which you requested our assistance in dealing with your tax.

As you know, the government has introduced a new tax system for people in your situation called 'Self-Assessment'. According to this system it is up to you to correctly assess the amount of tax that you need to pay. Every year the Revenue Commissioners will investigate in detail a certain number of returns made by this method. Those investigated which have underestimated the amount of tax they are required to pay will incur heavy fines.

Please ring our offices as soon as you can so that we may arrange an appointment for you. We will go through all your documents and we will be pleased to help you return the correct amount of tax.

Yours sincerely

John O'Brien
ACCA

# Exercises

1. Define 'non-verbal communication'.

2. Give examples of positive body language behaviour.

3. Why is it important that customer contact staff are clean and well presented?

4. What are the consequences of having poorly trained customer contact staff, with negative attitudes, dealing with customers?

5. How can the slovenly appearance of a staff member affect the perceptions of a customer towards an otherwise excellent hotel?

6. A customer has written to you complaining about a cooker that she bought in your shop. It has been giving her trouble since she bought it six months ago. Compose a suitable letter in reply.

7. What are proximics?

8. Why is it important to have clear, concise and accurate business letters?

9. Why use headed notepaper?

10. Outline briefly how you would go about compiling and structuring a report.

11. Assess the following means of transmitting information: mobile phone; fax; electronic mail.

# 3

# ON THE TELEPHONE

---

Topics covered in this chapter:

- Why good telephone behaviour is so important
- How to prepare for and make a call
- Answering the telephone
- Listening to the caller
- How to deal with bomb threats made by telephone
- Telephone technique role-plays
- Self-assessment – how good is my telephone behaviour?

## Good telephone behaviour

No matter what your role in an organisation is, you will have to use the telephone at some stage. It is important to be able to use it correctly. It is amazing how many people give a terrible impression of themselves to customers over the phone. They would probably treat the customer much better if they were standing right in front of them. The explanation for this is that when we are on the phone, we cannot see the customer – it is far easier to be rude to someone you cannot see or who will never be able to recognise you. Just look at the way people behave when they are cocooned in the anonymity of their cars. It is also difficult to appreciate the circumstances of whoever is calling. They may have a disability, be standing on a building site or have a child swinging from each arm. This, of course, works both ways. Customers may not realise that they are calling you in the middle of a meeting or during some crisis. Customers also tend to be ruder on the phone than in person. They are not representing your company, however, so it is up to you to be the bigger person. Here are some guidelines for using the telephone.

### Before the call

- Make sure your office environment is as conducive to work as possible.
- Sit upright in a comfortable chair with good back support. This will help prevent your voice sounding constricted.
- Be prepared. Always have a pen and pad at the ready. A special telephone message pad is very useful because it prompts you to ask all the right questions. It is also very useful to

have a notebook nearby containing all the extension numbers of people in your organisation, their names, skeleton schedules and responsibilities. If you deal with specific queries, for example orders or invoices, then relevant information should be close at hand.

## Making the call

- Get the name and number of who you need to call.
- Get any area codes or extension numbers that may be necessary.
- Try to ring at a time when you have a good chance of contacting them, not at lunchtime, when they will probably be out of the office.
- Have a back-up contact to ask for if your first choice is not available.
- Compile a list of the things that you need to say. This will ensure that you don't forget anything important. You can tick off each point as it is dealt with and if you leave some space between each point, you can make brief notes.
- Be polite, but firm, with whoever answers the phone. Make sure that they have your number and understand clearly the purpose of your call.
- Make sure you speak clearly. Avoid slang, jargon or technical terms that might confuse others. Make sure that what you say is not ambiguous so as to avoid misinterpretation.
- Repeat key information.
- Thank them for taking your call.
- Maintain courtesy throughout.

## Answering the telephone

- Answer the phone within five rings.
- Never answer the phone at work with 'Hello'. An example of a suitable greeting would be: 'Browne's Office Supplies, Accounts Department, Elizabeth speaking. How may I help you?' A greeting should begin by giving the name of the organisation the caller has reached, the department and/or extension number and the name of the person answering the phone. Write out and practise a suitable greeting for the company you work for.

## Listen to the caller

- Listen carefully to the caller. Give them your full attention. If another task or the people around you are distracting you, then you are not listening fully. As a result you may take a message incorrectly or misdirect a caller. The caller may also realise that they do not have your attention and may get annoyed as a result. It will certainly create a bad impression of you and your company. If it is impossible for you to concentrate at this moment, for example during an important meeting, explain this to the caller and arrange to call them back at a more suitable time when you can give them your full attention. Find out exactly what the caller wants. Do not send them on to another department until you are sure that it is the correct place for them to go. There is nothing worse for the caller, and for the impression that is created by your company, than when they are passed around from extension to extension.

---

**Sample telephone message pad**

### Telephone message

From: .............................................   Date: ...............................................

To: .................................................   Time: ................................... am/pm

Address: ...........................................................................................................

Message: ...........................................................................................................

...........................................................................................................

...........................................................................................................

...........................................................................................................

Taken by: ........................................................................................................

---

- Make a careful note of the caller's details on your notepad. Get their name, their telephone number and any other relevant information. Where necessary, make a note of what the caller is saying. Be sure you understand what they are saying. We hear faster than we speak so you have a chance to make sure that you understand. We write more slowly than we speak so make only brief notes. If you try to write out sentences in full you will be left behind. If you do not understand something or if what the caller said was ambiguous, ask for clarification. If this can wait to when the caller is finished speaking, then wait; interruptions will cause the caller to lose track of what they are saying. Try to avoid becoming too fussy about irrelevant details. This will only waste time and annoy the caller. If for some reason you cannot understand the caller do not pretend that you do. We may not to wish to embarrass someone with a strong accent, poor English or a speech impediment by asking them to repeat themselves but they will be far more annoyed when your politeness means that their call was ineffective or misinterpreted. Ask them politely to repeat slowly what they said. Be patient with the caller and do not assume that just because you are having difficulty understanding them that they have difficulty in hearing or understanding you. Resist the urge to shout or speak unnecessarily slowly down the line. If you feel that they have trouble understanding you, ask them diplomatically, then change your speech accordingly.
- Repeat key phrases back to the caller to make sure you got all the information right.
- Always repeat tricky information such as telephone numbers back to the caller for their verification.
- If you have to leave the caller waiting on the line, explain why. They will be far more understanding if they know why they are waiting.

- Offer to put the caller on hold or to call them back if necessary. Give them the choice. It can be very frustrating and expensive to be put on hold so always try to give the caller other options.
- If the caller opts to call or be called back, arrange a mutually suitable time and stick to it.
- If you tell a caller that you will call back at a certain time, then do so, even if you have failed to complete whatever task they had requested of you within the time. If you call back and tell them that you have been unsuccessful or that the task is incomplete, they will know that you have tried and that you haven't forgotten them. If you don't bother to call back, they will assume you didn't attempt to deal with their request. Therefore it is always good customer care practice to call back when you said you would even if the news is bad.
- If you leave a caller on hold, make sure that you service the call every 45 seconds. Don't leave them dangling on the line indefinitely.
- If, when you are dealing with their request, you find that it is taking longer than you had anticipated, again offer them the option of calling back.
- Never shout across the room at someone when you are on the phone.
- Never be over-familiar on the phone. Use your own judgment and discretion when it comes to using first names or being in any way familiar with regular callers.
- Do not use slang on the phone. For example, do not say 'hang on' or 'just a sec'.
- Do not talk on the phone while eating, drinking, smoking, chewing gum or even with a pencil in your mouth. These all impede your speech. They also give the impression that you are taking this call very casually.
- Smile while you are talking on the phone. It may not be seen but it warms the tone of your voice.
- Never lose your temper or be sarcastic on the phone. Do not take difficult calls personally. Anyone who uses the telephone professionally will inevitably receive difficult calls. Deal with them as politely as possible; remember to have a professional attitude towards them.
- Always thank the caller for their call. This might be hard sometimes, but it does end the call on a positive note.
- If you have listened to the customer's complaint fully and sympathetically and have tried to help, sometimes a customer will still go on dwelling on the initial complaint rather than co-operating with you in finding a solution. To stop them from going on, simply keep quiet. Make no more listening noises; if you have a mute button, use it. The caller will quickly notice and stop. This gives you an opportunity to take control of the call.
- Another way of getting their attention is by asking them a relevant question. This gets you back into a conversation with the caller.
- If a caller is angry and won't listen or acknowledge what you are saying, repeat your assurances and explanations until they are ready to listen.
- Try to maintain a positive attitude and be as helpful as possible. If the caller realises that you sincerely want to help them they will be more understanding.

## Self-assessment

It is hard for us to imagine the impression we give of ourselves on the phone. Often we are surprised when we hear a recording of our own voice. We wonder if we really sound like that and if our accent is that strong. The caller may also pick up on our attitude towards our work or our customers, though we may not realise it. The key to improving flaws in our telephone technique is continual assessment. As you begin to learn about the professional use of the telephone and as you develop your skills, constantly monitor your progress.

This chapter contains role-play telephone conversations for you to practise (see pages 66–80). The first section contains guidelines for the caller while the bottom section is for the candidate dealing with the complaint. The candidate should try to avoid reading the first section and should only respond to the information given by the caller. Where possible, record these conversations. It is the best way to discover where your weaknesses lie.

On page 81 there is also a self-assessment sheet. Use this as a model to monitor your progress.

## How to deal with bomb threats made by telephone

The following details were issued by the Crime Prevention Unit, Harcourt Square, Dublin 2. Keep them in your desk.

---

It is important that a telephonist, on receipt of a bomb threat, should not panic. So as to reduce confusion and assist the appropriate authorities, every effort should be made to obtain and record the information outlined below:
- Note the exact time of the call.
- Note the exact words of the threat, particularly the location of the bomb and when it is going to explode.

ASK:
- Where is the bomb now?
- What does it look like?
- When is it going to explode?
- Who planted it?
- Why was it planted?

- Note whether the voice is male or female.
- Note the accent of the caller.
- Note whether the caller sounds intoxicated.
- Note any background noises – traffic, music, voices, etc.
- Note if the voice is familiar – who?
- Note the time that the caller hung up.
- Notify your manager, security officer and the Gardaí immediately on receipt of the call.

---

## Exercises

1. Answering the phone – imagine you are working for the following organisations. Prepare what you would say if you were answering the telephone.

   a. Linda's Antiques (096) 43048

   b. Megavision Cineplex (567) 234 56710 – booking section

   c. VJ's Home Exercise Equipment Warehouse (01) 820 28035

   d. Abbey Business Machines (066) 501 172

   e. Dalumar Ltd (061) 546 4744

   f. O'Driscoll, Karen M., Barrister-At-Law, Courthouse Chambers (034) 27 51 51, Ext. 6786.

2. Compose answerphone messages for the following:

   a. Athlone College of Further Education

   b. Georgeson's Bank, 12 Adler's Street, Tralee

   c. Betty's Bookstore

   d. Lordan's pub, Main Street, Mallow

   e. Dr James O'Brien, dermatologist

   f. Tom Murray's cell phone

   g. Galway Regional Hospital's switchboard

   h. John and Clara O'Brien's house phone.

3. A customer rings up to complain about a day tour around Ireland organised by your bus company. Outline briefly the steps you would take to deal with that customer over the phone.

## Role-plays for practical skills test

*At the airport*

Mrs Veronica Murphy is a busy executive on a routine flight from London to San Francisco. She has to stop at Shannon Airport and at New York to change planes. Her schedule is as follows:

| | |
|---|---|
| Depart London 7.30am | Arrive Shannon 8.25am |
| Depart Shannon 9.40am | Arrive New York 10.25am (3.05pm GMT) |
| Depart New York 11.30am | Arrive San Francisco 3.30pm (6.30pm East Coast Time; 11.30pm GMT) |

Mrs Murphy has an important lecture to give to members of her company in San Francisco at 9am the next day. Her lecture is to be based on current European currency rates. She had information on these rates stored on her laptop and had intended to work on this information on the two connecting flights from Shannon to New York and from New York to San Francisco. As the flight from London to Shannon was so short, she decided that she would store the laptop in the baggage hold with the rest of her luggage and just relax. She had intended to spend her short stopover in Ireland buying Irish whiskey in the duty-free and having a full Irish breakfast at Bewleys. However, when she went to retrieve her baggage from the carousel at Shannon Airport, her laptop was nowhere to be seen. Subsequent searches by the ground staff have proven fruitless. She is very anxious when she contacts you. It is already 9.25am.

## Notes for candidates

*At the airport*

You work in the baggage department in Dublin Airport. You can contact the following:

- baggage handlers
- the information desk
- airport security
- first-aid and emergency services
- the restaurant
- other airports
- airport insurance
- customer complaints
- duty-free.

Your immediate superior is Elizabeth Greenway, head of the baggage department.

## Role-plays for practical skills test

*Faulty goods*

Thomas Connery is returning a pair of Italian leather shoes that he had bought in the luxury goods department of a large shop for €600. He says that the girl behind the counter promised him that they were waterproof. He has a receipt. He is very angry. He thinks that the salesgirl is a liar and he wants her fired. He remembers when a man could buy a decent pair of shoes for six shillings in a proper shoe shop, not like these ruddy department stores. In those days, only men served behind the counter and all shoes were made to measure. Things have gone downhill since women started all this feminism rubbish ...

The only thing wrong with the shoes is the fact that they were stained but he tries to make it sound worse. He had bought them for a social event but had worn them out in his farmyard. He has not tried to clean them, he's not a woman, you know ...

## Notes for candidates

*Faulty goods*

Your job is to deal with goods that are being returned. You can refuse a refund if the customer has no receipt, if the guarantee has run out or if the goods have been abused or tampered with. You can contact the following areas:

- the luxury goods department
- the manufacturer
- your immediate departmental superior, Mr Smith
- accounts
- security.

## Role-plays for practical skills test

*At the office*

Clare Sheehan has been trying to get in contact with Fred Murphy for the past three weeks. She wants to order some shelving for her new clothes retail outlet. Fred had promised her a discount. However, she cannot wait any longer and is frankly disgusted by Fred and the company that he works for. She wants shelving for a space 80 x 125 feet. The front wall will not need shelves. It is one of the shorter walls. Her floor is pinewood so she will want shelving that matches. She would like all fittings to be fully adjustable and to run on wheels for mobility. She would like a quote by this afternoon. Her office telephone number is 01-546 7732. Her mobile phone number is 087-976 4421 and the number of the retail outfit is 01-342 5678. She will be at the retail outlet until midday.

## Notes for candidates

*At the office*

You are answering the phones while everyone else is at lunch. You have a list of telephone numbers for all departments, including:

- sales
- despatch
- accounting
- marketing
- administration
- complaints
- stocks.

Fred Murphy is a sales rep with the company. His telephone number is 088-456 456. You also have a complete list of all your company's products in front of you. Your products are sold by metrical measurements. The price quoted on your list does not include labour, haulage or VAT.

TELEPHONE TECHNIQUES 4

## Role-plays for practical skills test

*At the restaurant*

Kevin Lynch rang Chez Maurice to book a table for 8.30pm on 1st September of this year. He had waited for two whole months for this table as it is a very popular and exclusive restaurant. He had intended to propose to his girlfriend, Valerie, there. On arrival, they were forced to wait for 40 minutes before they were seated. No explanation was given for this delay other than the waiter saying, 'If you want the best, then you should be prepared to wait.' They had to borrow a menu from another table and had to wait another ten minutes before anyone took their order. The starter took 25 minutes to arrive and all they had ordered was a salad. Valerie is a vegetarian and when she ordered the main course, she was told that they had run out of the vegetarian option as it was very popular. When she asked if she could have a baked potato instead, there was a grudging reluctance to prepare it. The main course took another 35 minutes to arrive. When the bill came, Kevin was disgusted to see that he had been charged €15.50 for Valerie's potato.

**TELEPHONE TECHNIQUES 4**

## Notes for candidates

*At the restaurant*

You are an assistant manager at Chez Maurice. Maurice is the chef and also your father. You can contact him or any of the staff.

## TELEPHONE TECHNIQUES 5

### Role-plays for practical skills test

*At the supermarket*

Gillian Doherty is a busy woman. She has a job and a young family. Her husband works very long hours. Last Saturday, she was forced to take her two small children shopping with her. When she arrived, she discovered that the crèche was being renovated. She could not find any trolleys with children's seats, as all of them were in use, and she had to put her children in a regular trolley. Her daughter hurt herself as a result. It took her two hours to do her shopping this way. Her groceries were squashed and melting by the time she had got them to the checkout. Then her son grabbed at a chocolate-covered apple that was displayed near the counter. It had no wrapping on it, which she found very unhygienic. Before she had a chance to stop him, he had stuck it in his mouth. Mrs Doherty was very upset as her son is allergic to chocolate, it gives him severe stomach pain and a rash. She had been bagging groceries by herself when this happened. The girl at the checkout insisted that she pay for the chocolate apple, something that she would not have given to her son even if it had been free. She is very unhappy with the treatment she has received. If she had known that the crèche was unavailable, she would have gone elsewhere. She suspects that that is the reason no notice to that effect was put up.

## TELEPHONE TECHNIQUES 5

### Notes for candidates

*At the supermarket*

You are dealing with all incoming telephone calls. You can contact any staff you choose, including maintenance men and your direct superior, Marion Boyle.

## TELEPHONE TECHNIQUES 6

### Role-plays for practical skills test

*At the gym*

Gerry Walsh joined the gym to get fit. His time is limited, but he was assured that he would be able to get a thorough workout. Everything was fine for the first month, but now he finds that he has to queue between pieces of equipment and as a result he cannot get a good workout. He warms up, but by the time he gets to the next activity, he has been waiting so long that he is cold.  Also, the trainer who is on hand is only interested in his most advanced clients. He seems irritated when Gerry asks him a question and makes him feel like a proper weed. It has put him right off all this keep-fit business, so he would like his money back. He would like to be fit, but he does not like being bored or embarrassed. Money is not a huge incentive for him, so he might be persuaded to stay.

## TELEPHONE TECHNIQUES 6

### Notes for candidates

*At the gym*

The gym has just been taken over by the company you work for.  Your job is to deal with all telephone enquiries.  You can contact any member of staff you like.  The old staff still work there. Management is keen to keep on all the gym's original customers. You are allowed to offer them a discount. It is up to you to use your customer service skills and powers of persuasion.

## TELEPHONE TECHNIQUES 7

### Role-plays for practical skills test

*At the garage*

Peter Green had booked his car in to be serviced at 9.30am. He had to drive to Galway in the afternoon for an important appointment. The garage assured him that it would be ready within two hours. They quoted him the price of €60 over the phone. Peter left his car with them and went for a stroll to kill time. There was no waiting area and when it rained Mr Green had to hover in one of the nearby sheds where cars were for sale. He was embarrassed when the salesman tried to sell him a car. When he returned to the garage, he found that his car had not yet been touched. It was now 11.30am. He had to leave for Galway by 2pm. They assured him that the work would still be done on time. He had to leave the garage again as there was no place for him to wait. He returned at 12.30pm. The car was now without tyres and mounted on a stand. The mechanics had all gone for lunch and the garage was empty. Mr Green discovered that his car had been left unlocked and that anyone could easily have stolen its contents. The mechanics returned at 1.15pm. They then began to work on the car, but were not finished until 2.30pm. Mr Green had been left hanging around the village for five hours even though he had been guaranteed that the job would only take two. He was late beginning his journey to Galway. To top all this, the final bill came to €95. The mechanics had changed his brake shoes and spark plugs without consulting him. He was in such a hurry at the time that he didn't have an opportunity to argue, but he is calling now to register his disgust.

## TELEPHONE TECHNIQUES 7

### Notes for candidates

*At the garage*

You work in the office of Smith's Auto Repairs and Car Sales. You are in charge of administration. You can consult the mechanics or your boss, John Smith.

## Role-plays for practical skills test

*At the dentist*

Mary Adams had no appointment but she was in agony. She rang her own dentist, Dr Howland, who performs her regular check-ups. Dr Howland's secretary was extremely unhelpful. She told her that the dentist was too busy to see her and that Mrs Adams should make an appointment like everyone else. When Mary started crying, the secretary snorted and slammed down the phone. Mary went to another dentist instead who dealt with her toothache immediately. She is now calling to have her dental files transferred to her new dentist.

## Notes for candidates

*At the dentist*

You work as a secretary for Dr Howland. The other secretary, who also works there, is a bit brusque. Try to persuade Mrs Adams to reconsider her decision.

## TELEPHONE TECHNIQUES 9

### Role-plays for practical skills test

*At the travel operators*

Jenny Dawson booked a holiday from Breakaway Travel. She picked out the holiday that she wanted from a brochure. When she arrived there, she was terribly disappointed. The hotel was much further from the sea than she had been led to believe. The view that she had admired in the brochure had been replaced by another big ugly hotel. There was no running water in her apartment except what ran from her broken fridge. She had repeatedly asked the staff to fix it but they did nothing. The noise from the hotel disco meant that she could never sleep. The hotel had boasted in the brochure that it had air-conditioning but it hadn't been installed by the time Jenny had arrived. She blames the travel agency and she is demanding compensation. She will take her business elsewhere in future.

## TELEPHONE TECHNIQUES 9

### Notes for candidates

*At the travel operators*

You work for Breakaway Travel. Your agency books accommodation and flight packages from the company who compiled the brochure. While you do have a responsibility to your client, you were acting in good faith and believed the brochure to be accurate. You can contact the brochure company or any member of your staff. Your priority is to retain your customer's good faith.

## TELEPHONE TECHNIQUES 10

### Role-plays for practical skills test

*At the concert*

Amy Kelly booked two front-row seats for a concert by Barbara Breisind.  They cost €50 each. It was supposed to be a two-hour concert. Barbara sang for 40 minutes and then left in a huff.  The management refused to refund Amy Kelly's ticket.  She is very angry. She rings up the customer service department of Concerts of Cork for help. She is so upset that she tends to waffle on a bit.

## TELEPHONE TECHNIQUES 10

### Notes for candidates

*At the concert*

You work for Concerts of Cork. Your company deals with quality assurance for all musical events in the Cork area.  You can contact the promoters of the concert or those of the singer.  You can also contact legal sources and other watchdog bodies.

## TELEPHONE TECHNIQUES 11

### Role-plays for practical skills test

*At the cinema*

Frank Touhy waited a week to get a ticket to see *Raise the Lusitania.* He was in the cinema watching the 'three-hour extravaganza' when the fire alarm sounded. It took the audience ten minutes to file out. He was then standing outside for another 15 minutes before the all clear was sounded. By the time he sat back down in his seat, 35 minutes of the film had elapsed. It had been playing away while Frank and the rest of the audience were outside. The projectionist wouldn't rewind it because it would interfere with the scheduling of later screenings that night. No refund was offered and Frank is very annoyed.

## TELEPHONE TECHNIQUES 11

### Notes for candidates

*At the cinema*

You work at the ticket desk of Megamovieplex. You can call any member of staff that you wish, except your manager, Mr Smedley, who is away on holiday. It is not in your power to grant refunds or complimentary tickets. However, you should be aware of company policy in these circumstances and be able to advise customers.

## TELEPHONE TECHNIQUES 12

## Dealing with queries

*At the train station*

Joan Foley has just arrived at Pearse Street railway station from Dublin Airport. She wants to spend the day in Dublin and needs a place to store her luggage. She also needs to know where she can convert some Australian dollars into euros. She is travelling to Cork this evening but needs to be there by 11.30pm. She telephones the tourist information office from the railway station.

## TELEPHONE TECHNIQUES 12

## Notes for candidates

*At the train station*

You work at the railway station, where you have a complete list of all the train timetables. You also have a phone and a telephone directory. Remember that good customer service means exceeding the customer's expectations.

## TELEPHONE TECHNIQUES 13

### Dealing with queries

*At the bank*

Lillian Kinsley is eighty-five years old and a bit hard of hearing. She has just acquired an ATM card. She has attempted to use it with no success. She isn't sure which way the card goes in, what a PIN is and what kind of account she has. She tried to withdraw €27.56 to pay for her bill without success. This much progress took several attempts.

## TELEPHONE TECHNIQUES 13

### Notes for candidates

*At the bank*

You are working in the main branch of the bank when this call comes through. Try to explain to Mrs Kinsley how to use the ATM card correctly.

## TELEPHONE TECHNIQUES 14

## Dealing with compliments

*At the bed & breakfast*

Kurt and Petra Schmidt have just spent a wonderful week at Rainview Guesthouse. They ring the following week to compliment the couple who run the guesthouse. They were delighted with their room, the friendly staff, the generous breakfast and the value for money.

## TELEPHONE TECHNIQUES 14

## Notes for candidates

*At the bed & breakfast*

You run Rainview Guesthouse with your spouse. Respond to Kurt and Petra's praise. Remember that you are running a business.

## TELEPHONE TECHNIQUES 15

### Dealing with praise

*At the French class*

Cyril has just swapped from his Thursday night intermediate French class to the Tuesday night one. He thinks that his previous teacher, Mr Farrell, was terrible and that his new teacher is fabulous. He rings his new teacher to pass on his feelings.

## TELEPHONE TECHNIQUES 15

### Notes for candidates

*At the French class*

You are Cyril's new French teacher. Mr Farrell is a colleague of yours. Respond diplomatically to Cyril's praise.

## Customer service

### Self-assessment for telephone techniques

Name of candidate: _____

Class code: _____

Please assess critically your own performance in dealing with customers on the phone over the course of your academic year. Take into account your specific telephone technique classes, any telephone technique assessments done in school and any telephone duties you performed during your work experience. Grade yourself as follows: 1 = very poor; 5 = satisfactory; 10 = excellent.

Did I answer the phone promptly? _____

Did I use the appropriate opening salutation? _____

Did I get the information I needed from the caller? _____

Did I get the information as efficiently as possible? _____

Did I repeat back key information and numbers to the caller
to ensure they were accurate? _____

Did I remember to use the caller's name? _____

Did I listen carefully to the customer? _____

Did I take notes and use appropriate listening noises? _____

Did I handle complaints in a positive manner? _____

Did I use an appropriate tone throughout? _____

Did I smile during the telephone call? _____

Did I thank the customer for calling? _____

Did I promise to take appropriate action? _____

Did I take that action? _____

How was my attitude throughout the call? _____

Did I promptly convey all information to the appropriate people? _____

Did I correctly convey that information? _____

Did I use the call-hold function with consideration for my callers? _____

What is my own opinion of my overall performance on the telephone? _____

Total _____

Comments _____

_____

_____

# 4

# TEAMWORK

## The characteristics of a successful team

A successful team is made up of individuals with different skills and aptitudes, different experiences and different personality traits that help the team deal with a variety of problems and situations. Each member understands and accepts the objectives of the team they are in and fully realises their role within the team. They understand the limits of their role and also its responsibilities. Thus, they do not seek to expand their role by encroaching on another team member, nor do they try to shift some of their responsibility onto another team member. Each member accords respect to every other member and each accepts responsibility for their own mistakes and failings.

A successful team also has a strong leader who respects and values each member of the team. The leader is willing to take advice from other members and does not always insist on having their own way. They will credit the individual efforts of all the team. In addition, a successful team has the tools and materials it needs to complete its task, whether this is money, information or a spade each.

### Team members

A successful team is greater than the sum of its members. In other words, a team should work more effectively than any individual alone and better than any group of individuals working independently of each other. Otherwise there is no point in forming a team. The key to a successful team is in the selection of its members. You need team members who are appropriate for the tasks that you hope you will achieve with them. They need to have relevant skills and suitable personalities. You might need a lot of people with specialist skills in a particular area. For example, you might be forming a team to develop a new drug. In such a case, you would need chemists with specialist skills quite specific to the aim of the team. On the other hand, if you were building a house, you might need a variety of skills, say, an architect, a bricklayer, a plumber, a carpenter, a painter and an electrician.

You also need to have different personality types within a team. While you need an effective leader, the important point is that you need only one effective leader. Otherwise it will be a case of too many cooks spoiling the broth. There are different personality types that contribute to the success of a team. In the initial stages of team formation, there may be some awkwardness as people find their role and position within the team. This will continue if you have too many similar personality types jockeying for the same positions. It will lead to a negative competitive situation within the team, which will distract the team members from their goals.

## What personality types do you need in your team?

### Leaders

First of all, a successful team needs an effective leader. It is important to choose carefully because the leader is crucial to the overall atmosphere and success of the team. You need to select someone with excellent leadership skills.

- *Perceptiveness.* A team leader should have the perception to realise when things are going wrong even if others do not yet realise it or omit to mention it.
- *Judgment.* A team leader should be an excellent judge of the character and skills of their team members. In that way the leader can get the most out of the team.
- *Fairness.* All members should be treated equally. No member should be privileged over the others. This will only end in resentment among the team members and will weaken the leader's authority as respect for the leader diminishes. It is not enough to be fair, however. The leader must also be seen to be fair. For example, if some special consideration is made for a team member then the reason for that concession should be made clear. If, then, in another situation further discretion is needed, members will understand because they will trust their team leader. Finally, remember that the team leader is also a member of the team. Therefore they should not let themselves off more lightly than the other members. A team leader who demands perfection from their team and then fails to do their own job satisfactorily is a hypocrite and will earn the contempt of the others.
- *Reasonableness.* There is a big difference between being fair and being reasonable. Being fair involves treating all members equally. Being reasonable means not asking for more than they can reasonably be expected to deliver. 'I want it yesterday' is an example of an unreasonable demand. It puts members under negative pressure because they know before they start that no matter how hard they work they will fail

to satisfy the unreasonable expectations set by their team leader. An unattainable deadline does not motivate people because they will feel they have failed before they have even tried. No matter how quickly they have completed the task, they will expect only criticism from the team leader.

- *Good communication skills.* Good communication is vital to the success of a team and it is essential that the team leader has strong communication skills. A team leader should be able to communicate clearly and effectively what the goals of the team are. They should be aware of the importance of keeping the entire team up to date with the latest developments at all times. This will prevent the need for team members to depend on rumour and speculation for their information. In large organisations this would form itself into an informal communication network, commonly known as the grapevine. The grapevine grows as information diminishes. Teams with the least information have the biggest grapevines. A big grapevine is a negative sign. It means that a team lacks information and is discouraged from acquiring any. A good team leader would not only impart information but would welcome questions. It is not enough to growl 'Any questions?' threateningly at the end of the meeting. That is bullying and people will be afraid to ask any. A good communicator is open to questions but also to comments. The other team members should feel that they can approach the team leader with problems and suggestions. If they are afraid to do so then the problem will go untended and may escalate as a result. Part of good communication is listening and team members will stop making suggestions if they are not listened to. The purpose of a team is that all contribute to its success. If the team leader oppresses the team then it becomes a team in name only.

- *Determination.* Leading can be hard. You have a responsibility to your team and also to achieve the task that you have been set. It can be difficult striking a good balance between the two. It can also be difficult dealing with external pressures. When problems occur, the team leader is expected to sort them out. Therefore it is important that the team leader is not someone who gives up easily.

- *Responsibility.* A team leader should be able to act responsibly and accept the benefits and disadvantages of the position. This may involve taking credit for a job well done but also accepting blame when an error has been made and working towards a solution.

- *Confidence.* To inspire confidence in your team, you must first have confidence in yourself. If the team leader is seen to be unsure then this will translate into panic among the other team members.

- *Human resource skills.* A good team leader should be able to deal effectively with people. This means being able to understand and respect their position within the team. It also means doing your best to make sure that others are happy and secure in their role within the team. This will boost team spirit and, as a consequence, productivity.

### Supervisors

The supervisor supervises the team and oversees the work being done, suggesting improvements to help quality and output. They put together the work of the entire team and retain an awareness of the tasks of the team through every stage of its development.

### Researchers

The researcher collects data related to the team's tasks. This can be general background information or it can be highly specialised.

### Analysts

An analyst collects information in relation to the team's task at every stage of development. Beforehand this person will perform a feasibility study to determine the value of achieving a certain goal and will look at various ways of working towards the goal.

### Communicators

A good communicator will ensure that all members of the team are kept up to date. They will also build a good rapport between team members. The communicator can also act as an external spokesperson for the team. This can be an important role as the communicator can strongly affect the way in which the team is perceived. A good communicator will be able to effectively use the many means of communication available, mainly the written and spoken word, the Internet and the mass media. A good communicator will know the value of good personal and environmental presentation as well as the effective use of body language.

### Performers

A performer is a person who gets things done, the one who works most directly towards the achievement of the goal.

### Instigators

The instigator is the person who gets the ball rolling. They come up with the ideas and inspire other team members.

### Motivators

The motivator helps other people perform better. They motivate by advice, support and by example. They are invaluable in the middle of a project, when enthusiasm is most likely to flag.

It is important to note that the qualities outlined above are not descriptions of individuals. They are qualities which will be found in different combinations and in various quantities within a team. For example, a person who is good at research might also be very good at analysis. A good communicator is often a good instigator. So you might have several qualities in one person. The trick is to select people so that you have all the team qualities that you need and in the right balance.

A successful team should have:

* respect for each member and credit for their individual contribution
* acceptance of the responsibility and limits of each role
* the necessary resources at hand.

## The stages in a team's life

B.W. Tuckman, in his paper 'Development sequence in small groups' (1965), recognised four key stages in a team's life. He referred to these as:

* forming
* storming
* norming
* performing.

### Forming

Forming is at the very beginning of a team's life when the members are unsure of their own role within the group and are wary of the other group members. This is the stage at which the goals and attitudes of the group are identified. Those who do not fit in with the developing identity of the group may choose to leave, may be asked to leave by other members or may simply feel unwelcome. The members who do fit in will have similar goals and may begin to gel as a cohesive unit. Sometimes it can be hard for new members to join a group after this forming stage.

To help the forming process, you can create leisure activities where the group can work together as a team and encourage informal social events where members can get to know each other better.

### Storming

Storming is the stage where people stop feeling the need to be polite to each other and is characterised by conflict as people struggle for position within the group. There may be conflict over the ultimate aims of the group and there may also be personality clashes. Through these confrontations the individuals will come to a greater understanding of the other personalities in the group. Hidden agendas may be revealed and a threat may be posed to the leader of the group. There may also be some changeover of team members at this stage.

It is important for the designated team leader to assert their authority at this stage, to use fairness and good judgment in assigning roles and goals to team members and in doing so take the basis for conflict out of the hands of individual members.

### Norming

This is the stage where norms are established and the pattern of the team is set. Everyone now knows what everyone else is capable of and, from that knowledge, realistic expectations for each team member are established. People may be shifted to different positions in the team once their true skills have been recognised and all the team will come to recognise what they as a unit can hope to achieve together. The particular strengths and weaknesses of the team and its members have been ascertained.

While a team may be flawed, as long as it is better than the sum of its parts, it is worth maintaining. A team that fails to move from the storming to the norming phase should be disbanded. To ensure that a team moves to this stage, support and encouragement should be offered. Otherwise the team may feel that it is getting nowhere. Norming also involves ensuring that a regular working routine is established for the team.

## Performing

Performing is the final stage in the development of a successful team. At this stage the team members settle into their roles and work productively together. Everyone feels that they are contributing to the team effort and that their work is recognised. No one is 'carrying' anyone else.

To get the best from your team allow them some measure of autonomy. A team that is confident and independent is more proactive and productive.

Clearly Tuckman's model of the stages in group development is a general one. Teams do not always form all at once. Many teams are constantly expanding or changing their members. This can mean that the forming, storming and norming stages may have to be continually repeated on a smaller scale. Too much of this can lead to team fatigue, where, because of the transitory nature of some of its members, the more established members of the team are no longer motivated to make an effort to get to know them. Clearly it is in the best interests of a team if the same members remain over a long period of time, so management should support and encourage the team every step of the way. Incentives should be offered to encourage people to remain within the team.

---

### Bullying

A bully is someone who uses a position of greater authority, physical and or mental strength to intimidate those in a weaker position.

There is no place for a bully within a successful team. They bully in order to increase their influence and/or to hide their own inadequacies. A bully doesn't necessarily hit or push a person around physically. They may use verbal intimidation. They may threaten violence or disciplinary action. They may threaten to spread rumours. They may deliberately invade the privacy or personal space of their victim. They may continually single out one person for special censure to not only intimidate that person, but to intimidate other team members. The days of the bully are numbered, however, as more and more legislation comes into place to deal with this sinister and cowardly practice.

## Identify your own weaknesses

As children, we imagine that we can do anything, or be anyone. As we get older we realise that we are better at some things than we are at others. Perhaps we realise that we are good at mathematics but bad at history or that we are good at football but bad at athletics. As we become more self-aware we may realise that we like subjects that we are good at because we are good at them and that if we tried harder at other subjects we might learn to appreciate them as well. We learn what our strengths and weaknesses are. We can then play to our strengths and work to improve our weaknesses. We might even turn a weakness into a strength. We can develop and improve ourselves with effort, but we cannot all reach the same level of achievement at everything. If that were possible it would be a terrible prospect; we would all be exactly alike. So while we should not be complacent about ourselves – 'I'm untidy, that's just the way I am' – neither should we expect perfection. When we reach our limit we should accept that we have done our best.

When you go out to the workplace, you will be putting into practice all that you have learned. School and work are two very different environments, however, and you will be learning a lot that you could not possibly have experienced in school. For example, in school many people of similar age and background with similar goals generally surround you. At work you might be the only beginner and you might be sharing your break with people far older or younger than you. The word-processing or accounting package you learned at school might be far newer or older than the one you now have to deal with and it might be your first experience at discovering what a temperamental machine the photocopier can be. You may find that your boss is lacking in understanding and/or is very demanding.

In this new environment it will be very useful to reflect on each day and to learn from your successes or failures. Here you will learn about your strengths and weaknesses. In many ways failures are more instructive because they can point to areas you need to improve on. There is a saying that 'the man who never made a mistake never made anything'. If you make a mistake, ask yourself why. Is it because you were disorganised? If you labelled documents and folders more clearly in future, for example, would it eliminate the possibility of you making that error again? Ask yourself how you behaved when you made the mistake. Did you sulk? Did you deny that it was your fault, either to yourself or to others? Did you develop a hostile attitude towards the person who pointed out your error? Could you have had a more positive response?

Look at the list of qualities needed by team members above and ask yourself the following questions:

- Which do you have and which do you lack?
- Do you think you have the right qualities to be a team leader?
- Would you like to take on any of the above roles?
- How close are you to being suitable for that role?
- What do you need to work on to make yourself suitable for the team role that you want?
- Do you think you are a team player?

- What would you like about being part of a team?
- What would you dislike about being part of a team?
- Can you handle constructive criticism?
- Are you a bully?

## The benefits of teamwork

By getting people to work in teams, communications are enhanced. People that would otherwise have little or no contact with each other – say, people from different departments – have the chance to develop a much greater understanding of one another's problems, and this will make them all more tolerant when there are inter-departmental difficulties or delays.

There will be a greater pool of ideas to work from. There will also be more immediate feedback. For example, a new idea can be evaluated immediately by all the people in the group from different departments rather than time and money being wasted developing a proposal and circulating information leaflets.

As everyone is communicating effectively there will be less danger of overlap where two or more people are working separately on the very same thing.

All this greater communication will lead to improved morale as people will feel they are being listened to and are contributing in a meaningful way to their organisation.

## Some final points about teams

- When selecting members be very careful to pick people who are receptive to the ideas of others.
- Remember that each team member is an individual with particular strengths, needs, goals and weaknesses. Treat each member as an individual and make sure they realise that their efforts are being recognised and appreciated.
- Be clear with your staff about what you want them to do.
- Be very careful when you select team goals. Too many small goals will fragment your work and lead to confusion. One large goal may cause the team to lose heart. Try to have long-term goals but divide them up so the team will feel a sense of progress at regular intervals but will still be clear as to what the final goal is. This will help keep the team focused and motivated.
- Recognise success and failure with equal measure within a team, otherwise resentment will set in.
- Don't let initial failures defeat you. If one idea doesn't work, then try another. Do not assume that the failure was the team's fault. Try and find out exactly where the problem lies.
- While team members are individuals they still have an obligation to work together. Individual members should not work against the team or use the team to pursue their own goals at a cost to the team. If team members fail to perform as team members, remove them.

- Encourage friendships to develop within the team through socialising. A good leader will know his/her staff well.
- Do not allow the leader or any other member to do everything. That is not teamwork and the talents of the other members will be wasted. People who feel they should do it all themselves because no one else can be trusted are not the best to do the job, they only think they are. The other team members will grow resentful and will withdraw psychologically from the team. Leaders must learn that they are there not to do it all for others but to show others how to do it for themselves.
- If someone makes a suggestion which is rejected, their effort should be recognised and they should be given solid reasons for the suggestion's rejection. People who have things explained to them are far more receptive than people who have their ideas dismissed out of hand. If you ask for advice, listen and act on it where appropriate. A leader should encourage both negative and positive comment from the team. Locking yourself in an ivory tower may be soothing to you, but it is not a good way to run a team. You will quickly become out of touch and team members will do their own thing while losing respect for you.
- No leader can lead without the respect of others. Too often leaders think that respect comes with authority. Untrue. Rather, authority comes with respect and respect has to be earned. Get to know all your team members. Analyse situations of conflict rationally and never be seen to give preferential treatment. Use compassion where needed and know when to use the stick and when to use the carrot. Assert your authority firmly, sparingly, but never aggressively.
- Communication, communication, communication: the key to an effective team. Make sure the leader is in constant communication with the team. Make sure the team members are in constant communication with each other. Make sure that the team maintains communication with important links outside the team. Make sure that the team has the latest information technology and communications systems that it can acquire. Keep the team nearby for ease of communication. Nip any communication problems between team members in the bud before they get out of hand. Make sure team members are kept well informed of all developments. Circulate agendas well in advance of meetings.

## Team members are internal customers

We identified two types of customer in Chapter 1: the paying customer who comes in off the street to buy or make use of a product or service; and the staff members themselves. We referred to the former as the external customer and the latter as the internal customer. We highlighted the importance of keeping the internal customer or staff member satisfied in order to maximise production, improve external customer care and reduce the costly problem of rapid staff turnover. In this chapter we have been looking at teamwork. Teams generally consist almost entirely of staff members – an exception to this is when outside consultants in effect become temporary members of staff. Teams need to function in an environment conducive to work in order to be at their most productive. In such an environment all members can pull their weight and fulfil their role within the team and neither management nor other team members will put pressure on them to take on unrealistic roles. The team should also be given a suitable physical environment to work in. Research into office environments has shown that a well-thought-out office and work area can lead to greater job satisfaction and creativity.

## How to create a good office environment

Conduct a survey. Ask your staff how they feel as they approach the building. Ask them how they feel about their work area. Use the following points as your guide and based on the results you find, make some moves to improve the work environment.

- *Clutter.* Untidy offices or workstations can have a depressing effect on workers. It can also make their job harder as they sift through mountains of paper to find some crucial note that they wrote on the back of an envelope three days ago. Clear away clutter. First of all make sure that all notices on the notice board have a 'remove by' date on them. The notices should then be taken down as soon as they are obsolete. As a result important new notices will not be buried in a sea of old notices and there will be enough drawing pins to hand; also, there won't be an avalanche of paper as a drawing pin gives way under the stress of holding ten notices on the board at once!

  Initiate a scheme whereby any paper found on the ground or on tables on a Friday evening will be dumped.

  Make sure that there are no deliveries of stationery, office equipment or water for the cooler clogging up any working or walking area. Have a separate storage area for them.

- *Noise.* It is impossible to work in noisy conditions. If there is a lot of noise, then soundproof the area. Turn down the volume on landline phones so they cause as little disturbance as possible above alerting the person who should answer it. Cover the floor with carpet to absorb the sound of people walking by. Partition work areas with some material that helps absorb sound. Put spring mechanisms on doors so that they close slowly rather than slam. Make sure there is a door between the work area and the hall and that it is closed. Make sure that there is a dedicated rest room and that there are dedicated conference rooms so that important conversations do not distract others from their work. Keep noisy equipment such as shredders, faxes and photocopiers in a separate room.

- *Temperature.* Make sure the temperature is comfortable to work in: if it is too warm then workers will become sleepy; if it is too cold they will be distracted.

  There are rules about acceptable temperatures which must be adhered to, but remember that sedentary occupations, such as computer programming, can leave a worker feeling much colder than active occupations like waiting on tables. Some buildings have heating systems that leave the air too dry. This can affect workers' health. It can also lead to a build-up of static in carpets resulting in workers getting mild electric shocks when they touch metal objects. This is part of a condition known as 'sick building syndrome' and can lead to greater instances of fatigue and illness among workers. Ensure that your staff are not working in a 'sick building' environment.

- *Light.* Seasonal Affective Disorder (SAD) is a condition where people become depressed during the winter months because they are not being exposed to sufficient amounts of natural sunlight. In severe cases the condition has been linked to suicides, particularly in countries with long dark winters. Sweden, for example, has a very high suicide rate. Even those of us who do not suffer from SAD know how a sunny day can lift our mood. Natural light therefore can be seen as being very important to our well-being and happiness. Try to expose staff to as much natural light as possible within the work area. As for artificial light, try to get the balance right. Too much bright light can glare and cause headaches. Too little light will lead to eye strain. Try to light the work area well and provide strong lamps to be used for close work. Any flickering or buzzing lights should be replaced immediately and it is important to light the office or work area in such a way that individual staff members can control the light in their own area.

- *Furniture.* Make sure that the furniture is clean, in good repair and ergonomically designed. *Collins English Dictionary* defines ergonomics as the study of the relationship between workers and their environment. Make sure that all seats have good back support so that people will not develop lumbar problems. Make sure that keyboards are sloped so that staff do not develop repetitive strain disorders in their wrists, such as carpal tunnel syndrome. Make sure that visual display units are the required size for work and that there is no flicker or glare from them. Provide special screens to reduce glare if necessary. Remember that your staff will be of different shapes and sizes and that a large minority of them will be left-handed. Bear that in mind when ordering furniture, hanging notice boards, whiteboards, blackboards, filing papers and assigning pigeonholes. Make sure that all areas are wheelchair accessible and have appropriately positioned sockets and light switches.

- *The appearance of the work area.* As discussed above, the work area should be neat and tidy with as little clutter as possible. However, it should not be a soulless place. Staff should be allowed to personalise their work area to some extent as long as this does not interfere with the general work environment. Plants can improve the appearance, as well as the air, of a place as long as they are cleaned and well looked after. The work area should be repainted regularly to keep it looking fresh. The colours should be selected with care. Green is generally considered the most soothing colour. It looks cool in summer, warm in winter and can have a calming effect. Blue is usually a cold colour, grey and black are depressing, while red can be very aggressive. Choose neutral tones for your work area and avoid primary colours. You can use blue, for example, but warm it up by mixing it with green or some other warmer colour. Avoid anything garish that could be hard to live with on a daily basis.

By looking after the work environment you are not only improving the quality of your staff's working day, you are also sending a clear message to your staff that you value them.

## Motivation

Motivation can be defined as the will to act. A good leader wants to motivate people. The key to motivating people starts with learning how to influence people's behaviour. Once you understand this, you will begin to become a good motivator. In 1943 Abraham Maslow published his paper 'A Theory of Human Motivation'. In it he theorised that people's needs increase as their circumstances improve.

Our most basic needs are our animal needs and they focus all our attention until they are satisfied. We need food, warmth and shelter. Until then, we are not too interested in promotion prospects. Maslow expressed his hierarchy of needs in a five-tiered pyramid, putting the most basic needs (the ones we must satisfy first) at the bottom. When these needs have been appeased, we move up a tier on the pyramid.

Maslow's hierarchy can be applied to any aspect of life. It can help a good manager motivate his/her staff by helping them meet those needs within the business environment. By addressing these needs you can help your staff become self-motivated. So rather than goading them on on a daily basis, you create an environment where not only is their job putting food on their table, but they also feel secure. They feel that they belong, that they are valued and challenged to achieve goals and gain bonuses, perks and promotion.

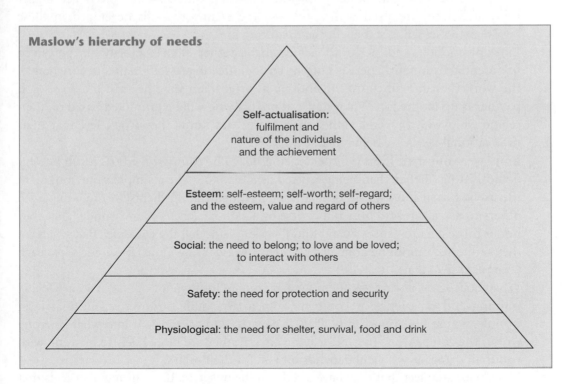

**Maslow's hierarchy of needs**

**Self-actualisation:** fulfilment and nature of the individuals and the achievement

**Esteem:** self-esteem; self-worth; self-regard; and the esteem, value and regard of others

**Social:** the need to belong; to love and be loved; to interact with others

**Safety:** the need for protection and security

**Physiological:** the need for shelter, survival, food and drink

## Needs at work

1. Salary
2. Benefits
3. Working conditions
4. Status
5. Job security
6. Interpersonal needs at work
7. Guidance and supervision versus autonomy
8. Personal life
9. Achievement
10. Recognition
11. Responsibility
12. Job interest.

- In order to maintain motivation, get to know your staff. This gives them recognition and also allows you to spot the first signs of demotivation. If you have good rapport with your staff they will feel happier bringing problems to your attention.
- Organise social events that have some sort of sporting or communal effort involved in them. These help staff bond with you and each other. People often get highly motivated when involved with sport and the teamwork skills developed in these leisure activities will also benefit their working life.
- Link promotion and perks to achievement rather than seniority or perceived preferential treatment. There is nothing so demotivating to staff than to realise that all the work they do will count for nothing at promotion time because the boss's golf partner is up for the job. When staff can predict who will be promoted based on their relationship with the boss rather than merit, you know they won't feel that their motivational needs are being met at work.
- Empower your staff. If every little decision has to be run past the boss it can be very demotivating. Rather than being trusted as adults to make a simple value judgment themselves, staff must waste time and energy, demeaning themselves queuing with others to ask a harassed boss if a course of action is okay. Is it any wonder that staff under those circumstances would find it easier just to tell the customer that whatever they requested cannot be done or obtained? I wonder how much business is lost each year because of that.
- When staff leave, always ask them why. If you are losing a lot of staff, you are losing training and experience. A company with a large staff turnover is one that is in trouble. So use the opportunity of their departure to gain insight into what is wrong within the company. As they are leaving anyway, they are more likely to be frank with you than someone who still depends on you for their salary.
- Make your staff feel that they have a stake in the business. If a staff member feels that

the business is partly theirs they will be far more motivated than if they realise that no matter how hard they work it has no effect on their salary or job security. One way to get staff involved is just by the way you treat them. Other incentives could be giving them shares in the company.

- Remember that your staff are more important than your customers. They are here every day, in places where you cannot be and their behaviour affects how your customers perceive your company. They can cost a lot to replace.

Motivation is the means by which people acquire the incentive to do something. For example, eating is motivated by hunger. Though we work to earn money it is never our only motivation. Otherwise no one would spend years studying medicine when other jobs can pay better and require far less study. When we work we can be motivated by many different things: professional pride, a sense of satisfaction, the knowledge that we are making a contribution, promotion prospects and the feeling that our work is being recognised and appreciated. When we start an important project we are often buoyed up by initial enthusiasm. As the task progresses we sometimes feel bogged down. We have put in so much work and yet there seems to be even more to do. In such circumstances, our enthusiasm can wane. When enthusiasm flags it is very important for the team leader to be able to motivate the team. Here are some ideas for building and maintaining motivation in yourself and others.

- *Think positive.* When you have a big task ahead of you, think of all the things that you have done well in the past. Think of the times when you had a great sense of achievement. This will help build your confidence. You will realise that you have felt daunted in the past and that you succeeded anyway.
- *Think of all the excuses you have made for avoiding this task.* Now eliminate them.
- *Face up to your fears.* It is probably a lot harder on you worrying about and avoiding a task that you have to complete than it is to actually begin the task. Once you make a start you will begin to feel more in control.
- *Set reasonable goals.* We eat pizza one slice at a time. We eat a slice one bite at a time. Break your task up into slices and bites.
- *Think of how you will feel when the task is completed.* Promise yourself a reward for finishing.
- *Do not be afraid to delegate.* There is only so much work any one person can do. When you have too much work, do not be afraid to delegate. People who try to do it all themselves spread themselves too thinly and the quality of their work suffers. This wears down motivation and in some cases can lead to burnout. It also demotivates the rest of the team, who feel that you think they cannot be trusted. So delegate, it benefits everyone.
- *If you have a lot of work to do, prioritise.* Divide your work into what has to be done now and what can realistically be done tomorrow and next week. By doing the urgent work first you will not become so stressed by the end of the day.
- *Relax.* If you are working hard then you deserve to reward yourself. Make sure that you

have some time to yourself to relax every day. It will help relieve stress and will help you feel more motivated tomorrow. Use exercise as part of your relaxation routine. It will help you sleep better and keep you fit. Sitting in front of the television thinking about work is not relaxation.

As team leader never forget the importance of motivation. Remember that motivated people are happy to put that bit extra into their work. Motivated people are proactive and enjoy their work. Management that is too controlling can demotivate people. Make sure you know what makes people happy at work. In general, people are happy at work if they get respect and recognition for what they have done. They like variety and challenges in their work to keep them interested. People like being trusted with responsibility and being able to make decisions without having to always ask the boss. People are happy when they know that they will be rewarded for their work through promotion, increased responsibility and influence, opportunities to learn new skills, bonuses or a salary rise. However, people who are very happy where they work are not necessarily as concerned about salary, as long as it is sufficient.

## Exercises

1.  Outline the main stages in the life of a team.

2.  How important do you think it is to have an effective leader in a team? Give reasons for your answer.

3.  You have been asked to form a team of five to live on a castaway island with you for a year. What criteria would you use when selecting your team?

4.  What are the characteristics of a successful team?

5.  Write a short history of a team that you have been in yourself or have had experience of. Mention what worked well and what conflicts there were. Did someone establish themselves as a leader, and if so, how? Were they successful as a leader? What was your role in the team? Were you a success? Were you involved in any conflicts within the team? Were there any other conflicts within the team?

6.  Write about a leader that you know about or have experience of. It could be a political leader, a boss or even a scout leader. What did you think of their leadership skills?

7.  What is 'ergonomics'?

8.  List three qualities that are important for a team leader to have.

9.  What do you understand by the term 'bullying'?

10. What is the role of the instigator within the team?

11. Why do you think good communication skills are important within the team?

12. Why is it important to select team members carefully?

13. What is the grapevine?

14. Comment on the following quotation: 'Of a great leader, the people will say, "We did it ourselves."'

15. Mulligan's off licence – Anne had been working at Mulligan's for two years. She rarely missed a day's work and was always on time. Mary has been working there for six months, but her record is not so good. She is missing regularly and is often late. One morning Mary is 20 minutes late for work but Anne is 40 minutes late. How would you deal with the situation?

   a. Scold both Mary and Anne severely. They were both late and you do not want to be seen having favourites.

   b. Scold Mary only, but in front of Anne. Anne is rarely late.

   c. Scold Mary, but be more severe with Anne as she was later.

   d. Call both into the office separately for a private word. Ask Anne why she was late. Give Mary a warning.

   Give reasons for your choice.

# 5

# QUALITY SERVICE

Now that everyone has realised the importance of customer care, the standards have risen considerably. Every large supermarket gives you a trolley, labels their aisles, prices their products and bags your groceries. These things have now become part of customer expectations. In order to win more customers, organisations are now forced to exceed customer expectations. They do this by offering more than their competitors.

Quality service can be defined as service to the customer that is of a consistently high and dependable standard. Three different features make up quality customer service:

- the environment
- the system
- customer staff interaction.

The *environment* is the surroundings and the atmosphere in which customer contact staff deal with customers. If we take the example of a restaurant, the environment could be divided into the dining room and the kitchen. The dining room has to be clean and attractive. If it isn't, people will not want to eat there even if the food is good. Even though the kitchen is not generally seen by the external customer it does affect the customer environment. It has to be clean and well organised. If it isn't, the staff (or internal customer) will be stressed and this will affect the atmosphere of the entire restaurant. A customer may not be able to enjoy their meal if there is tension between the staff.

The *system* is basically the method used by an organisation to provide their goods or services to their customers. For example, the standard practice of your milkman may be to pass your house at 5am, take your empty bottles and replace them with three pints of semi-skimmed milk as per your standing order. Systems can vary from organisation to organisation. So you might have two organisations providing essentially the same service, but the system they use to provide it can be completely different. For example, compare the system used at Argos with that of other stores selling similar products. In most stores, you go in, examine the product and take it yourself to the checkout. You pay for it and it is wrapped by the cashier and handed back to you. At Argos you make your selection from a catalogue either at home or in the store itself. You then go to Argos, type in the product code and a computer will check if that product is in stock and confirm the price listed in the catalogue. You then fill in a form and take it to the checkout where you pay for the product and get a receipt. You then proceed to a collection point where your purchase comes up from the store room and is given to you.

*Customer staff interaction.* Quality service depends on the way in which the customer contact staff deal with their customers:

- Is the receptionist hostile when you make a query and does she immediately get on the defensive when you make a complaint?

- Are you interrupting the sales assistant's social life when you walk up to the cash register?

- When you phone a company to make an enquiry, are you passed around like a hot potato from extension to extension?

- In a restaurant, is your meal placed carefully in front of you by the waiter smiling pleasantly, or is it slammed down in front of you? Either way, you are getting the same meal and just as quickly but in the latter case you are certainly not getting quality service.

## How is quality service measured?

Many goods and services now have grading systems. These can help the customer make an informed choice. A trustworthy grading system is a handy guide to what a customer can expect to get for their money. Here are some examples.

### Q Mark

This means 'quality mark'. It is an Irish mark but it is not used on Irish products only. It is granted to products that have reached a satisfactory standard in the Irish market.

### ISO (International Standards Organization)

The ISO 9000 system is concerned with setting, evaluating and maintaining the level of quality in systems and procedures, from initial design to after-sales care, and is divided into three sections: ISO 9001, ISO 9002 and ISO 9003.

- *ISO 9001.* This deals with the design and development of a product, its production, installation and servicing. It is used by organisations involved in design and manufacturing.
- *ISO 9002.* This is more specifically concerned with production and installation and would be used by organisations involved in manufacturing.
- *ISO 9003.* This quality assurance system is concerned with the final inspection and test. It is also used by organisations involved in design and manufacturing. However, this is used less frequently than the other two systems as it focuses on products whose conformance to the ISO standards can only be tested in the final inspection.

There are many other organisations that set standards in the area of design and manufacture. This can make the customer very confused; what one standard will accept, another will reject. In the 1970s an attempt was made to create a global standard in the form of the International Standards Organisation. Nowadays a company may apply for accreditation as an ISO standard company. They will be inspected and will have mounds of paperwork to do but, if accepted, the company will have certain advantages over non-accredited competitors.

1. Some customers will only deal with ISO-accredited producers and all customers will recognise them as quality producers. ISO is a globally recognised standard of quality.

2. The ISO offers guidelines that help companies understand how they can begin to operate to a higher quality.

3. Because of all the documentation involved and the fact that members must sign it, those involved in design and manufacture are forced to think more deeply about what they are committing themselves to during every stage of development.

There are some problems with the ISO system, however.

1. Some consultancy firms might be owned by people involved in organisations seeking ISO accreditation and they may therefore be tempted to grant ISO status where it might not be deserved. Similarly, they may thwart a rival's plans to get the same accreditation.

2. As the people who inspect and award ISO status vary, so too does the standard they expect. The ISO standard in Pakistan and the ISO standard in France may not mean the same thing, though they should if the ISO is to be a truly global standard.

3. Once an organisation has achieved ISO accreditation, there can be very little incentive to continue improving. An organisation might even let its standards slip though it still retains ISO accreditation. Also, it is the organisation and not the product that gets the accreditation. So an ISO company could start supplying a product that does not conform to the ISO standard and the customer might not realise the distinction. So as usual remember *caveat emptor,* 'buyer beware!'

## CE (Certification Europe)

This sets quality safety standards for products to be used in Europe.

## Hotel star ratings

The ratings ★, ★★, ★★★, ★★★★, ★★★★★ give the consumer an idea as to the cost and quality of accommodation within a hotel. Not all hotels that sport stars have had them awarded to them by any organisation and standards may vary from place to place. A global hotel star rating system has yet to be established.

## Michelin Guide

This guide was started by the French tyre manufacturers Michelin. It gave motorists information about the best places around France to eat and stay in. It also included a road map. This guide has become highly respected and has extended its range beyond France. A Michelin star is a recognised and much-sought-after mark of excellence within the catering trade. There have been occasions where hotels that have lost one of their stars have had their chefs resign in shame.

## Egon Ronay guide

Egon Ronay was an epicure who started compiling guides to good eating. His range now covers many countries, and restaurants hope to be acknowledged in his guide as places where a high standard of food is available.

## Fáilte Ireland-approved

Fáilte Ireland deals with hotels and guesthouses. It assesses the overall standard of accommodation, food and service. A bed & breakfast, guesthouse or hotel that fails to reach a satisfactory standard will not be included in Fáilte Ireland's approved catalogue which is widely on sale for the use of tourists and travellers.

## Skytrax

This is an airline review website that rates airlines from five stars down. It is an interesting site for anyone studying customer service because it not only rates airlines, but it also explains the methodology it uses for arriving at its scores and includes customer reviews.

## Good Salon Guide

This is a rating system that covers hairdressing and beauty salons in the UK and Ireland. Salons are rated as R (registered) and given three, four or five stars. A similar system is used by the Good Barbers Guide.

## What are codes of practice?

A code of practice is a document that outlines the standards of excellence of an organisation. It offers guidance on all aspects of the company's customer care as well as on strategies for dealing with complaints and returns.

## What are standards of excellence?

Standards of excellence are goals set out by the organisation for itself. For example, a gas company might set itself the standard of dealing with 80 per cent of its complaints within 24 hours of being called. A supermarket might set as a standard of excellence the goal of there never being more than three customers queuing at a till at any given time.

## What does TQM stand for?

TQM stands for Total Quality Management. This was a buzzword in the customer service world of the 1990s. It was felt that the key to customer acquisition and retention was to provide them with a product of the highest quality from start to finish, including after-sales service. While TQM still holds true, it is now taken for granted. In order to be at the cutting edge in the competition to win customers you have to do more than just provide a high-quality product and service. This leads us on to CRM.

## What does CRM stand for?

CRM is the abbreviation of Customer Relationship Management. It looks at the requirements and wants of customers and focuses on the need for customers to feel that the company regards them as individuals and that their custom is valued. So instead of pigeon-holing each customer into anonymous target markets, each individual is seen as a segment market of one and dealt with accordingly. At its most basic, CRM is the collection of all relevant information about your customers and the recording of all transactions the company has with those customers.

### What is the purpose of CRM?

The purpose of CRM is to build up an entire picture of your customer in order to serve the customer as best you can at present and enhance customer loyalty, to target the customer for cross-sales and to develop future products in an intelligent way that will appeal to that customer.

### What are 'cross-sales'?

Here 'cross-sales' means targeting an existing customer of one product and selling them another product. For example, if you sell a customer a digital camera, you may also be able to sell them a digital photograph printer at a later date. Likewise, if you use CRM you may learn that this customer loves to upgrade their technology on a regular basis and so you might be able to target them later and sell an even more advanced digital camera.

## How does CRM work in practice?

The salesperson, or whoever makes first contact with the customer, collects relevant details about the customer. Then each time an e-mail, visit, letter or phone call is received from or sent to the customer, that information is added to their details. All business transactions are recorded and, very importantly, integrated into one easily accessible file on each specific customer.

This information is stored using dedicated software, which allows the sales and marketing staff to analyse and use their information more easily. A full picture of the customer is developed and from that the staff learn when to target the customer and, more importantly, when *not* to.

When a customer rings up a company that they have dealt with previously and identifies themselves, the staff member would type in the person's name and call up a profile of that customer on the screen. Staff can then personalise the conversation as well as dealing more efficiently with the caller without having to ask basic questions.

For example: Mr Brown walks into the car showroom where he bought a car three years ago. He also has his annual service performed there. The salesman has made it his business to get to know his regular client. He strides quickly over to Mr Brown.

> *Salesman*: Jim, it's good to see you again. How are you?
> *Mr Brown*: Fine, and you?
> *Salesman*: No complaints. How's Sheila?
> *Mr Brown*: Very well, thanks. We've just had another child.
> *Salesman*: Congratulations! That's three, isn't it?
> *Mr Brown*: Yes.
> *Salesman*: A girl or a boy?
> *Mr Brown*: A girl.
> *Salesman*: Fantastic, Sheila must be thrilled to have a girl at last.
> *Mr Brown*: Yes, she was beginning to feel outnumbered.
> *Salesman*: Well, I guess you're here looking for a bigger car this time?
> *Mr Brown*: Well, I suppose so.
> *Salesman*: Well, Jim, why not take a look around with me and see if I can
> show you something that you and Sheila will like.

## Who are the CRM providers?

At the moment three of the most popular products in this area are by Peoplesoft, Oracle and SAP. Sage aims its products at smaller firms. Sugar CRM is free but consequently doesn't offer a lot of customer support. It has no real after-sales service, nor does it offer upgrades. As with a lot of things in business, you get what you pay for. Other specialist

CRM packages include Siebel Call Centre, Siebel Field Service and Siebel Sales. It is very important to shop around and pick the CRM product that best suits your company. (See Chapter 12 for more on CRM technology.)

## How to use CRM

The purpose of CRM is outlined above and all the data you accumulate should serve to attain that purpose. Do not burden the system with superfluous information that might come in handy. Most of it won't and any information that does eventually become useful can be collected again at the time.

## Advantages of CRM

It is a clean and efficient way to develop a total view of your customer. It allows you to target customers at specific times with specific products rather than continually harassing them by blanket bombing them with information about new and existing products they have no interest in.

In this way:

- You save money on unnecessary communication.
- The customer isn't put off by the company's 'hard sell' and will be more likely to take an open-minded approach to any product or upgrade suggestions your company does make.
- It will help you keep existing customers, making them feel more important.
- It will also allow you to deal carefully with them, especially if there have been problems in the past.
- It allows the marketing department to track more accurately which marketing strategies generate the most sales. Return on investment (ROI) is crucial to any business and CRM can help them gauge that.

## Disadvantages of CRM

It costs money to install, implement and maintain. The installation of CRM software can cause a lot of extra work and disruption initially. All this money and effort will be wasted if the staff is then reluctant to use this new CRM technology.

The collection of information on members of the public by companies is strictly governed by the Data Protection Commission. A company who uses CRM without fully understanding their legal requirements could easily get into legal difficulties.

## Easing the cost and disruption of introducing CRM into the company

Some companies offer CRM as one part of various inter-linked packages. Thus CRM becomes part of an enterprise resource planning (ERP) solution. This makes the installation process less disruptive as all your packages can come from the same vendor and are cheaper too, especially if you already use some products by that vendor.

To avoid getting into legal hot water, a visit to the Data Protection Commissioner's website at www.dataprotection.ie is recommended.

Some companies, by reason of the nature of their service, collect personal details of a highly sensitive nature, such as health history, criminal background or religious beliefs. They consequently have to register with Digital Rights Ireland. All Internet service providers are obliged to register. You can visit their website at www.digitalrights.ie

## Past, present and future CRM

CRM is nothing new; it has been around since the 1990s. However, Irish companies were slow to take an interest; that has now changed. Companies realise that the amount of customers out there is finite and new customers are expensive to attract. They see the potential of CRM in minimising customer attrition and in using it to develop new customer strategies. A simple example would be a customer loyalty card in a supermarket. If 65 per cent of your customers are buying nappies today, that means that in the next 3 to 5 years they will be in the market for buying school stationery, sports gear and backpacks. Also, governments are taking an interest in CRM, seeing its potential in being better able to cater for their citizens' needs now and in the future and also to be able to more accurately revise their legal and taxation structures.

## Customer loyalty

Customer loyalty is when a customer repeatedly uses the same organisation for goods or services. It is built by consistently providing value for money and by providing an excellent after-sales service. To achieve customer loyalty, you need to treat the customer as an individual and know the customer's needs and cater to them. Customer loyalty can be rewarded with Christmas cards, clubcards and preferential treatment.

For example: there was a global oil crisis in the 1970s and petrol was very strictly rationed. In Ireland, as elsewhere, there were enormous queues at petrol stations. Many petrol stations gave their long-standing customers preferential treatment. One petrol station did not. It was simply a case of first come, first served. When the petrol shortage ended, that petrol station found that they had lost their loyal customer base. The customers resented the fact that they were treated as strangers while other customers at other stations had their loyalty rewarded. They also feared that if another petrol shortage was to occur they had better have established themselves as loyal customers somewhere else.

Customer loyalty is the idea that a customer will support a certain product, company or service because they feel allegiance to it.

As we know, it is easier and cheaper to keep a customer than to try and win a new one. It is even better if you can develop a customer base that will stand by you through thick, thin and fashion changes. But how can you get loyal customers?

## What influences customers loyalty?

- Location
- Family connection
- The owners are friends/neighbours
- Racial/religious ties
- Value for money
- Atmosphere
- Service
- Tradition
- Memory
- Fairness
- Snobbery
- Fashion
- Rewards.

*Location*: A customer will visit the shop around the corner and support it because it's convenient even though it may not be the cheapest. Customers may even support it more if they fear that it might close.

*Support your own:* A customer will support a family enterprise even if its product is dearer or inferior. Likewise they may support a company or service where they have strong ties. Immigrants and *racial or religious minorities* will often band together and will support their own products or services. There is empathy within these groups, as well as particular practices that only they might fully understand, for example a kosher butcher.

A customer will remain loyal to a company that consistently offers *value for money*, but will that loyalty remain if prices rise?

A restaurant would be an example of a business that could maintain loyal customers through *atmosphere.* This atmosphere might supersede considerations such as price, service or quality.

A customer will remain loyal where they get consistent high-quality *service.* When there is an occasional glitch and it is dealt with positively, then their loyalty will only increase.

How many people buy the same washing powder that their parents used to buy? If there is no discernibly superior product on the market then we tend to *remain loyal to the products we are used to.* This is very apparent in food sales. The brown sauce on the table of our youth is the brown sauce we will most likely stick with. We develop eating habits as children that we generally maintain, unless we make a very conscious decision to change. This is why some fast-food outlets are so keen to recruit children as customers.

A product that was effective in the past will be *remembered* and recommended in the future. Likewise a company that exploited customers during a period of high demand will find that customers will remember that and support other companies when the market changes.

If a customer knows that a company will accept responsibility for its mistakes when it is to blame and will always treat its customers *fairly*, then he/she will be loyal.

Some customers shop in certain shops and keep the shopping bags and use them later. This allows them to send the message that they are the type of person who has the money and taste to shop there. *Snobbery* or image is very important in customer loyalty. Consider how many people buy expensive cars in order to present a certain image of themselves, either real or inspirational.

Customers are loyal to products that are in *fashion*. If a product remains fashionable over a long period of time, this can be construed/misconstrued as customer loyalty.

Customers will remain loyal to companies that reward them. A second-hand car dealer who will always throw in a free tank of fuel will gain loyalty from customers that far outweighs the costs. However, some customers in certain areas will only remain loyal as long as they are getting the rewards, for example buying a certain chocolate bar in bulk until all the golden tickets are won. Loyalty cards are fairly common nowadays and as with all new customer service innovations they lost their effectiveness as they became commonplace. Most of us have more than one supermarket loyalty card so we shop in the same ad hoc manner and merely whip out the appropriate card when we reach the till. In fact we are more likely to go to a particular shop because we mislaid the loyalty card for the other shop rather than out of a strong sense of loyalty.

### How can you win customer loyalty?

The first thing is to analyse what customer loyalty is and what makes customers loyal, and then ask how you can apply it to your own company, product or service.

## Customer-oriented organisations

A customer-oriented organisation will have a customer-oriented policy incorporating a policy of listening to customers and acting on their suggestions. This will lead to the formation of a policy statement that again is focused on the customer. The standard operational procedures will also have customer-focused bias.

For example: as its mission statement, a bank might express its intention to make a greater amount of money than its competitors. It will therefore streamline its policies and operational procedures to save money. This might mean having as few bank clerks working on the counters as possible in order to save money. The customer waiting area will be small, as for the majority of banks, customers generate the smallest amount of profit for the organisation. Operational procedures will then encourage clerks to devote most of their time to customers who have the greatest amount of money in the bank.

In contrast, a customer-oriented bank would have a policy that seeks to recognise the value of customers, no matter how small their accounts are. The bank's mission statement would reflect that; for example, 'We will welcome all savers, great and small.' Operational procedures would make customers a top priority, so staff might be taught to open another counter whenever there are more than four people queuing.

## What is a mission statement?

A mission statement outlines the basic function of a business or organisation. It shows us how the organisation sees itself now and how it hopes to be seen by its customers in the future. It maps out the vision the company or organisation aspires to and sums up some of the main principles put forward in the customer charter in just one sentence.

For example: a company might have a customer charter that emphasises value for money. Its mission statement might be:

*Smiths, the cheapest around or your money back.*

Mission statements can emphasise different things:

*Browns, for the finest things in life.*

*Jones Plumbers, at your door before you put your phone down.*

A mission statement might be aspirational in nature:

*Sullivans will be the biggest name in home furnishings by the year 2030.*

### Sample customer care policy – The Brown Thomas Group

The Brown Thomas Group issues these guidelines to their employees:

*Customer care standards.* Our customer care standards are based on our interacting with customers in a professional and consistent manner. Our professionalism includes presenting ourselves at work in accordance with business dress standards and maintaining our work area in perfect condition using the housekeeping check list and visual merchandising standards. The customer care standards are as follows:

- *Acknowledgement.* The customers must be acknowledged with a smile or eye contact or a greeting within one minute of entering a department.
- *Approach.* The customers should be approached in a professional and courteous manner using open-ended questions to determine their needs.
- *Product knowledge.* Customers should be provided with all product information they require and other information, for example, department location, or additional services, for example, gift wrap and delivery service.
- *Closing of sale.* Once the sale has been finalised the customer should be brought to the nearest cash point, thanked for their custom and provided with a business card where appropriate.
- *Cash point.* Customers should be acknowledged and thanked for their custom at the cash point. Sales transactions, that is, register procedures and

documentation, should be completed within three minutes.

- *Services.* Customers should be advised of the wide range of services provided throughout the store, for example, Mailing List, BT MasterCard, Personal Shopping and Wedding List Services.
- *After-sales service.* Outstanding queries, special orders, alterations, etc., must be followed through to the satisfaction of the customer.
- *Confidentiality.* Customer transactions should be treated in the strictest confidence and never discussed outside the store.
- *Telephone techniques.* All calls should be answered within six rings. All calls should be answered by using one of the following greetings: 'Good morning', 'Good afternoon', or 'Good evening'. Identify your department, give your name and say, 'How can I help you?' For example, 'Good morning, Menswear, John speaking, how can I help you?'

## Designing operational standards for front-line staff

When designing operational standards for front-line staff, be sure to consult the staff. They are the people who have the experience in this area and can point out to you what can realistically be done. Without contacting them, they could be resentful, seeing your input as an intrusion, and will be reluctant to put your suggestions into practice.

Start off with just a few operational standards. Too many will overstretch the staff and make them feel that your ideas are unworkable. A few smaller goals will give them an opportunity to quickly master the new ideas and these can then be added to while the staff's confidence grows.

Here is an example of operational standards for a takeaway restaurant:

1. Answer the phone within five rings.

2. Give the name of the restaurant, your name and ask, 'What would you like to order?'

3. Have the menu near you so that you can answer any questions.

4. Make sure you can always give them the correct price over the phone.

5. Make sure you have the customer's correct name and address.

6. Make sure that the meal is ready within 10 minutes for collection.

## The customer charter as a quality assurance mechanism

The purpose of a customer charter is to inspire trust. The charter tells customers what they can, at the very least, expect from the organisation. If the organisation fails to meet that expectation, customers know that they can complain and that their complaints will be dealt with competently. In this way, the customer charter encourages complaints from customers who are unhappy but who do not generally complain, feeling that it would be pointless or unpleasant to do so. This policy does not generate complaints, it just means that more complaints are heard by the organisation and can be dealt with. This leads to better customer service and to happier customers who know that their custom is appreciated.

## Sample customer charter – ESB

The ESB has issued a customer charter setting out 12 guarantees of customer service:

*Guarantee 1*: Network repair guarantee
If you contact the ESB when you lose power and you are not reconnected within 24 hours you can claim back €40 from your bill or €100 if you are a business customer. For every subsequent 12 hours that you are without power, you can claim back an extra €20.

*Guarantee 2*: Planned supply interruption guarantee
If the ESB plans to interrupt electricity supply they will give at least two days' notice or else you can claim €20 if you are a domestic customer or €100 if you are a business customer. Very short interruptions and interruptions caused by sources other than the ESB are not covered by this guarantee.

*Guarantee 3*: Main fuse guarantee
If you inform the ESB within four hours of losing power and that call is made between 8.30am and 11.30am, the ESB will deal with your complaint before 12.30pm the following day.

*Guarantee 4*: The meter connection guarantee
The ESB guarantees to install electricity meters in businesses within five days and domestic meters within three days.

*Guarantee 5*: Supply quotation guarantee
If you are starting a small business, you must send relevant details to the ESB. If they need to visit you, they guarantee a quotation within 20 working days. If no visit is necessary, they guarantee a quotation within 10 working days. If they fail to meet these targets, they will pay you €40.

*Guarantee 6*: Voltage guarantee
If you contact the ESB with concerns over voltage, they guarantee to investigate the matter and to contact you again within 10 days. If they fail to do this, they will pay you €20.

*Guarantee 7*: Meter accuracy guarantee
If there has been a mistaken meter reading taken, contact the ESB. They will reply within five days or else pay you €20.

*Guarantee 8*: Account guarantee
If you want to change your payments, the ESB will contact you within five

days or change the payments within that time. Otherwise they will pay you €20.

*Guarantee 9*: Appointment guarantee
If the ESB fails to keep an appointment with the customer, they will pay them €20.

*Guarantee 10*: Reconnecting supply guarantee
When outstanding bills have been paid, the ESB will reconnect power the following day or else €20 will be paid to the customer.

*Guarantee 11*: Refund guarantee
If the ESB fails to give a guaranteed refund within seven working days they will pay you €20.

*Guarantee 12*: Payment guarantee
If the ESB has failed to live up to one of their guarantees and payment is due to you under the terms of their charter, the ESB will pay you or credit your account within 10 working days. If they fail to do so, they will pay a further €20 to the customer.

In 1998 ELCOM was set up to provide an independent voice for ESB customers. If a customer feels unhappy about the way in which a complaint has been dealt with by the ESB, they can use the services provided by ELCOM.

## ELCOM
### ESB Customer Complaints Commissioner

*Terms of Reference*
An independent voice to resolve complaints about electricity service

### Summary

The Complaints Commissioner is appointed by ESB, following nomination by the Director of Consumer Affairs. The Commissioner will operate outside ESB but will have an independent contractual relationship with it. The contract, which has been drawn up in consultation with the Director of Consumer Affairs, guarantees the independence of the Complaints Commissioner.

This initiative provides for an independent voice in reviewing and making recommendations on certain types of unresolved complaints from customers or potential customers about ESB. The Commissioner will adjudicate on complaints about electricity supply connections, billing, metering, distribution network repairs, service levels, etc. Certain complaints, such as those relating to ESB Power Generating Stations, do not come within the scope of the Commissioner's remit.

The Commissioner has the power to issue binding recommendations to ESB Customer Services and may recommend that ESB follow a particular course of action or pay an ex gratia sum.

The service is free to customers and is in no way prejudicial of a customer's legal rights.

A complainant will first go through ESB's internal complaint resolution process in accordance with its published complaints procedure before referring the unresolved complaint to the Commissioner.

The Commissioner will have direct access to the Managing Director, ESB Customer Services and will submit a report annually to the Board of ESB on the incidence, nature and resolution of complaints. This report will subsequently be published. The Director of Consumer Affairs and Chief Executive, ESB, will arbitrate on any issue not mutually resolved between ESB and the Commissioner.

In the event of Government appointing a Regulator/Consumer Council of the electricity supply industry, the Commissioner's role will be reviewed to ensure there is no conflict between respective roles and responsibilities.

## Customer Complaints Commissioner

The Customer Complaints Commissioner is a contractually appointed arbitrator of customer complaints.

Appointed by ESB Customer Services, following consultation with and nomination by the Director of Consumer Affairs, the Commissioner is charged with the resolution of complaints about customer services provided by ESB when the complaint cannot be resolved directly with ESB.

## Reporting arrangements

Although funded by ESB, the Commissioner is an independent office holder with clearly defined powers to investigate and determine issues in dispute between ESB and customers. The Commissioner will be provided with the necessary resources and facilities to efficiently deal with the level of complaints from time to time.

The Commissioner has direct access to the Managing Director of Customer Services in ESB and presents an annual report to the Board of ESB. This report will be published subsequently. The Director of Consumer Affairs and the Chief Executive, ESB, will arbitrate on any issue not mutually resolved between ESB and the Commissioner.

## Scope of Commissioner's operations

The Commissioner deals with any and all complaints relating to:

- The service provided by ESB to the customer, including complaints concerning electrical supply connections, billing queries, metering, network repair service, supply outages, communications with customers and service levels.

- The Commissioner also has power to arbitrate on disputes concerning Customer Charter guarantees of service, including the application of exemptions under the 'small print'.
- Alleged maladministration or unfair treatment.

The areas outside the scope of the Commissioner include the following:

(a) Complaints already the subject matter of legal proceedings or those which are best addressed through defined legal proceedings (such as planning permission and way leave disputes).
(b) Complaints relating to the activities of ESB Retail (Appliance Sales), FinancElectric or ESB Electrical Contracts (including Public Lighting). These are separate business lines operating in a highly competitive environment and are the subject of separate complaints procedures. In addition, the sale of electrical appliances is governed by the Sale of Goods and Supply of Services Act 1980. FinancElectric activities are regulated by the Consumer Credit Act 1995.
(c) Complaints which relate to ESB Power Generation and National Grid (High Voltage Networks) businesses.
(d) Complaints which have not been processed initially through ESB's internal complaints procedure as published or the complaint was not initially lodged with ESB within 6 months of the action (or lack of action) giving rise to the complaint.

## The Commissioner's powers and duties

To receive and act on any complaint referred to the Commissioner by a customer or potential customer which comes within the scope of the Commissioner's Office and which remains unresolved after being through ESB's internal Complaints Procedure.

The Commissioner has discretion in determining whether a complaint comes within the scope of the Office.

The Commissioner will seek to promote a resolution of the complaint, will act impartially and fairly in all the circumstances and may make an ex gratia award in favour of the customer.

In assessing a complaint, the Commissioner may seek and be given all relevant documents and information on the matter and can seek such additional material as may be relevant. ESB will amend its registration under the Data Protection Act to include the Complaints Commissioner as a discloser of relevant customer information requested for the purpose of processing a complaint initiated by that customer.

If the complainant is being represented by a person, other than a legal representative, the Commissioner will seek the authority of the complainant prior to the disclosure of any relevant information to that third party.

The Commissioner may also seek and be given access to any ESB staff member involved in the circumstances giving rise to the complaint for the purposes of clarifying aspects of the complaint. ESB management and staff will co-operate fully with the processing of any complaint and will respond quickly to any questions raised by the Commissioner.

It will be a condition of the investigation of any complaint that the complainant will co-operate with the investigation and be available to the Commissioner if necessary.

The Commissioner's recommendation will be binding on ESB.

The Commissioner will not be bound by any previous decision made by the current office holder or any predecessor.

The Commissioner will endeavour to issue a final recommendation to both ESB and the customer within 10 working days of receiving details of a complaint, together with copies of related correspondence between both parties or any other information required by the Commissioner to deal to conclusion with the complaint. If the complaint takes longer to resolve, the customer will be given an initial response within the 10-day period.

## Limits to Commissioner's powers

Apart from the complaints (set out under 'Scope') which are outside the scope of the Office, the Commissioner cannot deal with complaints which while coming within the general scope of Customer Services relate to:

- An issue which is best resolved under another process including arbitration and the courts, or the subject matter has been, is or becomes the subject of legal or other proceedings.
- The commercial judgment of ESB relating to tariffs and conditions and terms for supply, unless the complaint relates to maladministration or unfair treatment.

In the event of Government appointing a Regulator/Consumer Council of the electricity supply industry, the Commissioner's role will be reviewed to ensure there is no conflict between respective roles and responsibilities of the ESB Customer Complaints Commissioner and the Regulator/Council.

## ESB internal complaints procedure

Before the Commissioner can adjudicate on a complaint, it will first have been referred by the complainant to ESB in accordance with ESB's published complaints procedure and, in particular, must have been the subject of a referral to senior management at ESB. A leaflet explaining the internal complaints procedure, including response times, will be circulated by ESB to its customers and copies will be available at all Service Centres.

That procedure requires the complainant to seek resolution of the complaint with the local ESB Service Centre. If it is not possible to resolve the complaint at this level, the matter should be referred to the appropriate Regional Manager. If still unresolved to the satisfaction of the customer, the matter may then be referred by the customer to the Commissioner.

## Notification of complaints procedure to customers

ESB will take steps to inform customers of the Complaints Commissioner's role and to explain how the complaints resolution process works. Details of the Complaints Procedure will be forwarded to customers. This Procedure will explain ESB's internal complaints procedure including response times together with the Complaints Commissioner's role and how, where and when to refer a complaint to the Commissioner.

## What does it cost to refer a complaint to the Complaints Commissioner?

This facility is free to ESB customers. The procedure does not make any allowance for reimbursement to customers of any expenses or cost incurred by them in processing a complaint.

## Protection of a customer's legal rights

The complaints procedure within ESB and the role of the Commissioner is an additional facility afforded to customers and is in no way prejudicial of a customer's legal rights (contractual or statutory). Likewise, the procedure does not impact on the legal relations between ESB and the customer under the General Conditions of Supply. Under the complaints procedure, ESB agrees to be bound by the findings of the Commissioner (on a without prejudice basis), while the customer is free to reject the finding and pursue other remedies. However, an award by the Commissioner will be made subject to such an award being in full and final settlement of the customer's dispute.

## Exercises

1. Explain the term 'quality service'.

2. What is the purpose of a customer charter?

3. Explain what the following represent:

    a. ISO

    b. CE

    c. Egon Ronay

    d. Q Mark

    e. Fáilte Ireland-approved

4. What is a mission statement?

5. What does CRM stand for?

6. Why is customer loyalty so important to business?

7. What are codes of practice for?

8. What is the function of ELCOM?

# MARKET RESEARCH

Topics covered in this chapter:

- **What is market research for?**
- **Market research defined**
- **How to undertake research**
- **Research methods**
- **Primary and secondary data**
- **Why should we listen to customers?**
- **Questionnaires**
- **Reports**
- **Market segmentation**
- **Examples of customer-oriented organisations**
- **Customer-oriented products**

Market research examines both existing and potential markets. It began in the United States with the use of primitive surveys and slowly developed into a very important part of every business in the last century. Nowadays, the bigger the company, the bigger the portion of its budget is spent on marketing. The marketing department of a company works to ensure that the goods or services a company produces will sell. In order to do that successfully the marketing department needs to ask, and have answers to, the following questions.

### What should I sell?

There is no point making beautifully crafted butter churns if no one is going to buy them. People buy in order to solve a problem or answer a need. In the past, people needed to make their own butter but unless butter churning becomes necessary or fashionable again, you will sell very few churns.

### Where should I sell it?

Location is very important. That is why there are far more skiing equipment shops in Switzerland than in the Canary Islands. You have to sell in or near the location of the people who will buy from you.

### Who will buy it?

It is rare, possibly even unheard of, that a product or service appeals to all people. You need to know your own market and sell to those who want your product. Knowing your market will profoundly affect the characteristics of your product and the quality of your service. For instance, look at the way certain ice creams are marketed towards children and contrast it with the way in which the same company might aim another line of ice cream at adults.

### What can I charge for it?

This depends on the reputation of your brand, the price the competition is charging and just how price-sensitive your particular target market is.

### Who is my competition?

Knowledge is power and the more you know about the competition, the better prepared you will be to take it on.

### How well am I selling at the moment?

Even if you are doing extremely well there is absolutely no guarantee that this trend is going to continue. Examine what is selling well and what is selling badly for you at the moment. If one of your products is doing badly, would it be wiser to discontinue it or try and push it harder in the marketplace?

### How can I ensure that what is selling well will continue to do well?

If a product or service is doing really well then there is someone out there who will try and do something similar in order to cash in. How can your original product maintain its market position?

### What future trends should I be anticipating?

Bill Gates anticipated a future where there would be a computer in almost every home and look what that did for him.

### What do I expect my competition to do in the future and how can I turn that to my advantage?

If, for instance, you know that a competitor is going to allow their product to be repackaged and sold as part of a supermarket brand, you could try and turn that to your advantage by emphasising your product's brand integrity.

Market research can be defined as the systematic collection of information through the use of recognised research techniques for the purpose of analysing and assessing the viability of current products and services and the feasibility of future ones. Market research's function is to find out what customers want, what they will want in the future and what they will buy.

## How to begin your research

- Be clear about your objective. What is the purpose of this research? What do I want to know at the end of this?
- What is the scope of your research? Are you going for breadth or depth?
- Know your audience. Who is going to read this? What do they want to know? Will they understand complex jargon? Will most people only read segments? Do I need an executive summary?
- Where will I get my information? Do I need it to be very up to date and localised, or is it generic?
- What methods of research should I employ? Should I interview local customers, clients, employees, residents, etc., or can I do most of my research from documents?
- Will my methods of research require gathering information that people might give me in confidence? Will I be able to ensure confidentiality?
- When is my deadline? How will that affect the choices I make in my research?

## Research methods

We perform research by experiment, observation, survey, consultation and library and Internet research.

We can *experiment* by introducing new initiatives into goods and services and noting the response. For example, a petrol station might offer a free car wash with every €20 of petrol sold.

*Observation* may involve changing the decor in a hairdresser's salon and noting the responses.

A *survey* may be made within the organisation, among its customers, on the street, on the Internet or by telephone. You would ask each person the same set of questions and note their responses. By grouping similar responses together and counting them, you can then express your findings in visual form, as in a bar chart or histogram.

You could *consult* experts within your particular area. Specialised consultants can be hired to analyse your particular situation and design a customer service plan specific to your needs.

*Library* and *Internet* research are self-explanatory, both being rich in literature on customer care.

## A breakdown of the most popular forms of research

### Observation

Observe a process or interaction as it actually happens, for example counting the amount of cars that use a car park in any given day.

*Advantages*
You can actually view the process as it occurs. You can adapt your observation as unforeseen events occur.

*Disadvantages*
People may behave differently if they know that they are being observed.
It can be expensive to do.
It can be hard to get an overview of what is happening when you are so close to the ground.

## Interviews
*Advantages*
You can get the specific information you require.

*Disadvantages*
The interviewee may feel inclined to tell the interviewer what they think the interviewer wants to hear.
The interviewer may bias the interviewee through leading questions or body language.
They can be expensive.
Sometimes it's hard to categorise and analyse responses.

## Questionnaires
*Advantages*
They are cheap.
They are quick.
They are anonymous so there is no pressure on the person filling in the questionnaire to impress or deceive.
You can target a lot of people.
They are easy to compile.
You can collect a lot of data.

*Disadvantages*
A lot of questionnaires are wasted, as people don't bother to fill them in.
People may not take care filling them in.
Some people might fill in the questionnaires inaccurately or might be deliberately misleading for their own reasons.
The questions might lead people towards certain answers.

## Secondary research, books and documents
*Advantages*
This is relatively inexpensive.
A lot of the work is already done for you. The research has been conducted and verified.

*Disadvantages*
This can be time consuming.
The documents might not exactly answer the questions you want to ask.
The research can be out of date.
Just because it's in a book doesn't make it necessarily true or unbiased.

## Focus groups

*Advantages*

This is a quick way to get information.

The interaction in the group may allow questions and solutions to come out that would never have surfaced through a more rigid method of information gathering, such as a questionnaire.

You get a sense of the prevailing attitude.

*Disadvantages*

It can be difficult and expensive to organise.

You need to select suitable people for the topic to be covered.

## Primary and secondary data

*Primary data* is collected through research methods that directly question or observe people, for example through interviews, surveys and so on. *Secondary data* is obtained by acquiring information from another party that has already done research, for example information in books or from a government body.

The most prevalent market research methods used are surveys and questionnaires, interviews, focus groups, suggestion schemes and customer hotlines, sampling and empirical research:

- A *survey* provides the means to find out the opinions of people on your chosen topic. You can conduct a survey over the telephone, through the post, publish it in a magazine or newspaper or you can conduct it face to face.
- *Questionnaires* are often used in surveys. They involve asking each person the same set of standardised questions, which makes it easier for you to analyse your results, but one disadvantage is that you cannot direct those completing the questionnaire in any way. Also, if one person gives you an intriguing response, you have no way of following it up.

  Questionnaires are cheap to make and distribute and the person targeted can complete it at their leisure. Unfortunately, because of this, the response level for questionnaires is usually very low, so in order to encourage any response at all, questionnaires must not be too long or detailed.
- *Interviews* are a discussion between two or more people in order to serve a specific function. They can vary in their degree of formality, depending on the purpose of the interview. A lot of very detailed information can be collected by interview. Because it is an open discussion on a specific theme, you can ensure that the interviewee fully understands and answers each question. You can ask them to expand on their answers. The interviewee may also throw up important points that you had not previously factored into your research. You can show the interviewee your product or service and get a clear reading of their immediate reactions and opinion.

  Unfortunately, interviewing can be an extremely costly and time-consuming endeavour and it is a lot harder to find potential interviewees because of the amount of time it generally takes. There is also the fear that a customer may be too embarrassed to answer some questions truthfully. If you conduct interviews over the telephone the interviewee will probably be less embarrassed and is likely to be more truthful. However, they will also be more likely to refuse to do the survey at all. They will also be less likely to give you their full attention. A telephone interview is best, therefore, if it is not very long, but it saves on travel and it means that you can question people from anywhere.

* *Focus groups* are groups gathered together to deal with a particular issue. They may be a random collection of people, for example a group of customers randomly selected to taste and comment on a new breakfast cereal, or they may be specially selected for their expertise in a specific area, say, electrical engineers gathered together to develop a better type of vacuum cleaner. A focus group has many of the same advantages and disadvantages as an ordinary interview. Individuals can be shown the product or service and in-depth responses can be obtained. However, you can also let the participants of the focus group talk among themselves and this can be a great way of getting more natural responses as well as lots of good ideas, as in a brainstorming session. Again, however, it is a very costly business and people will be less likely to agree to attend because of the time involved. Also, people may be reluctant to be totally truthful about some issues when they are confronted with a roomful of people and, inevitably, some personalities will dominate while others will say nothing so you will not necessarily get the opinions of the entire group.

* *Suggestion schemes* are methods used to encourage feedback. This could be a comment card propped up on a coffee table or a suggestion box where people can drop in ideas and criticisms, anonymously if they prefer. These are extremely cheap to organise but the responses can be varied and some can be far from helpful.

* *Customer hotlines* are telephone lines made available by organisations to their customers to provide easy access to the organisation whenever they have a problem or comment to make. This can be a useful way of assessing where the areas of least customer satisfaction occur.

* *Sampling* works on the premise that a sample can represent the whole. An opinion poll is a common example of sampling. The pollster may ask a random selection of a thousand people their opinion of the current government, for example. The answers will be seen as a reflection of the population as a whole. Another example of sampling would be to find a shop in a community you feel represents a fair profile of the consumer market and to start selling a new product or service there. From that you can make an assessment of how your product will fare in a wider market.

* *Empirical research* is the means of collecting data by experiment, measurement and experience. This could involve discovering which brand of cereal is more popular by physically counting the number of packets that are bought by people. Also, in-store loyalty cards can tell us a lot about the profile of our customers and what their shopping habits are, down to what brand of tea they have with what brand of biscuits and how much they buy of each in a week.

## The Internet

The Internet can be used as a means of primary and secondary research. It is cheaper than phoning people or printing questionnaires. It is also quick and convenient. You can reach a global audience from the comfort of your office and the information can be easily stored. Search engines such as Yahoo, Altavista, Google and Ask Jeeves make secondary research easier. You can also bookmark your favourite sites so that you can access them more quickly in the future.

However, there are some serious hazards attached to Internet research. You are potentially exposing your computer to viruses when you download information off the Internet. The response level for questionnaires on the Internet tends to be low and you have no idea who is answering your questionnaire. As your respondents are virtually untraceable, they can say whatever they like and there is no guarantee that they are being honest. There is also no guarantee that the same person is not filling in the questionnaire again and again. It would therefore be very easy for a rival to distort your results in this way. Once compiled and analysed your findings hold little weight because there is no way of verifying them. When undertaking secondary research on the Internet be wary of the information that you obtain. When you visit a site for the purposes of research, ask yourself who set up the site and why. Check a few related sites to see if the information that you are obtaining is consistent.

## Why should we listen to customers?

It is very important to listen to individual customers if you want to know what future customer trends will be. In satisfying a particular customer today, you may be anticipating what might be a common request in the short-term future. You also need to keep up to date with current customer service trends and theory in Europe and the United States as new practices tend to arrive in Ireland with increasing speed each year.

Listening to existing customers is also crucial in order to keep them. Think of the amount of effort each company or organisation puts into winning new customers and the large amounts of money spent on product development, market research and advertising. It has been estimated that it costs five times more to win a new customer than it does to retain an existing one. So if you spend all that money attracting a new customer and then lose them through poor service, all that expenditure is wasted. If you can reduce customer turnover by 10 per cent you stand to increase your profits by 30 per cent or more. Not only that, but a lost customer might tell other people how disappointed they were in you. It makes far better sense therefore to make a big effort to acquire new customers and an even bigger effort to keep them.

Ask your customers to give their general overall impression of your company. Remember, this is the impression that they will take with them and pass on to other potential customers. Get them to give an overall satisfaction rating. Then analyse that satisfaction rating in relation to more specific ratings. From their responses you can learn what attributes of your company your customers value most. For example, if a customer gives you a high general satisfaction rating, while giving a poor satisfaction rating for packaging and a high rating for value for money, then you can surmise that value is more important to customers than good packaging.

## What is a questionnaire?

A questionnaire can be defined as a data-gathering device that elicits answers from a respondent to pre-arranged questions in a specific order.

Questionnaires are a form of research which depend on the honesty of the respondents. They need to be designed carefully so that they are a genuine reflection of the attitudes of respondents.

There is always the danger that the respondent will either tell the questioner what they think they want to hear or try and give answers that make the respondent look good.

For example, who is going to tell an immaculate questioner that they shower once a week, eat cold pizza for breakfast and have never had a pedicure?

## Designing a questionnaire

We have seen above the sort of information market researchers wish to learn from customers. When designing a questionnaire you will have a specific brief. You will know what data is required and how the questionnaire will be used, for example in a telephone survey, a random street survey or posted to a target audience of existing customers. Its use will affect the length of the questionnaire. An existing customer with an already established relationship with the company is far more likely to take the time to fill in a lengthy questionnaire than a person on the street with no vested interest in your company, who may feel that they have better things to do with their time. Likewise, a person is less likely to spend 20 minutes on the phone answering questions for a stranger who may have interrupted their work.

When you have decided the target of your market research and the manner in which it will be employed, your next decision is what questions you want answered. The questions themselves can vary from product to product and service to service, but no matter what the product or service is and how you obtain the information, remember, you are essentially trying to assess satisfaction levels.

What you need to find out is: are your customers happy with the services that you currently supply? Are there any services your customers would like to see you supply in the future? What aspects of your services do they particularly value? Where do they see room for improvement? In what ways do your customers see you doing better or worse than your competitors?

### Types of question

To obtain the information you need, you have to decide on the type of question that will best serve your specific needs. Inexperienced researchers often ask the wrong questions.

Their mistake is apparent only after the survey, when the responses are found to be unusable. To obtain the information you need, you have to decide on the type of question that will best serve your specific needs.

Questionnaires should have specific objectives, so you must define those objectives before you design your questions.

### Closed questions

Closed questions are useful because they elicit only a short clear response, usually yes, no or one specific answer. For example:

> Do you smoke?
> Do you go to the cinema at least once a month?
> What is the highest mountain in the world?
> What age are you?

These answers are easy to tabulate but do not offer insight into what the customer is thinking. It is useful to know that your customers do not like your broccoli and parsnip soup but it would be even more useful to know why. Knowing that people dislike the soup means that you might discontinue the product, but knowing that the reason people dislike it is because it is too salty is more useful because now you can rectify the problem, repackaging it 'Now with less salt', and save yourself a fortune.

### Open-ended questions

Open questions are useful because they help you discover exactly *why* a customer is dissatisfied. An open-ended question allows people to make a fuller reply. For example:

> Why do you smoke?
> What would influence your decision to go to the cinema?

Sometimes a questionnaire will elicit a comment that pinpoints a problem you were previously unaware of. On the other hand, some people will be put off by having to write long explanations in questionnaires. Also, as answers will vary so much it will be hard to tabulate such information.

### Multiple-choice questions

These are quick and can be fun to fill in. They are easy to tabulate but have the same drawbacks as closed questions. For example:

> How often do you eat fruit?

> a. At least once a day.
> b. Twice a week.
> c. Once a week.
> d. Only when there is an olive in my Martini.

## Rating questions

You can use rating questions to evaluate the positive and negative aspects of something by awarding marks. These questions can be made enjoyable to fill in and the answers are also easy to tabulate. For example:

> How bad is noise pollution in your area? Rate the noise pollution in your area on a scale of 1 to 10 with 10 being extremely bad and 1 being non-existent.

With regard to your product or service and its image, you could list the most important elements of your goods or service and give your customer an opportunity to rate each one, or get your customer to rate each product and service on value for money, reliability and effectiveness.

## The format

Start your questionnaire with an easy question. If the question is difficult then people will lose interest. The questions should flow logically from one to the next as this will make it easier and more interesting for your respondents to answer. People hate having to refer back to previous questions. Save any difficult questions until the end when people will be more willing to answer them. Make sure the language is clear and simple. If people misunderstand the questions, this will damage the quality of the answers. Never ask a question out of curiosity or because it might be interesting to know in the future. This will make the questionnaire unnecessarily long.

When you are designing the questionnaire form make sure that all the questions are well spaced out and clearly marked, with enough space for answers to be made in full. Make sure that it is obvious where each answer should go. Leave space for comments, where appropriate.

## Sample questionnaire

---

### Smith, Smith & Smith Ltd
### Customer Survey

*Customer details*

Age category (please tick one):
(18 or under)          _____
(19–25)                _____
(26–35)                _____
(36–50)                _____
(51–65)                _____
(66 or over)           _____

→

---

*Questionnaire*

Please answer the following questions, circling the appropriate answer in each case (1 means poor while 5 means excellent).

1. What was your impression of the office environment?

   1      2         3         4         5

   Comments ————————————————————————————

   ————————————————————————————————————

2. How well did you feel staff at reception treated you?

   1      2         3         4         5

   Comments ————————————————————————————

   ————————————————————————————————————

3. How satisfactory was our sales representative?

   1      2         3         4         5

   Comments ————————————————————————————

   ————————————————————————————————————

4. How well do you rate our delivery service?

   1      2         3         4         5

   Comments ————————————————————————————

   ————————————————————————————————————

5. How do you rate our product for quality?

   1      2         3         4         5

   Comments ————————————————————————————

   ————————————————————————————————————

6. How do you rate our product for value for money?

   1      2         3         4         5

   Comments ————————————————————————————

   ————————————————————————————————————

7. How do you rate our after-sales service?

   1      2         3         4         5

   Comments ————————————————————————————

   ————————————————————————————————————

8.  How consistent are our different outlets?

   1    2       3       4       5

Comments ——————————————————————

————————————————————————————————

9.  How would you rate our organisation overall?

   1    2       3       4       5

Comments ——————————————————————

————————————————————————————————

What recommendations would you make to help us improve our service to you, the customer?

The data rated from 1 to 5 can easily be expressed in a bar chart or histogram. If the same questionnaire is used at regular intervals, it can become a useful tool in monitoring the progress of the company in customers' perceptions.

The comment lines are important so that you can learn what it is exactly that pleases and displeases your customers most about your company. Remember, one customer comment could be the key to opening up a whole new area in customer service that could give your company a commercial advantage.

## Analysing and presenting your findings

Information is processed data. It is useless until it is analysed and classified. That is why designing the questionnaire carefully is so important.

Keep each response separate and numbered. Then you can use one of the computerised analysis systems available more easily. By grouping and regrouping questions, you can spot trends. There are two main types of information that can be collected from people. You can get their *personal response*. This can be unreliable. For example, people often tell a waiter that they enjoyed a meal when they hated it. You can observe a *change in behaviour*. This is more reliable. For example, if the people who praised their meal never come back, then they may not have liked the meal. However there may be other reasons why they don't return, so there is still a margin for error.

Once you have your responses you must now decide how to present your findings.

It is often easier to absorb statistics if they are presented visually, so try and use graphs, charts and tables. Pie charts are an effective and attractive way of presenting findings where there were only a limited variety of responses.

You can also rank order your responses. For example, *alphabetically*:

What's your favourite fruit?

| | |
|---|---|
| Apple | 15 |
| Banana | 20 |
| Date | 1 |
| Lemon | 3 |
| Orange | 14 |

Or ranked in order of *popularity*:

| | |
|---|---|
| Banana | 20 |
| Apple | 15 |
| Orange | 14 |
| Lemon | 3 |
| Date | 1 |

## Reports

A report can be defined as the written findings of an individual or group following a research process.

## The structure of a report

Reports vary in length, from a half-page memo report to government reports covering several volumes. Within that, however, most reports follow the same basic structure though it may be expressed in many different ways.

Title
Terms of reference
Summary (optional)
Method of procedure
Findings
Conclusions
Recommendations (optional)
Appendices (optional)
Sources

### Title

This is the name you assign your report. It should be as plain and clear as possible. For example, if you want to write a report on who uses your business then call it that. The more clearly you title your research, the more useful it will be later.

### Terms of reference

This statement should answer the following questions where applicable:

Who commissioned this report?

What do they want to know?

What are the aims of this report?

What limitations are put on the report? For example, if you are asked to write a report on the feasibility of building an extension to your current premises, you might be limited to a certain budget. Also planning permission and health and safety concerns might limit you. These should be referred to in your terms of reference so that anyone reading your report will be aware of them.

When is the report due?

## Summary

A lot of people do not need to read an entire report. They just need to get a general sense of what is going on and then can focus in where necessary. A summary can be inserted into a report to give people that overview. It should be short and outline the main points of the report. Eliminate any repetition or unnecessary description. You also do not need to include procedures or proofs here. These can be found elsewhere in the report.

## Method of procedure

Here you explain how you collected the information that will appear in your findings. In a way it is a justification of those findings. For example, if in your findings you say that 3,000 vehicles used a certain car park over a ten-day period, your method of procedure will show readers that you got that number by observation, or by looking at the number of parking tickets that were bought during that period.

## Findings

This is a presentation of the information you gathered, uncoloured by your opinions. Just put the facts down here.

## Conclusions

There is the place for opinion. Here you use the information you gathered to come to conclusions.

## Recommendations

In some reports you need to make recommendations. Here you use your findings and conclusions to make suggestions to improve future products, procedures or services, etc. It is important to include all recommendations, not just the ones you favour. This prevents people from later claiming that they would have followed another recommendation if it had been presented.

## Appendices

If you have any information that is relevant to the report but it would not be of interest to all readers or would slow down the report, it can be included here. Blueprints, definitions, maps, statistical information, anything like that can be put in here if needs be. If you have used research methods such as surveys, interviews or questionnaires, you can include samples, transcripts or extracts here.

### Sources

Here you include a bibliography or other sources.

## Sample report

### Title

A Report into the Causes of a Water-Stained Ceiling in Room 343 of Smith's Hotel, Ballysomewhere

### Terms of reference

I was asked by the hotel manager, Mr Maurice Smith, to investigate the causes for the appearance of a water stain on the ceiling of room 343 and make recommendations to prevent it from recurring. The report must be submitted by March 12th next.

### Method of procedure

I visited room 343 and observed the ceiling. I then went to room 443 which is the room directly above it. I spoke to cleaning and maintenance staff.

### Findings

The room directly above the damaged ceiling is room 443. I went in there and observed that the floor was water logged. There was a sink in the corner with both taps on and the sinkhole was plugged. Water was streaming from the sink onto the floor.

### Conclusions

From my observation of room 443, I conclude that the ceiling became water damaged as a result of the taps being left on in room 443. This fell onto the floor and seeped down into room 343.

### Recommendations

*   Remove sink from room 443.
*   Remove plug from sink.
*   Put a sign up over the sink in room 443, asking people to turn off taps after use.
*   Get maintenance staff to check that the taps are off on a regular basis.

## Market segmentation

Market segmentation refers to the manner in which market research identifies different sections of the market requiring different marketing strategies. A market can be segmented by gender, age, geography, attitude, self-image, taste or purchasing style.

Thus, for example, car companies direct certain cars towards the male market, others towards the female market and others towards the family market. Travel brochures aim different holidays at different age groups and their marketing reflects that. Quieter resorts with good food and sedate leisure facilities in warm climates are used to attract middle-aged groups. On the other hand, some resorts constantly emphasise their wild nightlife to attract younger holidaymakers.

Advertisers will target different areas of a country for different things. A food product might sell well in one area of the country where it is an important ingredient in a popular local dish. It might sell badly elsewhere. International manufacturers of tea and soft drinks have found that different qualities in their products are valued in different parts of the world. Therefore their products are blended to suit local tastes.

Car manufacturers add certain features to their vehicles in certain parts of the world. For example, heated front seats and steering wheels are greatly appreciated in Sweden but not so much in Kenya.

Politics and religion can affect people's attitudes towards products. Newspapers are often tailored to reflect the attitudes of their target market.

Self-image is a very important part of marketing. Products are constantly pushed on us that pander to our desired self-image. If we see ourselves as discerning and sophisticated there is a whole range of products that allow us to do anything from drive our car to eat ice cream while maintaining and promoting that image.

Tastes vary, so products vary to encompass them. You can now select a computer, mobile phone and even a toothbrush to reflect your minimalist, kitsch or classical tastes or even your love for Elvis.

Customer purchasing styles have been identified as:

- the bargain hunter
- the indifferent shopper
- the health-conscious shopper
- the label-conscious buyer
- the impulsive buyer.

Marketing strategies, packaging and the layout of shops have been designed to target every kind of purchasing style. For example, many companies are currently developing strategies for mass specialisation.

As companies become more and more customer oriented each company that manages to exceed the expectations of its customers can only hope to keep an edge for a short time before it is copied. Today some companies are hoping that mass specialisation will give them that temporary edge while other companies rush to catch up. Mass specialisation offers the customer the opportunity to have goods designed specifically for them. It is already possible to log on to an Internet site and design a pair of trainers to your taste. The shoes you receive will be unique to your requirements. Mass specialisation could mean that you need never bemoan the fact that you are between sizes. The clothes you buy would be tailored to your exact measurements and you would have no problem obtaining matching accessories.

## MIS (Marketing Information Systems)

MIS is a market research management system that collects, checks and analyses market information before passing it on to the relevant people. In order for it to be a fully effective business tool it must be constantly updated and must constantly update its users.

## Customer-oriented organisations

### Disneyworld

Disneyworld is an example of an organisation that practises good customer care. Once you pay for your ticket, you are free to use the amenities as you wish. There are no hidden costs. Once in the door, children can go off and do what they want without having to constantly return to their parents for more money. There are excellent childcare facilities for the very young and loads of special rides for those not yet old enough or tall enough for the more challenging rides. The employees are encouraged to 'live the part.' They dress in the costume of famous Disney characters and many spend their entire working day just meeting and greeting small children. They are happy to pose for photographs, again, with no hidden charges.

Though Disneyworld originated as a theme park aimed at children, they have ensured that adults and older children also enjoy their visit. This is a classic example of customer service generating more customers. Firstly, by entertaining the adults, you ensure that they will be more willing to come along with their children, who otherwise might not be able to go; and, secondly, by providing entertainment for adults successfully, you actually garner an even larger and more lucrative customer base. Disneyworld have introduced so many rides and attractions for older customers that they are more of a target market than the young children. It is quite common to see adults visiting Disney theme parks without any children in tow and the park is so safe and self-contained that those who do bring children can happily, once there, abandon their children and enjoy themselves. The parks are uniform, all divided into five recognisable sections, each concentrating on a different theme to cater for different ages and interests. These are called Main Street, USA; Frontierland; Adventureland; Fantasyland; and Discoveryland.

Upon entering, each visitor is given a complimentary map and there is even a train constantly circulating the perimeter of the parks to save your legs and confusion. All the more challenging amusements have firmly enforced age and height restrictions. For the adults, cabaret-style entertainment is provided as a respite from the theme-park atmosphere. A large variety of eating establishments is provided, from fast-food outlets to full menu restaurants. The prices vary to suit all tastes and pockets.

As with all successful customer-driven companies, Disneyworld never rests on its laurels.

As rival theme parks are developed worldwide, the excellent customer service that Disneyworld provided yesterday is commonplace today. In order to keep one step ahead of the competition, the visitor is given opportunities to talk to workers and make suggestions. The Disney organisation is constantly upgrading and updating the parks, adding new and exciting attractions based on the latest crazes and blockbuster movies. These attractions always incorporate cutting-edge technology and astonishing graphics.

In 1992 they opened the EuroDisney resort at Marne-la-Vallée, 32km (20 miles) east of Paris. It covers 600ha (1,500 acres) and took almost four years to build. Since then they have added hotels to their parks, allowing families to completely escape from the outside world. Their ongoing success is such that they have now built their own town in America and there is a huge list of prospective residents. It gives a whole new meaning to the name 'Disneyworld'.

Recently, in response to the growing queues for the main attractions, Disney has adopted a booking system. You go to the attraction you want and you are given a time at which to return. This means that you only have to queue for a short time before you enjoy the amenity of your choice. It frees up your time to get around and see more attractions.

## Superquinn

Superquinn is an excellent example of an organisation that provides good customer care. This organisation is one of the earliest examples of a consciously customer-driven company. It has a strong philosophy, instilled by its founder Fergal Quinn, of listening to its customers and acting on their suggestions. Managers are actively encouraged to spend their time on the shop floor, talking to customers. Their offices are designed to be small and pokey, so that they will not be tempted to linger in them. The philosophy of the company is that the shop floor with the customers is where the real action is. Managers are also encouraged to help customers by performing some of the day-to-day functions of the store, such as bagging groceries. While doing this, the managers get a chance to listen to the customers and learn what they want. As a result, Superquinn was a pioneer in such initiatives as crèches, sweet-free checkout counters, salad bars, in-store bakeries and butchers. Superquinn was also one of the first to help people to their cars with their shopping, lend umbrellas, offer a wide range of fresh and exotic fruit and vegetables and provide community noticeboards.

Superquinn realised that though you may have the customer service edge today, some other company will take your idea and build on it tomorrow. The key to good customer service is to never be complacent. Therefore Fergal Quinn made sure that he was up to date in all the customer service initiatives that were developing around the world. He would take out subscriptions to relevant trade and business magazines around the world and give subscriptions to various employees so that they would read them and report back any ideas that would be of use to Superquinn, such as the concept of loyalty cards. This achieved the dual role of keeping Superquinn at the forefront of customer service and also of making the employees feel they had a genuine voice in the running of the company. Employees who feel that they are valued are more productive and better able to deal with customers and fellow employees (the internal customer) themselves.

Superquinn also invites groups of customers to come in at regular intervals and talk about what they like, dislike and would like in the supermarket. These focus groups are not paid because Fergal Quinn felt that if they were paid, they would be less likely to be critical about the supermarket and the company needed to hear what was wrong with the company so that it could put it right. However, the participants are given something nice from the supermarket at Christmas as a mark of gratitude for all the help they have given throughout the year.

## Customer-oriented products

Think of your customers when you create a product. Make sure that it is easy to use and that the instructions are easy to follow. If a product is created without regard to the needs and desires of customers, it will not sell. Here are some 'dos' and 'don'ts' of product design:

- Don't make products that are messy to use, such as milk cartons that are difficult to open and explode all over you.
- Don't make products that make customers feel wasteful. Many people are concerned about the environment and do not enjoy throwing out lots of unnecessary packaging.
- Customers don't like wasting products. They don't like to buy a pre-packed Caesar salad, only to find that they must throw away most of the salad dressing each time.
- Inadequate packaging can cause as much waste as too much, for example some pasta packaging is so fragile that it splits in two and covers the floor with pasta; or some packets of biscuits can't be resealed, so the next day the biscuits have gone soft, creating more waste.
- Customers don't like to feel misled. A customer may buy a frozen dinner once because of the appetising image on the box but if the actual meal itself is inadequate there won't be a repeat sale. A cake mix, for example, might fail to make it very clear that other ingredients will also need to be bought.
- Try to standardise your sizes, measures and grades. Do all factor 15 sunscreens offer the same protection? How is it that some total sunblocks have a higher SPF rating than others if they all totally block out the sun? It can be very time-consuming trying on three or four different sizes of each outfit because you can't trust sizes to always be the same. If a customer knows their usual size in your product range, they should be able to go in and just try on one shirt or one pair of shoes. The time saved may mean that the customer may try on and buy other outfits rather than being forced to take three sizes of the same shirt into a changing room. It would also mean that the customer would have to use the changing room less for each purpose. If it took less time to shop and try on outfits, people could shop more frequently.
- Customers don't like to be frustrated with meaningless information. Does a customer really care if a product is recommended by the *Newfoundland Journal of Animal Healthcare*? Should I believe the endorsement of Mary Smith from Berks? Does she even exist?
- Do not cheapen a good product once it becomes established. Take as an example an

ice cream brand that markets itself as a luxury quality product. To begin with, it uses only the finest ingredients. Its vanilla ice cream has little black dots in it because it is made with real vanilla pods. Then when the product is established, the flavour changes and the dots disappear. Your product will quickly lose its reputation as a quality product. Sometimes when a product is established its volume is reduced slightly while the price remains the same. That jar of hand cream is now 100ml not 125ml. There are now only eleven toffees in the packet, not twelve. Customers notice these things.

A brand name might try to branch out into another area. A trusted brand name for bread might move into frozen foods. The idea is that the good reputation of the brand will attract customers. If the frozen foods are not great then they might undermine the established reputation of your brand name. In most cases it is not worth the risk of cheapening your good product, you will only lose your loyal customers.

## Exercises

1. A housewife, a retired, elderly man, a man with three young children and a builder on his lunch break all visit their local supermarket at lunchtime. Make a list of what their different needs and wants might be.

2. How are your own customer perceptions formed? What factors would affect your perceptions if you were a customer dealing with the following situations?

    a.  Buying a second-hand car
    b.  Getting a haircut
    c.  Booking a holiday
    d.  Buying clothes
    e.  Getting a burst pipe mended
    f.  Ordering a taxi

3. Pick three local organisations, all offering the same service, and where you have been a customer. They could be supermarkets, banks, hairdressers, pubs, restaurants, etc. List them in order of preference and consider the reasons why you favour one over another. Now show that same list to friends, colleagues and family. Note how they order the same businesses and what reasons they give. You can then compile a bank of qualities that influence customer perception for that particular type of organisation.

4. Give an example of when a company exceeded your expectations. Outline the reasons why you were impressed.

5. Give an example of an occasion when you were unhappy with a service and say why.

6. You work for a local coffee shop. Decide on the best method of monitoring your customers' satisfaction levels. Justify your choice.

7. Draft a customer satisfaction comment card for a local pizza delivery company.

8. Draw a diagram delineating the internal/external customer roles within an organisation that you have knowledge of.

9. You have been put in charge of reorganising and redecorating the student canteen. How are you going to decide what to include? What improvements do you think are necessary?

10. People change as they get older. How do you think time will affect your perceptions, needs and wants as a customer?

11. Alicia is a trendy clothes store for males and females aged between 18 and 35. Its clothes go from the mid-price range to expensive. It is generally very busy at weekends. There are three cash registers on one long counter on the ground floor. Ann has been in a very disorganised queue for about 15 minutes. She and two other customers have become aware of another woman jumping into the middle of the queue. One of the other customers gets served and then this woman jumps in front of Ann in full view of the cash register. Ann objects but the woman just shrugs. Then Ann says loudly, 'Well, if you are that ignorant, then go ahead.' The woman is served by one of the girls and then Ann takes her turn. The girl behind the counter makes no acknowledgment of what has happened. Ann is annoyed and leaves. She has not shopped there since.

    a. Why do you think Ann was annoyed with the shop?

    b. In what ways could this incident affect future business?

    c. Imagine that you are Ann. Write a letter of complaint to the store.

    d. What recommendations would you make to the store so that this incident didn't recur?

# 7

# CASE STUDY – FORD

F ord is one of the largest and most famous car manufacturers in the world. Innovators from the start, the early Model T was the first mass-produced car, so reasonably priced that those who built it could own it. In 2000, the Ford Focus was the best-selling car globally and in 2006 continued to be the best-selling car in its class. Ford also owns Mazda, Land Rover, Jaguar, Aston Martin and Volvo. In America, they own Lincoln and Mercury. In addition, they have become involved in the car rental business with a majority interest in Hertz. All this success has not made them complacent and they have a highly developed customer care system called Customer Viewpoint. In this chapter we will examine the philosophy behind this programme and see how it works in practice.

Ford believes that the key to a successful business is a satisfied customer. All other considerations lead to that. A great product is a big part of customer satisfaction, but so are a positive sales experience, value for money and an excellent after-sales service. Customer Viewpoint aims to cater for the customer at every stage of the car-ownership experience and so encourage that customer to buy from Ford again and perhaps even become an enthusiastic advocate for the company. Ford also recognises the need to make internal customers a willing part of this process and puts a great deal of effort into explaining how this programme will benefit everyone within the company. For example:

> The purpose of Customer Viewpoint is not to compare and rank dealers but to encourage dealerships to improve their customer handling processes and thereby the satisfaction and loyalty of individual customers.

> Achieving customer satisfaction and loyalty is a team effort and no individual should be held responsible for poor performance.

> Your Sales Zone Manager or FCSD Business Manager will be able to help you and answer any questions that you may have.

> (Extracts from page 35, *Customer Viewpoint Programme Overview*, Ford)

This is Ford's strategy pyramid which is available online. To learn more about their strategy you simply click on any heading within the pyramid and and a more detailed explanation will appear next to the pyramid.

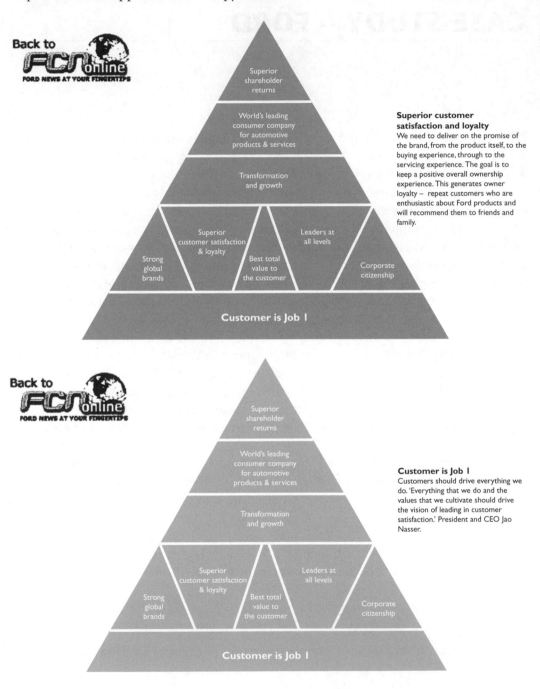

**Superior customer satisfaction and loyalty**
We need to deliver on the promise of the brand, from the product itself, to the buying experience, through to the servicing experience. The goal is to keep a positive overall ownership experience. This generates owner loyalty – repeat customers who are enthusiastic about Ford products and will recommend them to friends and family.

**Customer is Job 1**
Customers should drive everything we do. 'Everything that we do and the values that we cultivate should drive the vision of leading in customer satisfaction.' President and CEO Jao Nasser.

(This information was obtained from the Ford website http://www.fcn.ford.com.)

## Ford's mission statement

Our Vision. To become the world's leading consumer company for automotive products and services.

Our Mission. We are a global, diverse family with a proud heritage, passionately committed to providing outstanding products and services that improve people's lives.

Our Values. The customer is Job 1. We do the right thing for our customers, our people, our environment and our society. By improving everything we do, we provide superior returns to our shareholders.

## How the Customer Viewpoint Programme works

Once the vehicle is handed over to the customer a staff member of the Ford dealership will fill in the Vehicle Customer Service Record (VCSR). This information is recorded on computer by Ford and then e-mailed to Lorien. Lorien is an independent research agency that has been hired by Ford to administer the programme on their behalf. This ensures that Lorien can objectively and uniformly assess all information on the programme.

One month after obtaining the vehicle, the customer will receive the first survey from Ford (see pages 141–44). This detailed questionnaire focuses on the Purchase Experience and seeks to learn the customer's views on the purchase and delivery process as well as their satisfaction with the car so far. The questionnaire tries to ascertain the vehicle selection criteria of its customers by asking about previous vehicle ownership and why they decided to buy a Ford car at a particular dealership. It is also the first chance that the company has of ascertaining whether the customer will buy from Ford again. When a customer changes from Ford to another car manufacturer for their next purchase it is referred to as customer defection. Ford, like all organisations, seeks to reduce customer defection for the simple reason that it is more economical to retain customers than it is to attract new ones. This questionnaire asks for personal customer details and any recommendations that the customer may wish to make that would enhance the purchase experience.

The second customer survey measures the Service Experience (see pages 145–8). Questionnaires are sent out after 13 months or, if the customer has had warranty work carried out in this period, at 3–12 months.

This questionnaire checks that the car is still owned by the same customer and asks how long they intend to continue owning it. If the customer has changed their vehicle and bought one from another manufacturer, they are asked why they changed. It then asks about the type of service contact the customer has had with the dealership and their level of satisfaction with it.

Customers who have responded to either of the two previous surveys will be sent a third questionnaire at 24, 36 or 48 months. If a customer has not responded to previous surveys they will not be sent this one, as the company has no wish to irritate customers who dislike surveys. As we saw in Chapter 6, questionnaires can suffer from very few being completed and returned. However, Ford have enjoyed a high 24 per cent success rate in receiving completed questionnaires. This third survey measures customer satisfaction with all aspects of the Ownership Experience and gathers important information such as the likelihood of the customer buying another Ford vehicle, and when. It also asks defectors what made them decide to change, and invites the customer to offer their own opinions in spaces provided within questionnaire.

Lorien processes the information from each completed survey and the results are given to the dealers in two types of report, the Weekly Customer Response Report and the Monthly Dealership Report.

## Weekly Customer Response Report

> This report summarises key loyalty and satisfaction information and provides individual customer comments. It enables you to respond quickly to the needs of individual customers and take remedial action where necessary. Importantly, it also provides quick feedback of potential new vehicle sales prospects for salespersons to follow up.

Note how the programme clearly outlines to the dealer the benefits of this report. It is important to do this because it shows to the dealer the value of customer care and helps eliminate any fear or hostility individual staff may be feeling. In situations where companies foist unexplained customer care programmes on their staff, there can be a lot of resistance through fear of the unknown. By constantly showing the purpose and advantages of each step in the Customer Viewpoint programme Ford avoids such problems. Transparency is the key to a successful customer care programme.

*(Some text is deliberately obscured here at the request of Ford Ireland.)*

**Ford**

Henry Ford & Son Limited
Elm Court, Boreenmanna Road, Cork

**FORD TRANSIT**

PURCHASE EXPERIENCE

Please make any necessary changes here:

Name:

Address:

Delivery Date:
Telephone:

Dear

Thank you for your recent purchase of a Ford Transit (99D46989) from …Dennehy's Cross Garage.

As a valued customer, your opinions about your vehicle and dealership experiences are extremely important to us. Please take a few moments to complete this survey. The information you provide will be used by Ford Motor Company and Dennehy's Cross Garage to continuously improve the products and services provided.

If you would like to give more detail about your vehicle or experiences with the dealer there is space on the back page to write your comments. For your convenience, a postage-paid reply envelope is enclosed.

Thank you in advance for your time in completing this survey.

Yours sincerely,

501    0000167411

P.S. This survey should be completed by the person most familiar with the purchase and use of the new Ford Transit.

## SATISFACTION WITH YOUR NEW FORD TRANSIT

Please mark the relevant box with a ☒

**1**    How satisfied are you with the following aspects of your Ford Transit.

| | Completely Satisfied | Very Satisfied | Fairly Well Satisfied | Somewhat Dissatisfied | Very Dissatisfied | | | Completely Satisfied | Very Satisfied | Fairly Well Satisfied | Somewhat Dissatisfied | Very Dissatisfied |
|---|---|---|---|---|---|---|---|---|---|---|---|---|
| **a.** Your vehicle overall | ☐ | ☐ | ☐ | ☐ | ☐ | **j.** Comfort - front seats | ☐ | ☐ | ☐ | ☐ | ☐ |
| **b.** Body workmanship and finish | ☐ | ☐ | ☐ | ☐ | ☐ | **k.** Luggage capacity | ☐ | ☐ | ☐ | ☐ | ☐ |
| **c.** Quality of interior workmanship and finish | ☐ | ☐ | ☐ | ☐ | ☐ | **l.** Acceleration | ☐ | ☐ | ☐ | ☐ | ☐ |
| | | | | | | **m.** Braking | ☐ | ☐ | ☐ | ☐ | ☐ |
| **d.** Mechanical reliability | ☐ | ☐ | ☐ | ☐ | ☐ | **n.** Ease of handling | ☐ | ☐ | ☐ | ☐ | ☐ |
| **e.** Interior roominess | ☐ | ☐ | ☐ | ☐ | ☐ | **o.** Gearchange | ☐ | ☐ | ☐ | ☐ | ☐ |
| **f.** Level of equipment | ☐ | ☐ | ☐ | ☐ | ☐ | **p.** Quality of ride | ☐ | ☐ | ☐ | ☐ | ☐ |
| **g.** All round visibility | ☐ | ☐ | ☐ | ☐ | ☐ | **q.** Fuel economy | ☐ | ☐ | ☐ | ☐ | ☐ |
| **h.** Safety | ☐ | ☐ | ☐ | ☐ | ☐ | **r.** Quietness when driving | ☐ | ☐ | ☐ | ☐ | ☐ |
| **i.** Accessibility of the driving controls | ☐ | ☐ | ☐ | ☐ | ☐ | **s.** Heating and ventilation | ☐ | ☐ | ☐ | ☐ | ☐ |
| | | | | | | **t.** Value for money | ☐ | ☐ | ☐ | ☐ | ☐ |

IR 1 CSP 99 NS 30/12/98 V3

## YOUR OVERALL SATISFACTION

**2** **How satisfied are you with ...**

| | Completely Satisfied | Very Satisfied | Fairly Well Satisfied | Somewhat Dissatisfied | Very Dissatisfied |
|---|---|---|---|---|---|
| **a.** Your overall purchase and delivery experience | ☐ | ☐ | ☐ | ☐ | ☐ |

## YOUR PURCHASE EXPERIENCE

Based on the visit(s) you made to arrange the purchase, how would you rate Dennehy's Cross Garage in the following areas?

**3** **Treatment on arrival at the dealership**

| | Excellent | Very Good | Good | Fair | Poor |
|---|---|---|---|---|---|
| **a.** Promptness of acknowledgement | ☐ | ☐ | ☐ | ☐ | ☐ |
| **b.** Treating you as a serious prospective customer | ☐ | ☐ | ☐ | ☐ | ☐ |
| **c.** Giving you the level of attention you required | ☐ | ☐ | ☐ | ☐ | ☐ |

**4** **Your salesperson**

| | Excellent | Very Good | Good | Fair | Poor |
|---|---|---|---|---|---|
| **a.** Professionalism and courtesy | ☐ | ☐ | ☐ | ☐ | ☐ |
| **b.** Knowledge of the products and dealership services | ☐ | ☐ | ☐ | ☐ | ☐ |
| **c.** Ability to meet your requirements | ☐ | ☐ | ☐ | ☐ | ☐ |
| **d.** Conducting your purchase without making you feel pressured | ☐ | ☐ | ☐ | ☐ | ☐ |
| **e.** Offering you additional products and services without making you feel pressured (e.g. accessories, Extra Cover, Ford insurance) | ☐ | ☐ | ☐ | ☐ | ☐ |
| **f.** Honesty and sincerity | ☐ | ☐ | ☐ | ☐ | ☐ |

| | Yes | No | I didn't want one | I wasn't offered one |
|---|---|---|---|---|
| **g.** Were you satisfied with the test drive? | ☐ | ☐ | ☐ | ☐ |

**5** **Financial arrangements**

| | n/a | Excellent | Very Good | Good | Fair | Poor |
|---|---|---|---|---|---|---|
| **a.** Ability to provide a suitable finance plan | ☐ | ☐ | ☐ | ☐ | ☐ | ☐ |
| **b.** Providing clear and thorough explanations of the finance plans | ☐ | ☐ | ☐ | ☐ | ☐ | ☐ |
| **c.** Honesty and sincerity of the person who helped with your finance arrangements | ☐ | ☐ | ☐ | ☐ | ☐ | ☐ |

**6** **Taking delivery of your new vehicle**

| | Excellent | Very Good | Good | Fair | Poor |
|---|---|---|---|---|---|
| **a.** Having your vehicle ready for you when promised | ☐ | ☐ | ☐ | ☐ | ☐ |
| **b.** Overall cleanliness of your vehicle | ☐ | ☐ | ☐ | ☐ | ☐ |
| **c.** Making sure everything was in working order | ☐ | ☐ | ☐ | ☐ | ☐ |
| **d.** Explanation of vehicle features and operating controls | ☐ | ☐ | ☐ | ☐ | ☐ |
| **e.** Explanation of vehicle warranty | ☐ | ☐ | ☐ | ☐ | ☐ |
| **f.** Explanation of service schedule | ☐ | ☐ | ☐ | ☐ | ☐ |
| **g.** Amount of fuel in the tank | ☐ | ☐ | ☐ | ☐ | ☐ |

| | Yes, and I accepted | Yes, but I didn't accept | No |
|---|---|---|---|
| **h.** Were you offered an introduction to the Service and Parts departments? | ☐ | ☐ | ☐ |
| **i.** Did the dealership offer to schedule your 12 month/10,000 mile service? | ☐ | ☐ | ☐ |

| | Yes | No |
|---|---|---|
| **j.** Was your vehicle handed over using a delivery checklist? | ☐ | ☐ |

| | Yes | No | None ordered |
|---|---|---|---|
| **k.** Were all the options and accessories fitted satisfactorily? | ☐ | ☐ | ☐ |

**7** **After purchase contact**

| | Yes | No | |
|---|---|---|---|
| **a.** Have you been contacted, either by phone, post or personally, by anyone from the dealership since taking delivery of your new vehicle? | ☐ | ☐ | If no go to 8 |

| | n/a | Excellent | Very Good | Good | Fair | Poor |
|---|---|---|---|---|---|---|
| **b.** Timeliness of this contact | ☐ | ☐ | ☐ | ☐ | ☐ | ☐ |

IR 1 CSP 99 NS 30/12/98 V3

## YOUR PURCHASE EXPERIENCE (cont.)

**8. Handling of questions or concerns**

| | Yes | No | Didn't have any | |
|---|---|---|---|---|
| a. Have you let the dealership know about any questions or concerns you have had? | ☐ | ☐ | ☐ | If you **didn't have any** go to 9 |

| | Yes, first time | Yes, but not first time | No | |
|---|---|---|---|---|
| b. Have these questions/concerns been resolved to your satisfaction? | ☐ | ☐ | ☐ | |

| | n/a | Excellent | Very Good | Good | Fair | Poor |
|---|---|---|---|---|---|---|
| c. Ability to answer your questions or resolve your concerns | ☐ | ☐ | ☐ | ☐ | ☐ | ☐ |
| d. Helpfulness in responding to your questions/concerns | ☐ | ☐ | ☐ | ☐ | ☐ | ☐ |
| e. Follow-through on any promises made to help you | ☐ | ☐ | ☐ | ☐ | ☐ | ☐ |

## RECOMMENDATIONS/INTENTIONS

**9. Based on your experiences at the dealership, would you:**

| | Definitely Would | Probably Would | Maybe Would Maybe Not | Probably Would Not | Definitely Would Not |
|---|---|---|---|---|---|
| a. Recommend your salesperson | ☐ | ☐ | ☐ | ☐ | ☐ |
| b. Recommend this dealership as a place to purchase a Ford vehicle | ☐ | ☐ | ☐ | ☐ | ☐ |
| c. Recommend a Ford vehicle | ☐ | ☐ | ☐ | ☐ | ☐ |
| d. Recommend your Finance Company, if applicable | ☐ | ☐ | ☐ | ☐ | ☐ |
| e. Use this dealership for service or repair work | ☐ | ☐ | ☐ | ☐ | ☐ |

## CHOOSING YOUR VEHICLE

**10. About your previous vehicle ...**

| | Yes | No | Didn't have one | |
|---|---|---|---|---|
| a. Was it purchased from the same dealer as this new one? | ☐ | ☐ | ☐ | If you **didn't have one** go to 11 |

b. Was It a Ford vehicle?   Yes ☐   No ☐   If No, what was it?

**11. If you seriously considered any other vehicles, which ones were they?**

1   2   3

**12. What were the three most important reasons that made you purchase a vehicle from this dealership?**

| a. Dealership was recommended/word of mouth | ☐ | f. Dealership's ability to provide financing | ☐ |
|---|---|---|---|
| b. Dealership location | ☐ | g. Selection of vehicles | ☐ |
| c. Previous experience with dealership | ☐ | h. Price or deal offered by the dealership | ☐ |
| d. Vehicle availability | ☐ | i. Dealership advertising | ☐ |
| e. Information provided on the Internet | ☐ | j. Trade-in value | ☐ |

**13. How was your new Ford Transit paid for, excluding any deposit or trade-in?**

Cash only ☐   Ford Credit ☐   Ford Options ☐   Finance company (arranged by the dealership) ☐   Bank/finance company (arranged by you directly) ☐   Other ☐

| | 1 year | 2 years | 3 years | 4 years | 5 years or more | Don't know |
|---|---|---|---|---|---|---|
| **14. How long do you expect to keep this vehicle?** | ☐ | ☐ | ☐ | ☐ | ☐ | ☐ |

## ADDITIONAL INFORMATION

**15. How would you rate Dennehy's Cross Garage in terms of ...**

| | Excellent | Very Good | Good | Fair | Poor |
|---|---|---|---|---|---|
| a. Opening hours | ☐ | ☐ | ☐ | ☐ | ☐ |
| b. Ease of parking | ☐ | ☐ | ☐ | ☐ | ☐ |
| c. Exterior appearance | ☐ | ☐ | ☐ | ☐ | ☐ |

IR 1 CSP 99 NG 30/12/98 V3

## IMPORTANCE OF THE PURCHASE PROCESS

**16** Which, if any, of the following areas of the purchase and delivery process should the dealer improve (Please mark all that apply)

**a.** Treatment on arrival at the dealership ☐

**b.** Your salesperson ☐

**c.** Financial arrangements ☐

**d.** Taking delivery/vehicle condition ☐

**e.** After-sales contact ☐

**f.** Handling of questions/concerns ☐

## YOUR COMMENTS

**17** If you have any comments about your purchase or delivery experience, particularly concerning any areas you suggested the dealership should improve, please write them here.

Please tick this box if you do not wish these comments to go to Dennehy's Cross Garage. ☐

## YOUR PERSONAL OPINIONS

**18** Please let us know your personal attitude towards Ford and its products by rating your level of agreement with the following statements.

| | Strongly Agree | Agree | Disagree | Strongly Disagree | No opinion |
|---|---|---|---|---|---|
| **a.** I am an enthusiastic advocate of Ford products | ☐ | ☐ | ☐ | ☐ | ☐ |
| **b.** Price is the most important factor when buying a vehicle | ☐ | ☐ | ☐ | ☐ | ☐ |
| **c.** I would have bought a different manufacturer's product had it been 5% cheaper than my Ford | ☐ | ☐ | ☐ | ☐ | ☐ |
| **d.** I would have bought a different manufacturer's product had it been 10% cheaper than my Ford | ☐ | ☐ | ☐ | ☐ | ☐ |
| **e.** My choice of vehicle is influenced by the motoring press | ☐ | ☐ | ☐ | ☐ | ☐ |
| **f.** I will always buy a Ford if I can | ☐ | ☐ | ☐ | ☐ | ☐ |
| **g.** Ford designs and produces innovative products | ☐ | ☐ | ☐ | ☐ | ☐ |
| **h.** My dealings with this dealership will positively affect my future purchases from Ford | ☐ | ☐ | ☐ | ☐ | ☐ |
| **i.** I like to vary manufacturer irrespective of how satisfied I am with my current vehicle | ☐ | ☐ | ☐ | ☐ | ☐ |

## TELL US ABOUT YOURSELF

**19** Your gender?

| Male | Female |
|---|---|
| ☐ | ☐ |

**20** Age group?

| Under 20 | 20-24 | 25-29 | 30-34 | 35-39 | 40-44 |
|---|---|---|---|---|---|
| ☐ | ☐ | ☐ | ☐ | ☐ | ☐ |

| 45-49 | 50-54 | 55-59 | 60-64 | 65 or over |
|---|---|---|---|---|
| ☐ | ☐ | ☐ | ☐ | ☐ |

Your Ford dealership is also interested in your individual opinion. Would you therefore agree to us sending the information you have provided in this questionnaire to your dealership?

Yes ☐  No ☐

*Thank you for your time. Please return in the postage paid envelope provided.*

IR 1 CSP 99 NS 30/12/98 V3

*Again, some text is obscured here at the request of Ford Ireland.)*

**FORD TRANSIT**
SERVICE EXPERIENCE

Henry Ford & Son Limited
Elm Court, Boreenmanna Road, Cork

Please make any necessary changes here:

Name:

Address:

Delivery Date:
Telephone:

I am writing to ask for your help with a survey concerning your experiences with your Ford Transit (99D46989) that you purchased from Dennehy's Cross Garage about a year ago.

Because we, and your dealership, value your business, your opinions throughout your ownership of the vehicle are important to us.

You may have received a survey from us before, concerning previous experiences, but on this occasion I would like to ask you about any service experiences you may have had with the vehicle mentioned above.

If you would like to give more detail about your service experience there is space on the back page to write your comments.

Please take a few moments to complete this survey.

The information you provide will be used by Ford Motor Company and your dealer to continuously improve the products and services that are available. For your convenience, a postage-paid reply envelope is enclosed.

Thank you in advance for your time in completing this survey.

Yours sincerely,

Please mark your answers with a [X] in the relevant box.

## ABOUT YOUR VEHICLE

**1** Do you or someone else in your household still own this Ford Transit?

Yes ☐   No ☐   If no   go to 16

**2** When do you expect to replace this vehicle?

Within 3 months ☐   Within 6 months ☐   Within a year ☐   More than a year ☐   Don't know ☐

## SERVICING DEALERSHIP

**3** Where did you go for your most recent service or repair work?

Name:

Address/Town:

**4** When was this visit?

Within 1 month ☐   2-3 months ago ☐   4-6 months ago ☐   More than 6 months ago ☐

**5** Why do you use this dealership for service or repair work? (Mark all that apply).

Selling dealership ☐     Availability of parts ☐     Price (if applicable) ☐

Location ☐     Previous experience with dealer ☐     Recommended by someone ☐

Alternative transport arrangements ☐     Convenience of appointment ☐     Opening hours ☐

Other (please write in)

## YOUR OVERALL SATISFACTION

**6** How satisfied were you with ...

| | Completely Satisfied | Very Satisfied | Fairly Well Satisfied | Somewhat Dissatisfied | Very Dissatisfied |
|---|---|---|---|---|---|
| **a.** Overall experience of your recent visit | ☐ | ☐ | ☐ | ☐ | ☐ |

## YOUR SERVICE EXPERIENCE

How would you rate your servicing dealership in terms of ...

**7** Convenience of appointment

| | Yes | No | n/a | | |
|---|---|---|---|---|---|
| **a.** Did the dealership confirm this appointment | ☐ | ☐ | ☐ | | |

| | Excellent | Very Good | Good | Fair | Poor |
|---|---|---|---|---|---|
| **b.** Ease of arranging the appointment | ☐ | ☐ | ☐ | ☐ | ☐ |
| **c.** Getting your service appointment on a day and time that was convenient for you | ☐ | ☐ | ☐ | ☐ | ☐ |
| **d.** Alternative transportation arrangements | ☐ | ☐ | ☐ | ☐ | ☐ |

**8** Service reception

| | Excellent | Very Good | Good | Fair | Poor |
|---|---|---|---|---|---|
| **a.** Parking facilities | ☐ | ☐ | ☐ | ☐ | ☐ |
| **b.** Promptly acknowledging you when you arrived at service reception | ☐ | ☐ | ☐ | ☐ | ☐ |
| **c.** Attending to you within a reasonable amount of time | ☐ | ☐ | ☐ | ☐ | ☐ |
| **d.** Ability to understand and record your needs correctly | ☐ | ☐ | ☐ | ☐ | ☐ |
| **e.** Providing you with a price estimate, if applicable | ☐ | ☐ | ☐ | ☐ | ☐ |
| **f.** Provision of an accurate estimate of when the work should be completed | ☐ | ☐ | ☐ | ☐ | ☐ |
| **g.** Treating you as a valued customer | ☐ | ☐ | ☐ | ☐ | ☐ |
| **h.** Overall appearance of service department | ☐ | ☐ | ☐ | ☐ | ☐ |

| | Yes, and I accepted | Yes, but I didn't accept | No |
|---|---|---|---|
| **i.** Prior to the start of work, did they offer to inspect the vehicle with you? | ☐ | ☐ | ☐ |

IR ST CSP 99 NS 30/12/98 V3

## YOUR SERVICE EXPERIENCE (cont.)

**9   Completion of work**

a. On your most recent visit, did the dealership complete all the work requested first time?

| Yes | No |
|---|---|
| ☐ go to 9d | ☐ go to 9b |

b. Why was the work not completed first time?

| They couldn't find the fault ☐ | Required parts were not in stock ☐ |
|---|---|
| Not enough time ☐ | Same fault developed again ☐ |

c. What type of work did you have carried out?

| Routine Service ☐ | Electrical Repair ☐ |
|---|---|
| Mechanical Repair ☐ | Bodywork/Paintwork ☐ |

| | Excellent | Very Good | Good | Fair | Poor |
|---|---|---|---|---|---|
| d. Quality of work carried out | ☐ | ☐ | ☐ | ☐ | ☐ |
| e. Completion of all work requested | ☐ | ☐ | ☐ | ☐ | ☐ |
| f. Notifying you of any extra work required, if applicable | ☐ | ☐ | ☐ | ☐ | ☐ |
| g. Notifying you of any changes when your vehicle would be ready, if applicable | ☐ | ☐ | ☐ | ☐ | ☐ |

**10   Collection of vehicle**

| | Excellent | Very Good | Good | Fair | Poor |
|---|---|---|---|---|---|
| a. Having your vehicle ready when promised | ☐ | ☐ | ☐ | ☐ | ☐ |
| b. Length of time taken to complete the work | ☐ | ☐ | ☐ | ☐ | ☐ |
| c. Ability to collect your vehicle at a time convenient to you | ☐ | ☐ | ☐ | ☐ | ☐ |
| d. Cleanliness of vehicle on return | ☐ | ☐ | ☐ | ☐ | ☐ |
| e. Explanation of the work carried out and charges (if any) | ☐ | ☐ | ☐ | ☐ | ☐ |
| f. Advice on future service needs | ☐ | ☐ | ☐ | ☐ | ☐ |

| | Yes, and I accepted | Yes, but I didn't accept | Already booked | No |
|---|---|---|---|---|
| g. Did the dealership offer to schedule your next routine service | ☐ | ☐ | ☐ | ☐ |

**11   After-service contact**

a. Have you been contacted, either by phone, post or personally, by anyone from the dealership since completion of this recent work?

| Yes | No |
|---|---|
| ☐ | ☐ If no   go to 12 |

| | Excellent | Very Good | Good | Fair | Poor |
|---|---|---|---|---|---|
| b. Timeliness of this contact | ☐ | ☐ | ☐ | ☐ | ☐ |

**12   Handling of questions or concerns**

a. Have you let the dealership know about any questions or concerns you have had regarding your most recent visit?

| Yes | No | Haven't had any |
|---|---|---|
| ☐ | ☐ | ☐ If you **haven't had any**   go to 13 |

b. Have these questions/concerns been resolved to your satisfaction?

| Yes, first time | Yes, but not first time | Not yet resolved |
|---|---|---|
| ☐ | ☐ | ☐ |

| | Excellent | Very Good | Good | Fair | Poor |
|---|---|---|---|---|---|
| c. Ability to answer your questions or resolve your concerns | ☐ | ☐ | ☐ | ☐ | ☐ |
| d. Helpfulness in responding to your questions/concerns | ☐ | ☐ | ☐ | ☐ | ☐ |
| e. Follow-through on any promises made to help you | ☐ | ☐ | ☐ | ☐ | ☐ |

## ADDITIONAL INFORMATION

**13   How would you rate the Service staff in terms of ...**

| | Excellent | Very Good | Good | Fair | Poor |
|---|---|---|---|---|---|
| a. Appearance and dress | ☐ | ☐ | ☐ | ☐ | ☐ |
| b. Courtesy when serving you | ☐ | ☐ | ☐ | ☐ | ☐ |
| c. Concern for your time | ☐ | ☐ | ☐ | ☐ | ☐ |

## RECOMMENDATIONS / INTENTIONS

**14   Based on your experiences at this dealership, would you?**

| | Definitely Would | Probably Would | Maybe Would Maybe Not | Probably Would Not | Definitely Would Not |
|---|---|---|---|---|---|
| a. Continue using this dealership for service or repair work | ☐ | ☐ | ☐ | ☐ | ☐ |
| b. Recommend them as a place to have a vehicle serviced | ☐ | ☐ | ☐ | ☐ | ☐ |
| c. Recommend a Ford vehicle | ☐ | ☐ | ☐ | ☐ | ☐ |

IR ST CSP 99 NS 30/12/98 V3

## RECOMMENDATIONS / INTENTIONS (Cont.)

**15** Which, if any, of the following areas of the service process should the dealership improve (Please mark all that apply)

a. Convenience/timeliness of appointment ☐
b. Service reception process ☐
c. Completion of work ☐

d. Timely service/collection of vehicle ☐
e. Follow-up call after service ☐
f. Handling of any questions/concerns ☐

If you still own the vehicle mentioned in the letter, please go to Q19

## ABOUT YOUR NEW VEHICLE

Please only answer questions 16-18 if you no longer own the vehicle mentioned in the letter.

**16** What did you replace it with?

**17** If you bought another Ford, did you buy it from Dennehy's Cross Garage?

Yes, new ☐ go to 19 — Yes, used ☐ go to 19 — No ☐ go to 18

**18** If you **didn't** buy another Ford, could you please indicate the main reasons why? (Mark all that apply)

Price or deal offered ☐
Product range ☐
Competitive advertising ☐
Finance package ☐
Information provided on the Internet ☐
Wanted a different make of vehicle ☐

Previous experience with the dealership ☐
Advice of motoring press ☐
Previous vehicle experience ☐
Dealership location ☐
Another dealership was recommended ☐
Other (please write in)

## YOUR COMMENTS

**19** If you have any comments about your recent service visit, particularly concerning any areas you suggested the dealership should improve, please write them here.

Please tick this box if you do not wish these comments to go to the dealer you mentioned at Question 3. ☐

## TELL US ABOUT YOURSELF

**20** Your gender? —

Male ☐ Female ☐

**21** Age group? —

| Under 20 | 20-24 | 25-29 | 30-34 | 35-39 | 40-44 |
|---|---|---|---|---|---|
| ☐ | ☐ | ☐ | ☐ | ☐ | ☐ |
| 45-49 | 50-54 | 55-59 | 60-64 | 65 or over | |
| ☐ | ☐ | ☐ | ☐ | ☐ | |

Your Ford dealership is also interested in your individual opinion. Would you therefore agree to us sending the information you have provided in this questionnaire to your dealership?

Yes ☐ No ☐

*Thank you for your time. Please return in the postage paid envelope provided.*

**customer viewpoint**

# New Vehicle Delivery Response Report
## Peter Casey & Sons Ltd – Roscommon (015)

| **Customer Data** | **Vehicle Data** | |
|---|---|---|
| | Reference number | |
| | Registration number | |
| | VIN | |
| | Model | Ford Focus |
| | Registration date | |
| Home: | Date analysed | |
| Work: | Salesperson code | |

## Key Loyalty & Satisfaction Indicators

| | |
|---|---|
| Vehicle satisfaction | Completely satisfied |
| Purchase/delivery satisfaction | Completely satisfied |
| Recommend you as a place to buy | Definitely would |
| Recommend salesperson | Definitely would |
| Use you for future service | No answer |
| Timeliness of contact | Excellent |
| Satisfied with test drive | Didn't want one |
| Options/accessories fitted satisfactorily | Yes |
| Concerns resolved | Didn't have any |
| Offered introduction to service/parts | Yes, but I didn't accept |
| Offer to schedule 1st service | Yes, and I accepted |
| Previous vehicle: Ford | Yes |
| Bought from your dealership | No |
| Expected replacement period | 5 years |
| Predicted loyalty | Advocate |

## Customer Written Comments

### YOUR COMMENTS

17    If you have any comments about your purchase or delivery experience, particularly concerning any areas you suggested the dealership should improve, please write them here.

———→

| Predicted Loyalty | |
|---|---:|
| Vehicle satisfaction | Completely satisfied |
| Purchase/delivery satisfaction | Completely satisfied |
| Recommend salesperson | Definitely would |
| Recommend you as a place to buy | Definitely would |
| Recommend a Ford vehicle | Definitely would |
| Previous vehicle: Ford | Yes |
| If you seriously considered any other vehicles, which ones were they? | |
| I am an enthusiastic advocate of Ford products | |
| Price is the most important factor when buying a vehicle | |
| I would have bought a different manufacturer's product had it been 10% cheaper than my Ford | |
| I will always buy a Ford if I can | |
| Ford designs and produces innovative products | |
| My dealings with this dealership will positively affect my future purchases from Ford | |
| I like to vary manufacturer irrespective of how satisfied I am with my current vehicle | |

## 'What your customers really think'

The Customer Response Report (see pages 149–150) enables the dealership to see themselves through the eyes of their customers. It provides crucially important information about what they are doing right and where to take action in response to the needs of individual customers, which is what building long-term loyalty is all about.

The dealership receives a copy of the one-page Customer Response Report for each customer who has returned a completed survey. It tells them:

- how they are perceived by individual customers
- whether customers are 'in-market' for a particular service
- if customers are potential defectors
- if there are any unresolved concerns
- specific information on sales and service processes
- the likelihood of referrals/repeat business
- customers' attitudes and exactly what they think of you from their additional comments.

## Action

Having studied and assessed the priorities of the reports, it is important for the dealership to act on this information. Understanding customers' needs and wants is futile unless the lessons learned are applied in real life. Here Ford offers their dealers some concrete suggestions:

### Immediate follow-up

Give the Customer Response Reports to the relevant department managers and advise them to contact customers who require immediate attention. This could be because there is an unresolved concern causing dissatisfaction that could make the customer a potential defector. Or a prompt response is needed because the customer has requested you contact them. Obviously, if a customer has indicated that they are 'in-market' for a new vehicle or other dealership service, then they should be immediately followed up.

### Own the problem

Staff contacting a dissatisfied customer should familiarise themselves with possible concerns by looking up the customer's sales/service records and cross-checking comments from the report against the customer order or job card. Most importantly, the person who contacts the customer must 'own the problem' and be in a position of authority to handle the concern. As well as providing reassurance that everything possible will be done to resolve the situation, it treats the customer as an individual and builds loyalty.

### Quality control

Always make sure that staff record the date and details of the contact and the outcome. It's a good idea to use the back of the Customer Response Report so that all information is kept together. And, for added quality control, carry out spot checks to ensure that customers are being contacted. Remember, it's vital to address the causes and not the symptoms of any problem to prevent it happening again.

### Tracking improvements

Similarly, each time you introduce an improvement action check the Customer Response Reports to see whether it achieved the desired effect. For example, if you offer every customer a test drive, or provide every service customer with a price estimate prior to starting any work, you can identify the impact of these actions using the Customer Response Reports.

### Spreading good news

Compliments count for a lot. They show recognition for effort and are powerful motivators. They make your staff proud of doing a good job. So whenever a customer shows thanks or comments favourably, make sure all the staff hear about it and always display the letter or remarks on the noticeboard.

This sample report opposite details the responses to questions in the one-month survey. It covers the key loyalty and satisfaction indicators, including:

- overall satisfaction with purchase/delivery experience
- recommendations/intentions
- likelihood of using dealer for services
- unresolved concerns
- repurchase intention
- predicted loyalty.

## Voice of the customer

In Section D, space is available for customers to comment on where they believe improvements could be made. These remarks are very important as they tell Ford dealers how their customers really feel, in their own words. Very often, responding to these comments can be one of the most constructive ways to enhance customer loyalty.

**(A) Customer Data**

Mr J. Sample
4 The Avenue
ANYTOWN
Cheshire
TA13 2DG
Home 01478 632378
Work 01478 368923

**(B) Vehicle Data**

| | |
|---|---|
| Reference Number | xxxx |
| Registration Number | xxxx |
| VIN | xxxx |
| Model | Ford Escort |
| Registration Date | xxxx |
| Date Analysed | xxxx |

(C) Key Loyalty and Satisfaction Indicators

| | | | |
|---|---|---|---|
| Vehicle satisfaction | **Very satisfied** | Concerns resolved | No |
| Purchase/delivery satisfaction | **Completely satisfied** | — | — |
| Recommend as a place to buy | **Probably would** | Scheduled 1st service | No |
| Recommend salesperson | **Probably would** | Previous vehicle | Vauxhall |
| Use for future service | **Probably not** | Bought from your dealership | No |
| Timeliness of contact | **Not contacted** | Expected replacement | 3 years |
| Satisfied with test drive | Yes | Predicted loyalty | Possible defector |
| Options/accessories | None ordered | | |

**(D) Customer Comments**

*The man at the dealer was quite helpful but as I live about 50 miles away it's unlikely I'll go there for a service. By the way, they still haven't phoned me about my handbook that I never received.*

## Monthly Dealership Report

Key data from the Purchase, Service and Ownership Experience surveys are analysed and correlated. The findings highlight every dealership's strengths, weaknesses, opportunities and threats. This information enables each individual dealership to focus on important areas for improvement specific to them. The Monthly Report also tracks trends, which can be invaluable when it comes to developing business plans for the dealership.

## Programme benefits

### Focus on building loyalty

Each survey question provides actionable feedback so you can fine-tune improvements to meet individual customer needs. Overall, the programme is more responsive, more precise in identifying areas of concern and it's easier to measure whether your dealership is achieving the levels of customer loyalty that will grow with your business.

### Customer expectations and customer satisfaction standards

In order to achieve customer satisfaction a company has to first determine what the customer expects. In order to do this Ford used focus groups all over Europe. As customer expectations are always changing Ford wanted to know if the Customer Handling Standards they introduced in 1993 were still viable. Ford learned that while these standards were still useful they did not meet all the rising expectations of the twenty-first-century customer. One message that came across loud and clear was the need for customers to feel that they were being treated as individuals by the company. In response to this and other developments in customer care Ford revised their Customer Handling Standards and renamed them Customer Satisfaction Standards. They are reproduced on page 157 next to the Customer Expectations. The Customer Expectations list what the customer wants and the corresponding Customer Satisfaction Standard illustrates the procedure by which that expectation can be met.

### How to reach customer expectations

Ford issued a detailed document in January 2000. It gives the dealer practical advice on how to deal with the 15 expectations that were detected.

The president of Ford is Alan Mulally and he is extremely committed to customer care. Every week he sends messages to his workforce around the world where he highlights that week's priorities. In these messages he continually reinforces the importance of customer care.

Finally, to keep customer care to the forefront of employees' minds, a newsletter, *Customer Viewpoint News,* is issued at regular intervals (see pages 159–160). This newsletter restates the objectives of the Customer Viewpoint Programme and reminds employees of their goals. In addition, it looks at how the programme is being applied. In the issue that is reproduced here there is an interview with a dealer who has had great success with the programme, as well as an article on female customer satisfaction.

### Putting it all together

All the information gleaned from the questionnaires is put together to form a National Summary. The national summaries of every country can then be compared and Ford can get a global view of their performance. So far the results have been good. Customer

Viewpoint is working well as customers are responding favourably. There is always room for improvement, however. The National Summary highlights what is going well and what is not by a traffic light system. Statistics are often expressed in graph form and are colour-coded, with red indicating the areas that need the greatest attention.

In conclusion, Customer Viewpoint is an extremely well-organised and cohesive customer care programme. Its success lies in its simplicity. It is based around three main questionnaires to obtain information from the people who count – the customers. It is applied through 15 points of customer expectations, which each employee works to achieve. Its greatest strength in my view, however, lies in the ongoing support that the programme gets from management. So many customer care programmes are researched and developed at great expense only to end up as dead documents gathering dust in some forgotten drawer. Ford employees on the shop floor are constantly being encouraged to adopt and maintain strong customer-driven values. Information prepared for employees has the same high production values that customer-oriented material has. This shows employees that they are valued team members and they are being persuaded of the advantages of this programme, rather than simply being ordered to get on with it. Finally, the Ford customer care programme can be regarded as a good one because it is constantly evolving and adapting to the changing market trends and the growing sophistication of the buying public.

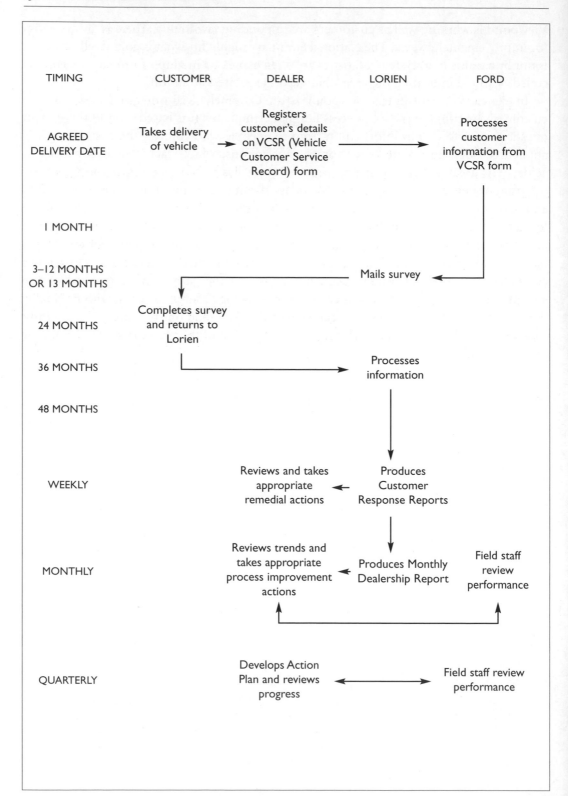

| Customer Expectation | Customer Satisfaction Standard |
|---|---|
| 1. Treat me as a valued customer when I arrive at your dealership. | 1. Customers will be courteously, professionally and promptly acknowledged and advised that a salesperson will be available on request. |
| 2. The salesperson should establish a relationship with me that is built on respect for me as a customer with individual needs. | 2. The salesperson will demonstrate genuine interest in the customer and establish an advisory relationship built on trust. |
| 3. The salesperson should offer me a test drive. | 3. All customers will be offered a test drive. |
| 4. Make it easy for me to finalise the finance or leasing arrangements. | 4. Salesperson and F&I personnel will provide all customers with thorough explanations and a pleasant, non-pressured purchase experience. |
| 5. Deliver my new vehicle at the promised time, in perfect condition. | 5. Using a checklist the salesperson will deliver the vehicle in perfect condition when promised. |
| 6. Call me within a reasonable amount of time after I've taken delivery to ensure that I'm completely satisfied. | 6. The salesperson will introduce the customer to members of the Service/Parts team to provide reassurance that the customer will be cared for during ownership of the vehicle. |
| 7. Be responsive to questions or concerns I bring to your attention. | 7. The salesperson will contact all customers within one week of delivery, resolving any concerns and will follow up on any promises made. |
| 8. Make it convenient to have my vehicle serviced at your dealership. | 8. Provide convenient appointments for the customer. |
| 9. Provide me with alternative transport arrangements when my vehicle is serviced at your dealership. | 9. Provide courtesy services. |
| 10. The Service Advisor should demonstrate a genuine concern for my service needs. | 10. Start the reception process within four minutes and inspect every vehicle prior to start of any work, with the customer when possible. |
| 11. Fix it right the first time. | 11. Provide a price estimate prior to the start of any work. |
| 12. Complete servicing my vehicle in a timely and professional manner. | 12. Service the vehicle right first time, with an effective fallback procedure. |
| 13. Provide me with a clear and thorough explanation of the service performed. | 13. Customer's vehicle will be ready at the agreed time. |
| 14. Call me within a reasonable amount of time after my service visit to ensure that I'm completely satisfied. | 14. Thorough explanation will be provided of the work done and related charges, with advice on future service needs. |
| 15. Be responsive to questions or concerns I bring to your attention. | 15. Dealer will contact customers within one week of completion of work, resolving any concerns and will follow up on any promises made. |

# 1 Treat me as a valued customer when I arrive at your dealership

## Customer Expectation

- Promptly welcome me to your dealership
- Take me seriously
- Give me the level of attention I desire

## Objective & Motivation

Not every customer appreciates a sales pitch immediately after arriving; some people would rather browse around first. But nobody minds being greeted in a correct and friendly manner, e.g.: 'Welcome, how can I be of service?' Furthermore, a customer who wants to be helped immediately, does not like to be kept waiting.

A prompt acknowledgment of the customer is a sign of the organisation's alertness. Empty showrooms and absent salespeople make the dealership seem sleepy and inactive!

## Employees involved

- Everyone in the dealership who can see customers arriving

## Optimal Process

- Proper use of the showroom schedule guarantees that someone is always present in the showroom
- Greet each customer when he enters the showroom. The exact moment of greeting depends on the individual customer
- Ask the customer how you can be of service
- Determine who is the best person to help the customer, and introduce this person to the customer
- Present customer with your business card
- While helping the customer, give him your full attention

## Tips & Traps

- Showroom lay-out must lead customer to the central reception (red carpet)
- Special parking facilities for showroom visitors
- Sales desks facing showroom entrance
- One showroom entrance, clearly indicated
- If showroom does not have security guard, use warning bell near door/under carpet
- Add greeting of customers to list of duties/job description
- Every dealership employee must be able to properly greet and attend to customers until a salesperson is available

## Progress Control

- As the dealer principal, give the correct example in the showroom. Make sure that everyone else follows your lead
- Have employees from other departments perform random checks to see whether showroom staff are present as scheduled
- Check progress via monthly dealer report

## Tools

- Ideal showroom lay-out
- Showroom schedule
- Business cards of salespeople
- Name badges of salespeople
- Welcome script

## How to Implement

- Examine showroom lay-out and discuss changes
- Introduce showroom schedule
- Train receptionist/telephonist and salespeople

# CustomerViewpoint News

| Issue 2 | July 2000 |

## Increasing your Customers' Intention to Repurchase

**Research has shown that at 24 MIS or later, completely satisfied service customers are much more likely to consider a Ford for their next purchase**

We recently carried out a study to examine the relationship between satisfaction with the customer's recent service visit, and their likelihood to consider a Ford for their next purchase.

The results of this study, illustrated in the table below, allow us to conclude that a respondent's level of satisfaction with their recent service visits is directly linked to their likelihood of considering a Ford for their next purchase.

The study revealed that 94% of respondents who were Completely Satisfied with their recent service visit tell us that they are considering a Ford for their next purchase. Of these owners, 80% are considering a Ford **only**.

Conversely, over half of Very Dissatisfied owners will not consider buying another Ford, whereas less than one in ten of those Completely Satisfied with their last service visit will not buy another Ford.

| Vehicles considered for next purchase: | Ford | Ford/Other | Other |
|---|---|---|---|
| **Level of satisfaction with recent visit** | | | |
| Completely Satisfied | 80% | 14% | 6% |
| Very Satisfied | 63% | 24% | 13% |
| Fairly Well Satisfied | 49% | 28% | 23% |
| Somewhat Dissatisfied | 35% | 29% | 36% |
| Very Dissatisfied | 25% | 22% | 53% |

## Dealer Interview on After Sales Satisfaction!

We interviewed Ron Skinner, Dealer Principal at Lincoln Ford, in which he outlines their main initiatives for improving After Sales customer satisfaction which has seen a rise in satisfaction ratings of 29.2 percentage points over a 3 month period.

He discusses some of the main reasons behind their recent improvement, and offers his view of the general business environment over the past 12 months.

He also looks to the future, and shares his internet-based initiatives, which he hopes will make life easier for his customers.

### This Issue

Female Customer Satisfaction          Page 2

Dealer Principal Interview          Page 3

Viewpoint Q & A / Top Tips          Page 4

GLOBAL CONSUMER INSIGHTS

IRL

*Ford* CustomerViewpoint News **P2**

# Gender Analysis : Female Customer Satisfaction

### Sales Experience
Female customers appear to be more satisfied than males with most aspects of their purchase and delivery experience. The only significant gaps being that fewer women than men are:
- Introduced to the service department
- Offered to have their first service scheduled

### Service/Warranty Experience
Female customers do not receive as high a level of service from the dealerships as their male counterparts, and are less satisfied with the event driven warranty experience. This is clear across almost all aspects of the dealer experience. The key influences driving female customers' satisfaction with warranty and service are:
- Ease of arranging an appointment
- Ability to resolve concerns
- Follow-through on promises made
- Helpfulness in resolving concerns
- Parking facilities
- Prompt acknowledgement
- Overall appearance of service department
- Courtesy when serving you
- Timeliness of after-visit contact

The table below shows the results for the four customer service issues relating to contact from the the dealer. It is clear that females are not receiving the same level of treatment as males. This is most evident where 20.6% less females than males are offered scheduling of their next routine service.

### Improving female satisfaction
**Sales Experience:**
- Introduce the female customers to the parts and service department representatives
- Offer to schedule the first routine service at new vehicle delivery

**Service/Warranty Experience:**
- Ensure that service reception personnel have received training in dealing with the needs and expectations of female customers
- Review dealership parking facilities
- Establish a process for tailoring after-service contact to meet individual customer needs
- Establish follow-up process to ensure customer concerns are resolved

**Ownership Experience:**
- Contact female customers with new finance offers prior to existing customer finance completion

Results from other sources also reveal that less females:
- Receive contact from the dealer
- Are offered to inspect their vehicle

### Ford Credit
Females are far more likely to recommend their finance company than males. This is evident at both the sales and ownership stages of the Viewpoint survey. This fact is reinforced when you reconsider that significantly more female respondents used Ford Credit to pay for their vehicle.

### Customer Behaviour
Female customers consistently report being less price-sensitive when it comes to the Ford brand. Less females than males:
- Agree that price is the most important factor in their vehicle purchase
- Would have bought another manufacturer's product if it had been 5% cheaper
- Would have bought another manufacturer's product if it had been 10% cheaper

| Customer Service Issues | | | | |
|---|---|---|---|---|
| **% Yes** | **Male** | **Female** | **F+/-M** | **%(F+/-M)** |
| **Confirmed appointment** | 85.1 | 78.2 | -6.9 | -8.1% |
| **Offered to inspect vehicle** | 45.0 | 36.6 | -8.4 | -18.7% |
| **Offered to schedule next routine service** | 36.0 | 28.6 | -7.4 | -20.6% |
| **After-service contact** | 35.1 | 29.8 | -5.3 | -15.1% |
| | | | | |
| **% Excellent** | **Male** | **Female** | **F+/-M** | **%(F+/-M)** |
| **Treated as a valued customer** | 45.4 | 42.8 | -2.6 | -5.7% |

# 8

# DEALING WITH DIFFERENCE

## Discrimination

The Equal Status Act 2000 makes it illegal to discriminate against anyone on the basis of disability. If you are providing a service for the general public, you must make it accessible to people with disabilities. Ignorance of the law will not be accepted as a defence.

I think that we all like to believe that we are different. However, a lot of the time we also just want to fit in and be the same. Schoolchildren often hate their school uniforms and try to put their own individual twist on it. Ironically, however, after school they try to fit in as much as possible with what the other members of their group are wearing – it's a kind of 'after-school uniform'. So though we may express a desire for individuality, a lot of us want to conform. This is not a big problem for most of us. If we want to be different we can dress up and when we are tired of that we can return to more conforming attire. But it's not that easy for everyone. If your colour, shape or medical condition makes you stand out from the crowd then you have to deal with being an individual all the time, without the luxury of being able to shrug it off.

This chapter deals with problems encountered by people in an environment where they are perceived to be different. It examines how this affects their choices as consumers. It looks at the legislation that is in place to protect people from discrimination. It also looks at how customer contact staff can meet the challenges of dealing with customers who have specific needs.

The *Collins English Dictionary* defines discrimination as unfair treatment of a person, racial group, minority, etc. based on prejudice.

Discrimination is based on difference. People discriminate against people who are different from them and as each person on the planet is different, then the potential for prejudice and discrimination is as great as the number of people alive. People discriminate against each other on the basis of gender, age, race, skin or hair colour, height, weight, religion, sexual orientation, occupation, disability, nationality, marital status, wealth, education, etc.

Discrimination can take many forms. It can be individual, where one person decides that all fat people are lazy, or it can be collective, as in a group of people beating up someone of a different religion to them. It can also be institutional, as in a male-only golf club, or constitutional, as in apartheid. In some instances, it can come from within a group, for example when a woman believes that women are not smart enough to hold important jobs and is severely critical of women who do so.

Discrimination can be conscious, as in refusing to hire a person because they are black, but it can also be subconscious, as in thinking someone is unsuitable for a job without realising that that judgment has been based on the fact that they are very short. In the past, many studies have been undertaken to examine the way we prejudge on the basis of appearance. One such study came to the conclusion that if two equally qualified and experienced men went for the same job and if one was tall and the other was short, the tall man would get the job. The reason for this may be that most of us are prejudiced into thinking that height carries age, experience and authority and it hearkens back to our childhood when we judged each others' age and experience on how much we had grown.

The ways that discrimination manifests itself can take many forms. They can range from something as simple as choosing not to sit next to someone on the bus because of our prejudices, to genocide as witnessed in World War Two. In the workplace, it can hinder job prospects and promotion. It can lead to sexual harassment and bullying.

As a customer, a victim of discrimination may be denied entry into a building and they may find that there are no products or services available to cater for their particular needs. In order to help deal with the problem of discrimination towards our customers we first have to identify who those customers may be.

They may have learning and intellectual difficulties:

- dyslexia
- illiteracy
- low intelligence quotient
- learning difficulties brought about through accident, illness or genetic inheritance, which can lead to memory loss, inability to absorb new information, language or numeracy loss and problems with depth perception and spatial reasoning
- phobias or manias, for example hydrophobia, agoraphobia, claustrophobia, ablutomania and kleptomania.

They may have sensory impairment:

- deafness
- blindness
- loss of the sense of smell
- nerve damage

- colour blindness
- loss of peripheral vision.

There are also disabilities related to sensory malfunction:

- tinnitus
- heightened sensitivity to bright light.

Other conditions may be induced through the senses, for example:

- epileptic attacks, which may be provoked by strobe lighting.

There may be physical difficulties, for example:

- a person who has lost one or more limbs through illness or accident
- a person with a condition which has resulted in restricted movement
- a person with respiratory problems.

It is important to provide a customer environment that sensitively accommodates the difference in individuals. For example, wheelchair access is considered essential in new buildings and older buildings can often be adapted, or ramps provided. Also, some customers – those who are easily tired, have respiratory problems, are in pain or are prone to seizures, for instance – may appreciate knowing a rest place is available.

Care should be taken to ensure that the customer environment is sufficiently clean, which will help to avoid provoking asthma attacks, and the composition of materials used or sold should be clearly marked or listed to help prevent allergic reactions. Strobe lighting effects should be avoided as it can bring on epileptic fits. Staff should be encouraged to take first-aid training courses and should be rewarded for their efforts.

If you have problems understanding a customer because of a communication difficulty, you should remember to be patient. The customer should never be patronised. You should use judgment in deciding what the best approach in the individual circumstances are. Speak clearly and, if you feel it is necessary, speak more slowly. If a person has a hearing impairment, for example, look directly at them to allow them the chance to lip read. Use hand gestures and body language to get your message across. If someone has a speech impairment, make every effort to understand what they are saying, but if you do not follow them, politely ask them to repeat themselves or to write down what they want to convey to you. Alternatively, you could write down what you have understood and ask them to check that you have got it right. Do not be embarrassed to seek clarification.

You could learn advanced communication skills yourself to help when meeting people with disabilities; for example, you could learn sign language or Braille. Braille menus, maps and guidebooks should be provided where appropriate to assist the blind and partially sighted.

A knowledge of foreign languages will help you to communicate with tourists, but be aware that the customs of other countries may create communication problems. A simple example is that in some countries nodding and shaking your head have the opposite meanings to the meanings we are used to.

## How to assist a customer or client with sight loss

Sight loss affects people in different ways. In fact, most people with vision impairments have some sight. This can range from distinguishing light from dark, to being able to see everything but in a very blurred way and with no detail.

Just as the amount of sight varies from person to person, so too does a person's ability to carry out everyday tasks independently. It stands to reason that a person who loses their sight suddenly in adulthood might have more difficulty managing and adjusting than someone who has had vision impairment since birth. On the other hand, a person who loses sight later has a memory of sight, whereas a person who has been blind all their lives might have no concept of colour. A person who gradually loses their sight may have more time to adjust. Therefore it is very important to be sensitive to the individual needs of customers. Assume nothing.

Here is some advice provided by NCBI (National Council for the Blind of Ireland) on how you can assist a person with sight loss:

- Greet the person by saying your name and role.
- Always ask the person if they would like assistance before giving it.
- Talk directly to the person rather than through a third party.
- There's no need to shout.
- In a group situation, introduce the other people present and address the person with sight loss by name when directing conversation to him/her.
- Make sure to let the person know if someone joins or leaves the group.
- When guiding a person with sight loss, offer your elbow. The person will hold your arm just above your elbow. Keep your arm by your side so that the other person can walk a little behind you.
- When guiding, it is helpful to give commentary on what is around, such as steps and stairs up and down.
- If you have been guiding a person with sight loss and have to leave, bring them to some reference point that they can feel, like a table, a wall or a chair. To be left in an open space can be disorienting.
- If you are giving directions, don't point! Give clear verbal directions or offer to guide the person.
- Don't assume that a person using a white cane or guide dog is totally blind.
- Never distract a guide dog that is in harness.
- Close all doors and cupboards to avoid the possibility of someone banging their head.
- If you see head-height obstacles ahead of a person using a white cane or guide dog, warn them. Such obstacles include truck wing-mirrors, overhanging branches, low shop awnings and unprotected scaffolding.

## Making written information accessible

A person with sight loss may be unable to see a poster on a wall or read a leaflet in small print. All relevant information should be made available in a format that customers with sight loss can use. These formats include Braille, audio cassette, clear print, large print and on your website. Ensure that your website is accessible to screen reading software used by people with sight loss. NCBI's Centre for Inclusive Technology can offer specialised advice on accessible website design (see www.cfit.ie).

Leaflets should be produced in a well laid out and simple format using large print, minimum 14 point font size. NCBI can also provide advice on the layout and design of publications. NCBI's Library and Media Conversion Service converts written material into Braille and audio formats.

## Completing forms

If you are assisting a person with sight loss to fill in a form, read the questions aloud and write down the answers on the person's behalf. If necessary, find a quiet and private place to do so. Show the person where to sign, guiding their hand to the correct line. Signature guides can also be used and are available from NCBI. Any long or complicated forms should be produced in an accessible format so that the customer can bring them home to read.

## Access to a building

Low-cost, simple adaptations can be made which will make a building more accessible to all customers. These include:

- Marking glass doors, providing an appropriate handrail on staircases, effective use of colour contrasting and tactile markings to highlight steps, edges and obstacles.
- Lighting levels should be even throughout the building. Changes from bright to dark can make it more difficult for the customer to see. Use matte paints to minimise glare.
- Signs should be large and clear, using good contrasting colours. They should also be well positioned and provided in tactile form as well as in large print and Braille wherever possible.
- People with sight loss often find wide-open spaces difficult to navigate. They often use walls and edges to find their way. Make sure that there are no protruding head-height hazards on the walls, such as fire extinguishers, that may obstruct them as they make their way.
- Where possible use contrasting colours on handrails, doorframes, door handles and edges of steps.

NCBI can provide further advice and assistance on the most effective way to do this.

## Shopping

There are lots of practical ways to make shopping easier for customers with sight loss.

Shop assistants can provide assistance by reading labels, checking sell-by dates and helping customers to find exactly what they want on the shelves. It is also important to ensure that customers are aware of the choice of products available, the range of prices and any special offers. You could also help a customer with sight loss to find their way around the shop or guide them to the door if necessary (see above).

## Hotels, bars and restaurants

There are simple ways in which customers with sight loss can feel welcome within a hotel, bar or restaurant.

- Offer assistance and always start by introducing yourself.
- Where appropriate, provide other staff with details of the guest's requirements.
- Offer an orientation tour of the hotel, giving a brief description of the layout of the building and their room.
- Accept guide dogs in bedrooms and public areas.
- Discuss evacuation procedures in the event of an emergency.
- Escape route maps and procedural information should be provided in accessible formats, such as Braille, audio, large print (using a minimum of 16 point font size).
- Menus and price lists can be offered in Braille and large print. Otherwise, you could offer to read the menu to the customer.

## Hospitals, surgeries, clinics and dentists

As well as the guidelines that are outlined above, there are ways in which medical staff can provide assistance to patients with sight loss.

- Patients with sight loss may prefer to be reminded of appointments by telephone, as well as with appointment letters or cards.
- When the patient is next in line in a waiting room, call them by name rather than saying 'next'. Let the patient know if there is a ticket system and digital display. Ensure that the patient knows what their number is and inform staff that a person with sight loss is in the waiting room and may need to be guided from the waiting room to another room.
- When changing shifts inform other staff of assistance the patient might require.
- If a patient is being admitted to a ward, it would be very helpful to arrange for a member of staff to greet them at reception, guide the patient through the building and help them settle into the ward.
- In the ward, it is important to introduce the patient to other patients and staff on the ward. Remember to be sensitive to the patient's privacy; the person might not want other patients to know that they have sight loss. You should ask what the person prefers.

- Familiarise the patient with their immediate surroundings, for example the position of the bed in relation to the entrance to the ward. Describe the room from left to right. It may be necessary to help the patient to locate the light switches, call system, bed and bedside locker and to tell them what exactly is on top of the locker.
- It is important to show the patient the route to the exit and to the toilet. Also show them the route to the public telephone and day room.
- Place any medication in the patient's hand.
- When the patient is going home, ensure that they know the date and time of any future appointments, have information about medication they are to take and can distinguish different medicine bottles and tablets.

## At the gym

As all people with sight loss are different you should ask the customer what assistance they require.

- If your gym or fitness centre meets health and safety requirements, a person with sight loss will have few difficulties using your facilities.
- Provide a comfortable place with a mat and a water bowl for guide dogs to wait for their owners.

For more information contact NCBI. NCBI is a non-profit charitable organisation, which offers support and services nationwide to over 10,000 people experiencing difficulties with their eyesight. About 18 per cent of people using NCBI's services are completely blind, while 82 per cent have varying degrees of usable vision.

The NCBI provides a variety of useful guidelines.

- *Meeting and Greeting People with Sight Loss*
- *How to Guide a Blind Person Safely*

  This gives tips on how to guide a person with significant sight loss up and down stairs, through narrow spaces, through doors, to a car, to a chair, etc.

- *Recommendations for Signage*

  This offers advice on the design and positioning of signs to make them easier to locate and read.

- *Guidelines for Access to the Built Environment for People with Vision Impairments: A Safer Environment for All*
- *Checklist for Accessibility for People with Vision Impairment – Indoors*

  These leaflets offer guidelines on how best to create a safer built environment for everyone.

- *Make It Clear*

  This leaflet advises on the clear layout and design of written information to make it easier to read.

- *Sport and Fitness for People with Vision Impairments*
- *Fitness Centres and Gyms*

You can find these leaflets on the NCBI website: www.ncbi.ie
For further advice the NCBI can be contacted at:
NCBI
Whitworth Road,
Drumcondra,
Dublin 9
Locall: 1850 334353
Fax: 01 830 7787
Email: info@ncbi.ie

## How to assist a customer or client with hearing difficulties

Again, it's important to remember that not all people with hearing difficulties are completely deaf. They range from the hard of hearing to the profoundly deaf. There are also sufferers of tinnitis, a distressing condition characterised by a persistent ringing in the ears. Some people have had hearing problems from work and this may have affected their speech, whereas other people may have developed hearing problems later in life and might sometimes find it hard to adapt. As result the amount of assistance required differs from person to person.

Here are some general guidelines on how to help customers who are deaf or hard of hearing.

- First of all, get the person's attention without startling them, for example tap them gently on the arm or shoulder.
- Identify yourself to the person. Show them your name badge or, if desired, write it out on a piece of paper.
- Ask if the person would like to communicate by writing or by using a computer.
- Make sure the person can see your face clearly by facing the light and removing anything that might obscure your face and mouth, such as a scarf. Keep your hands down from your face as well.
- Speak clearly in a normal tone of voice using short, simple sentences.
- If the person uses a sign-language interpreter, speak directly to the person, not the interpreter.
- If possible deal with important business matters in a private room where there is less noise distraction. This means that if you need to speak loudly, you are not broadcasting your customer's business all over the premises.

## How to assist customers with mobility impairments

- There is a lot you can do to make your premises more 'user-friendly' for people with mobility problems. Provide parking, a system of ramps and elevators, a wheelchair-accessible toilet and provide other facilities, such as desks and counters, at a lower level.

- Make sure that all pathways, corridors and gangways are clear.
- Get in contact with the Irish Wheelchair Association at www.iwa.ie for advice on this matter.
- Offer assistance in opening doors, moving furniture, etc. if the customer seems to be having difficulty. If the customer uses a walker, Zimmer frame, crutches or other assistive equipment, offer assistance with coats, bags and other belongings.
- Make sure there is a suitable chair available for the customer if they wish to sit down. Some people find low and soft furnishings difficult to get up out of.
- Do not assume your customer wants to be pushed, ask them first.
- Put yourself at your customer's eye level.

## How to assist a customer who has difficulty with speech

- Be patient with the person. Having a speech impairment is a very frustrating condition, and do not compound their stress by being impatient. Give them as much time as they need.
- If you do not understand what they are saying, do not pretend that you do. This is false kindness at best, patronising at worst, and will be very irritating for the customer when they realise what you are doing. Ask the person to repeat what they said and repeat it back.
- Try and use closed questions. These are questions that require only a nod or a yes or no answer. For example, instead of 'Which would you prefer?' use 'Would you like the porridge?', 'Would you like the cornflakes?'
- Look directly at the customer and focus on what they are saying. Sometimes it just takes a little time to get attuned and then you find that you can understand them more easily.
- Eliminate anything that may impede communication. Turn off the radio, take the person into a quieter part of the premises and remove any glass partitions.
- If you are still having difficulty communicating, ask the customer if they would mind writing it down.
- If this isn't acceptable or feasible, suggest getting someone to interpret for you, e.g. someone with keener hearing or someone who knows the customer, etc.

## How to assist a customer with cognitive disabilities

- Again, patience is the key. Your customer naturally will become distressed if they cannot make themselves understood or cannot understand what you are saying.
- Be prepared to repeat yourself and to simplify what you are saying until the customer understands.
- Offer assistance with the completion of forms, the following of instructions and with making decisions.

- Be aware that 'cognitive disabilities' is a very general term and some customers will need a lot of assistance, whereas others will need little or no help. So don't patronise them or shout at them as if speaking loudly will drive the message in.
- Take the person to a quiet part of your premises to help them focus on their business.

## How to assist elderly and child customers

These two groups may seem at opposite ends of the pole, but they have more in common than you think. Neither is generally listened to. We all have memories of going into a shop as a child and being ignored or treated with impatience because our purchases were small and picky, 10 cent worth of those, 5 cent worth of that, etc. Also, we often notice staff being impatient with elderly customers as they slowly and carefully count out their pension. But it is a mistake to discount any customer, especially a member of either of these groups. The nine-year-old who spends a few coins today is the customer of the future, your future. He may remember the shoddy treatment that he received by you, and who knows how much this could ultimately affect your business. Also, children have parents and guardians who note the way in which staff have treated their charges. Likewise, though the octogenarian may dole out his money slowly, it's still money; and as the population ages, there are more and more like him. It is a foolish businessperson indeed who ignores a growing market. If we look at the range of products available today and the style of marketing, you would be forgiven for thinking that anyone over fifty is only interested in stair lifts, easy access baths and leaving money to their loved ones to cover funeral expenses. Films, cars, holidays and clothes seem to be primarily geared at young people or young families.

- Don't assume anything about your customers because of their age. Neither youth nor advanced years mean that a customer is inept. Treat each customer as an individual and cater to their specific needs without preconceptions.
- As with other groups of customers, treat these customers with respect. A young person who is treated respectfully will often appreciate it and respond in kind. He or she is also more likely to return to your business. Elderly people also deserve our respect and staff shouldn't assume that they know more just because their reactions are quicker.
- Not all children like having their hair ruffled, and elderly customers do not necessarily enjoy being called by their first name or being spoken to in a way that takes away their dignity. Never patronise your customers.
- Have patience with your customers. Do not rush elderly customers. They will not return if they cannot use your services without being harried along. Some children can be very nervous in their first dealings with staff and you might lose them if you scare them.
- Explain procedures, options, etc. to your customers. Never let them feel inadequate for having to ask. Be approachable.

## How to help a customer who does not speak your language

As Ireland becomes a multicultural society, staff and customers increasingly find themselves dealing with people who have trouble understanding them because of a language or accent barrier.

The easiest solution is to learn the language, not all of it, but enough for you to discharge your business. I remember visiting a silk market in China recently and seeing the stall owners haggling with customers. They had enough English, French and German to sell their products. They recognised that they would lose customers to the competition if they didn't try to breach the language barrier.

Failing that, the most important rules in dealing with a language barrier are:

- *Talk slowly.* Obviously, the more slowly you speak and the more carefully you enunciate, the more likely the customer is to understand you.
- *Do not shout.* They are not deaf and shouting loudly won't make you understood.
- *Keep it simple.* Avoid long, complicated sentences. Avoid colloquial expressions. Simplify as you explain:
  'Tint' = 'We will colour your hair.'
  'En suite' = 'A room with your own bathroom.'
  If necessary, break the sentence into smaller pieces.
- *Ask simple questions.* Keep them short. Ask closed questions. Closed questions require only a yes or no answer.
  'Do you want a room in a hotel?'
  'Is the room for just one person?'
  'Do you want to smoke in the room?'
  'Do you want a shower in your room?'
  'Do you want breakfast in the hotel?'
  'Do you have a car?'
- *Be patient.* Give the customer time to gather their thoughts and express them. Anyone who has ever been through a language oral will remember how much harder it is to speak when under stress. If you give them time, they will relax and be able to explain themselves better. Also they will be more likely to revisit your business because they know that you will give them the time they need.

Remember that language barriers can be frustrating for both sides. Also the customer may have had to deal with the language barrier on several occasions that day/week and could be very stressed already.

- *Listen carefully.* Try and make out what the customer is trying to say. Do not laugh or deride the customer's attempts to speak your language.
- *Use gestures.* Pointing, miming or using facial expressions can help both sides get their meaning across.
- *Summarise the conversation.* If you have managed to communicate with the customer, try and repeat the main details as simply and clearly as you can. This is to make sure that the customer fully understands what has been agreed upon.

Accent and meanings vary from country to country. George Bernard Shaw once said, 'England and America are two countries divided by the same language.' Take for example the following sentence: 'He had a flat in the city so he had to use the underground.' Here, a flat can mean an apartment and the underground can refer to a metro system, specifically the London Underground. However, American English only uses the term 'the underground' to denote a secret society, such as resistance fighters, and a 'flat' is a flat tyre.

Some other words that differ in meaning are:

| English | American English |
|---|---|
| Jelly | Jell-O |
| Jam | Jelly |
| Biscuits | Cookies |
| Chips | French fries |
| Crisps | Chips |
| Lift | Elevator |
| Petrol | Gas |
| Plain | Homely |
| Handbag | Purse |
| Solicitor | Door-to-door salesman |
| Barrister | Attorney |
| Estate agent | Realtor |
| Car boot | Trunk |
| Tap | Faucet |

A very important difference between both sides of the Atlantic is the fact that in the United States dates are written: month, day, year. In Europe we write it: day, month, year. Thus, 06/07/08 is the 7th of June in the US, but the 6th of July in Europe.

## Making all customers feel welcome

Because it is difficult to anticipate all areas of difficulty that you might encounter, service providers should ensure their customers know they would be happy to help those customers who feel they are not being accommodated. As always, comments and suggestions for service and product enhancements should be welcomed and this should be made clear.

Beyond providing a service for people with specific requirements, any service we provide must be a quality service. To do that we must identify what customers' needs are. Customer needs are different from customer requirements. A customer may require a pair of trousers with a 64" waist but they need to be treated with dignity. Customer needs can be difficult to determine as every customer is an individual and their needs will vary dramatically. However, the needs of the majority of customers can be found in the following list:

- Customers need to feel their custom is welcome.
- Customers need to feel their satisfaction is important to the organisation and that it will make a sincere effort to accommodate them.

- Customers need to feel they are being listened to and understood.
- Customers need to feel they can rely on the service provider.
- Customers need to feel that the service provider knows what they are doing.
- Customers need to feel secure and happy with the service provider.

We satisfy those needs by making the customer feel welcome. Greet them in a friendly manner as soon as they come into your office or service area and ask them if they need your assistance. Tell them to let you know whenever they have a query. Remember to smile. Be just as courteous and welcoming to those who phone.

If there is a problem, make every effort to solve it. Never allow the customer to feel that you are grudgingly going out of your way to help them. Even if the customer feels that you have exhausted all the possibilities open to you without solving the problem and thanks you for your efforts, don't stop. If there is another possible solution, try it. That is the difference between good service, which meets a customer's expectations, and excellent service, which exceeds it.

Show that you are listening by giving the customer your full attention, repeating key phrases and asking for clarification. Make notes if necessary. If you are interrupted, apologise and remind the customer where they had got to before they were interrupted.

Show that you are reliable by your actions. If you said that you would ring back on Thursday then ring back on Thursday. If you said that the sofa would be delivered on Friday morning, then deliver it on Friday morning.

Know your area. If you work in a DIY shop learn as much as possible about the products you are selling. People will often ask you for advice so it is good customer service to be able to provide it. Know the prices of the goods or services that you are selling. Know a bit about each product in order to allow customers to make a more informed decision. Know about the people you work with. Know who they are, what their area is and where they can be reached during office hours.

Obtain qualifications for the area you are in and display them. They may be ISO certification or personal qualifications, such as a degree or diploma. If you have won any service or hygiene awards, display them. Demonstrate good practice in front of the customer. Keep yourself and your customer contact environment clean and tidy.

If you do all this for every customer you encounter you will have gone a long way towards eliminating discrimination in your area and your customers will be grateful. As with all customer service issues, however, do not grow complacent. Be constantly alert to ways you and your colleagues might still be discriminating against customers. This will benefit both your customers and your organisation.

An organisation formed either for an altruistic purpose or for profit cannot survive without customers of some variety or another. To that end, it is logical that the organisation that designs its customer care policy to avoid the exclusion of any potential customer by reason of race, religion or disability, for example, will profit by increasing the number of its potential customers. There will be customers who have had to forgo services or goods in the past because they were unavailable, for example a diabetic who had to do without chocolate until their local supermarket started to stock a suitable kind. Such people might potentially transfer more of their custom to the supermarket as a result because the supermarket has taken the time to cater for their specific needs. The benefits could be even greater as friends and relations of customers with special requirements may also bring more custom. For example, a disabled worker may find a coffee-shop with decent wheelchair access and will bring not only their own custom, but that of their colleagues as well.

Such innovations and a positive approach generate goodwill among customers, leading to increased customer loyalty and tolerance when things go wrong. In addition, loyal customers are less price-sensitive. For example, the disabled worker and their friends are hardly likely to transfer their custom to a restaurant with steps at its entrance just because coffee is a little cheaper.

## The Employment Equality Act 1998

This Act was designed to help prevent discrimination in the workplace because of sex or marital status. It supersedes the 1977 Employment Equality Act.

The Employment Equality Act 1977 distinguished between direct and indirect discrimination. Direct discrimination is when an employer distinguishes between employees because of their sex or marital status, favouring some groups over others. Indirect discrimination is when an employer imposes an irrelevant regulation on employees which by its nature excludes groups on the grounds of sex or marital status. There were exceptions though. The Garda Síochána, Defence Forces and prison services were excluded from the Employment Equality Act 1977. Also positions where the gender is essential to the job were excluded.

Under the terms of the 1998 Employment Equality Act neither sex nor marital status should preclude a person from being employed in any position. It should not affect their training or the conditions of their employment, including pay. In addition, sex or marital status should not impede promotion prospects in any way. The Act also deals with harassment in the workplace, including sexual harassment. Harassment can be physical or psychological and can relate to anything spoken, written or graphically depicted. If an employee feels that they have been discriminated against, they can take their case to the Equality Tribunal.

There are some exceptions to the Employment Equality Act. For example, there is positive discrimination towards females in relation to maternity leave. Employers can decide on the grounds of gender and other factors whether to grant compassionate leave in some circumstances.

## The Equality Authority

*'The Equality Authority seeks to achieve positive change in the situation and experience of those groups and individuals experiencing inequality, by stimulating and supporting a commitment to equality:*

- *Within the systems and practices of key organisations and institutions.*

- *As part of the cultural values espoused by society.*
- *As a dimension to individual attitudes and actions.'*

Mission Statement of the Equality Authority (www.equality.ie)

The Equality Authority is an independent body set up under the Employment Equality Act 1998. It replaced the Employment Equality Agency and has a greatly expanded role. The Employment Equality Act 1998 and the Equal Status Act 2000 outlaw discrimination in employment, vocational training, advertising collective agreements, the provision of goods and services and other opportunities to which the public generally have access on nine distinct grounds: marital status, family status, age, gender, disability, race, sexual orientation, religious belief and membership of the Traveller community.

Discrimination is defined by the Act as the treatment of a person in a less favourable way than another person is, has been or would be treated on any of the above grounds.

The Equality Authority sponsors research in areas of equality. It also provides public information on the workings of the Employment Equality Acts 1998 and 2004 and the Equal Status Acts 2000 and 2004. The Public Information Centre also makes information available on Maternity Protection Acts 1994 and 2004, the Adoptive Leave Acts 1995 and 2005 and the Parental Leave Acts 1998 and 2006.

This information can be accessed by telephone (Locall 1890 245 545 or 01-417 3333), by textphone (01-417 3385), using an online enquiry form, email (info@equality.ie) or letter to:

The Public Information Centre,
Equality Authority,
2 Clonmel Street
Dublin 2

Significant information is also available from their website, which I have used as my source here. There is also a pre-recorded telephone message service outlining the basic features of the five pieces of legislation mentioned above.

The Public Information Centre is not in a position to offer legal advice but the Equality Authority has an in-house Legal Service that may, at its discretion, where the case is of strategic importance, provide free legal assistance to those making complaints of discrimination under the Employment Equality Act 1998 and the Equal Status Act 2000.

## Equality Tribunal

This is a completely separate organisation to the Equality Authority, which has no power to decide a case. The Equality Tribunal investigates or mediates claims of unlawful discrimination under equality legislation. A tribunal mediator will facilitate parties to reach a mediated agreement, which is legally binding. Where parties object to mediation, a case will be heard by a Tribunal Equality Officer, who will hear evidence from both parties before issuing a legally binding decision. The Equality Tribunal can only act on a complaint made in writing and must be made within six months of the alleged act of discrimination. Complaints about discrimination in pensions must be brought not later than six months after leaving the job.

For further information contact:

The Equality Tribunal
3 Clonmel Street
Dublin 2
01-477 4100

This information was taken from their excellent website www.equalitytribunal.ie, which contains details of the whole complaint application process.

## The Unfair Dismissals Act 1977 and the Unfair Dismissals Amendment Act 1993

Before these Acts were promulgated employees had very little job security. An employee could be hard working and competent and still be fired. Until the Minimum Notice and Terms of Employment Act 1973, the employer wasn't even obliged to give reasonable notice to an employee before they were let go. Under these circumstances it was very easy for employees to be discriminated against. For example, an employer could fire a woman who had recently become pregnant or replace an unqualified person with a relative who had just qualified. An employer could exchange a competent worker of one race for another, and so on.

This changed with the 1977 Act, which stated that an employee had a right to security of employment in that they could not be dismissed unfairly. The Act goes on to define 'dismissal' as when:

a. an employer terminates a contract with an employee who has been working continuously for them for over a year before the end of the agreed contract
b. where a contract reaches the end of its fixed term but is not renewed by the employer
c. where an employee's contract is terminated because of that employee's conduct.

The 1977 Act then puts the onus on the employer to prove that they had just grounds for dismissal. Just grounds for dismissal would be if the employee was unqualified for the job they were employed to do or simply proved to be incapable of performing the duties of the job. The employee may be incapable because of poor physical or mental health and a lack of physical or mental skill or ability. An employer may also dismiss an employee if continuing to employ them would be breaking the law. For example, a stockbroker cannot continue to employ a trader in the stock exchange who has been caught breaking the laws against insider-trading. A doctor who has been struck off the register for negligence can no longer continue to be employed as a doctor; nor can a barrister who has lost his licence through misconduct be employed to practise law.

Serious employee misconduct can be grounds for dismissal but again the onus is on the employer to prove it and not on the employee to disprove it. The employer would need documented proof that the misconduct was of such a serious and ongoing nature that it warranted dismissal.

An employee can be dismissed on the grounds that the organisation they are working for is no longer large enough to maintain the current size of its staff throughout the organisation or in a particular area. For example, a clothing manufacturer might find that while business is okay in other areas, the demand for hats has diminished and so it has no work for its trained milliners. An employee may be dismissed on the grounds that the company they work for has ceased to exist. For example, a cashier might be dismissed when the jewellery shop they work for winds up on the retirement of its owner. On these occasions dismissal is no reflection on the competency or conduct of the employee and they are said to be dismissed on the grounds of redundancy.

## Exercises

1.  Explain the term 'discrimination'.

2.  What is the purpose of equal status legislation?

3.  Outline the current equal status legislation.

4.  Describe a range of disabilities that can interfere with a customer's ability to access different goods and services.

5.  Name five disabilities and suggest improvements and innovations that would help the customer get a better service.

6.  In what way does assisting customers with special needs benefit an organisation?

7.  How can we be aware of discrimination in customer care and what can be done to avoid it?

8.  Find out what 'ablutomania' is and say how you think it might cause problems for your customers.

9.  You see an elderly lady fumbling with her money at the checkout of the supermarket that you are managing. Some coins drop and fall to the floor. The shop assistant rolls her eyes and tells her that she now doesn't have enough to pay for her groceries. The queue behind her is growing longer and more impatient. How would you resolve the situation?

10. Based on what you have learned about customer needs in this chapter, comment on the following situations:

    a.  Mrs Feeley has just bought a new house in a half-built housing estate. The house will be painted in the colours of her choosing as part of the deal. She tells the painter, Mr Smith, what she wants.

*Mrs Feeley*: I want the bathroom to be aquamarine.

*Mr Smith*: Uh huh.

*Mrs Feeley*: The main bedroom should be cedar green with a lime ensuite.

*Mr Smith*: Uh huh, uh huh.

*Mrs Feeley*: The other bedrooms should be fuchsia, lilac and buttercup.

*Mr Smith*: Uh huh, uh huh, uh huh.

*Mrs Feeley*: Are you getting all this?

*Mr Smith*: Of course, Madam, er, you were saying buttercup . . .

*Mrs Feeley*: Yes, and the hall should be a rich yellow, harvest sunlight.

*Mr Smith*: Uh huh.

*Mrs Feeley*: The kitchen should be oyster and the living room mustard.

*Mr Smith*: Uh huh.

*Mrs Feeley*: I'm not sure about the sitting room, how about a spring green?

*Mr Smith*: Uh huh . . . Oh yeah right, lovely . . . great choice, great choice. I'll get on it right away.

*Mrs Feeley goes upstairs.*

*Bob*: So, what do you want me to order?

*Mr Smith*: Oh, seven tins of yellow, five of green, four blue, four pink, three purple and fourteen white.

b.  A woman walks into a boutique where two assistants are talking at the till. They briefly glance in her direction and then turn away. The woman begins browsing round the empty store and kneels down to inspect some shoes on the bottom rack. Suddenly there is a pair of shoes beside her. She quickly stands up and the assistant immediately begins to tidy the shoes that she was examining. Eventually she approaches the till with a skirt. Before she opens her mouth the assistant at the till says, 'Sorry, Madam, we don't have that in your size.'

c.  Tom rings up a car insurance hotline. He is looking for a quote for his 1.6 litre hatchback. He is 23 years old. The insurance company refuses to give him a quote.

d.  Margaret wants to book a holiday. She goes into a travel agency in the local shopping mall. There is only one man there, working behind the counter and munching his way through a bag of crisps. The office has not been painted and the floor is bare. There is one torn seat for Margaret to sit at. He puts down the crisps and wipes his hands on his trousers before he turns his attention to Margaret. He is interrupted constantly by the telephone. She tells him that she is interested in going to Barbados in June. It takes him five minutes to move the mounds of paper on his desk before he finds the right brochure. It is last season's brochure and is covered in coffee stains. Margaret selects one hotel from the brochure and asks if it has air-conditioning. The man behind the counter doesn't know. She asks if it is safe to go scuba-diving there. The man doesn't know. She asks if there are any sights of historical interest in Barbados. The man says that he will look all that up for her. He asks her name, address and telephone number. He looks for a pen and paper. Eventually he finds a pen in his breast pocket and writes her details on the inside of his cigarette packet.

e.  A woman tries on a brown woollen dress in the ladies department of a large store. The assistant tells her that she looks fantastic in it. She then tries on a red silk dress. The assistant says it is the perfect colour. The woman then picks a size 12 dress. She asks for it in size 14. The assistant looks but cannot find any. She then urges her to try it on saying that it is a large size 12.

# 9

# CONSUMER LEGISLATION

Topics covered in this chapter:

- The Data Protection Act 1988
- The Sale of Goods and Supply of Services Act 1980
- The Liability for Defective Products Act 1991
- The Consumer Credit Act 1995
- The Consumers' Association of Ireland (CAI)
- The Advertising Standards Authority of Ireland (ASAI)
- The Consumer Protection Act 2007 and the establisment of the National Consumer Agency
- The small claims procedure
- The Financial Services Ombudsman
- Employment legislation
- Health and safety
- The European Union

*Note: In the following chapter amounts given in euro have been converted from the Irish currency quoted in the relevant Acts or reports.*

This chapter deals with the legislation passed in Ireland to protect the consumer and the seller. It also deals with the rights of individuals regarding information that is stored about them on computer.

In accordance with the Data Protection Act 1988:

- A data controller is a person who has access to and control over the information stored on computer.
- The data subject is a person who has had information stored about them electronically.

## The Data Protection Act 1988

The Data Protection Act was promulgated as a response to the Council of Europe Data

Protection Convention which was concerned with the possible infringements on personal privacy that the then relatively new and quickly expanding computer technology threatened. The council wanted control to be imposed over any personal data that was processed electronically. That included its collection, processing, storage and divulgence. Personal information that is not processed electronically, that is, anything not processed by computer but processed manually, is excluded from this Act. Therefore, this Act does not give a person access to paper files stored traditionally or to legal entities such as businesses and organisations.

Anyone who has information stored electronically about them by someone else has the right to be given, on request, a copy of that information. If they suspect that an organisation has information stored about them electronically, they have the right to find out from that organisation if that is so. They can demand to know what sort of information it is and why it is being stored by the organisation. If it is a mailing list used for marketing purposes, then they can ask to be removed from that list. The data controller has to respond appropriately in writing within 40 days of receiving the request. If the data is incorrect, the data subject has the right to compel the data controller to correct or delete the inaccuracies. If this is not done or if a subject feels that the Act is not being complied with in some other way, the subject has the right to complain to the Data Protection Commissioner. If the data subject has been damaged through this inaccurate information, for example was unable to get a loan because of an alleged poor credit record, was falsely imprisoned or missed a job opportunity, the data subject has the right to claim compensation in court.

The data controller is obliged by law to ensure that:

- All data is honestly and justly obtained.
- All data is honestly processed.
- All data serves a lawful function.
- All data that is acquired for one specific purpose is not used for another; for example, a doctor's patient list cannot be used for marketing holiday brochures.
- All data gathered is relevant, adequate and in proportion – for example, (a) 'has six toes on left foot' or 'owns two radios' would be irrelevant to financial records; (b) because it is a broad term, 'criminal record' may not be adequate for certain records, more detail would be needed; records which contained details of your income, holiday preferences, blood group, dependants and banking arrangements would be out of proportion for, say, a library card.
- All data is disposed of when no longer needed; for example, if you borrow money, any specifically related banking information should be deleted once the loan has been repaid.
- All data is protected from being read by unauthorised people.
- The data subject is given a copy of all data upon request.

To ensure that companies comply with the provisions of the Data Protection Act, the Office of the Data Protection Commissioner was established in 1988. The Data Protection Commissioner reports to the houses of the Oireachtas annually. It is up to the Office of the Data Protection Commissioner to ensure that a register of all data controllers is kept and that processors adopt good data protection practice. If good practice is not followed, the Office of the Data Protection Commissioner has the following powers:

- To authorise entry into any premises where data is stored electronically and to retrieve the relevant data.
- To issue information, enforcement and prohibition notices.
- To force data controllers to issue data subjects with a full copy of the information about them that is stored electronically.
- To force data controllers to correct errors, delete unnecessary information or add data to the files of data subjects where the existing information is insufficient.
- To prohibit the export of such data.
- To prosecute those who fail to honour their obligations under the Data Protection Act.

## The Sale of Goods and Supply of Services Act 1980

The Sale of Goods and Supply of Services Act 1980 is simply an update on the Sale of Goods Act 1893. As commercial transactions have grown more sophisticated, legislation must be developed in response. Over the years the Sale of Goods Act has been continually added to, though the original principles hold true. It is significant that the phrase 'and Supply of Services' has been added as the 1980 Act now provides protection for those involved in supplying or receiving services as a business transaction.

Under the terms of the Act the consumer has the following rights:

- Goods must be of merchantable quality. This means that the product must be able to do what it was made to do and it must continue to operate for a reasonable amount of time.
- Goods that are sold by description must match that description.
- When goods are sold by sample, the sample should be an accurate reflection of the rest of the goods.
- If the seller agrees to deliver the goods but omits to do so, the buyer has the right to sue the seller.
- The buyer should be given enough time to examine the goods.
- If the buyer examines the goods and finds them unacceptable with good legal cause, they must inform the seller. The buyer does not have to send the product back to the seller unless such an agreement has been made. If the seller is in breach of contract in supplying his buyer with unacceptable goods, the buyer has the right to sue the seller. The buyer may revoke the contract as the other party has already breached it. The name, address and duration of whatever guarantee accompanies the goods should be clearly stated in writing.
- A guarantee can in no way be used to diminish the consumer's statutory rights. If a supplier tries to replace the consumer's statutory rights with the guarantee, the guarantee is void.
- If whoever supplies the guarantee fails to honour it they can be sued.
- A supplier who offers a service rather than goods will need to use materials to provide

the service. Those materials must be of merchantable quality. The supplier must be qualified or at least, depending on the nature of the service, be competent to provide the service offered and must provide the service competently. The materials, service and equipment must conform to safety guidelines.

- If the seller does not rightfully own the goods they are selling, the goods must be returned to the lawful owner. The exception would be if the owner had given the seller the impression that the seller had the authority to sell the goods. In such a case, the owner cannot later dispute the seller's authority to sell.
- The buyer who has bought goods from a seller who sold goods without having good title to do so has the right to be refunded with the entire price they paid for the product even if the product has depreciated through wear and tear.
- Any goods to the value of €12.70 or over must be accompanied by a signed written copy of the contract, otherwise the contract cannot be enforced.
- The seller cannot charge the buyer for the services of a third party if the buyer had not been informed of this until after the contract was agreed.

## The Liability for Defective Products Act 1991

This Act is for products only and excludes services and unprocessed products such as agricultural produce. The Act clearly states that if a product is defective, the producer is liable, regardless of whether the production process was defective or not. The producer is liable to compensate anyone who may have incurred personal injury or damage to private property because of the defective product. There is compensation for damage in excess of the value of €442.03. There is no limit for personal injury claims. It is up to the injured party to justify their claim. The Act offers no compensation for damages done to the defective product itself. The producer is not liable if they can prove that there was no scientific proof available at the time that this product could cause the damage to person or property that the plaintiff is alleging. Nor is the producer liable if the defect is as a result of conforming to European Union safety standards. In addition, the producer is not liable if the alleged product has been available and in use for 10 years or more before the claim against it was made. Conversely, if a product was never made available, the producer is not liable for the damage caused.

## The Consumer Credit Act 1995

This Act protects consumers. The Act defines consumers as people acting in their own interests. This means people who are in a credit transaction for their own personal use and not for the benefit of any business, profession or trade they might be involved in.

In accordance with this Act, the following terms apply:

- The annual percentage rate (APR) must be clearly displayed on all advertising material and contracts. The APR is the amount of interest that the consumer will pay on any borrowed money.

- If the consumer is being offered a hire-purchase scheme, information should be clearly displayed outlining how much the product or service costs, the amount of credit offered and information on how much the consumer must pay and when. For example, some hire-purchase schemes offer as much as one year of free credit before repayment begins or they may offer a very low repayment scheme but will want a large payment at the end. All these criteria must be displayed to consumers so that they are aware of them before they enter into any agreement.

- Information about any other charges other than those of repaying the capital and interest must be contained in all advertising material.

- If there are any factors that might affect the availability of credit or if security is requested before the consumer is granted the credit, these conditions must also be displayed.

- If you are refused credit, you have access to the credit information that influenced that refusal. By the terms of the Data Protection Act 1988, you have the right to have any incorrect information about you that is electronically stored corrected or deleted.

- An agreement must be in writing and must contain the names, addresses and signatures of all parties involved in the transaction.

- An agreement must state the penalties on the consumer in the event that they fail to honour the agreement.

- The consumer must receive a copy of the signed document within 10 days.

- The consumer is allowed 10 days to change their mind about the agreement.

- All correspondence relating to a credit agreement should be addressed only to the consumer involved, unless they have instructed otherwise.

## The Consumer's Association of Ireland (CAI)

The Consumers' Association of Ireland was established in 1966. It is an independent, non-profit and non-government association with the objective of ensuring that consumers are protected from any bad practice, shoddy goods or poor service. Its stated purpose is 'to independently protect, promote and represent the interests of consumers'.

It publishes a monthly magazine, *Consumer Choice Magazine*, to educate consumers, enabling them to make informed decisions about goods and services. It compares products for value, performance and reliability. It also updates consumers on changing consumer law.

The CAI website (www.consumerassociation.ie) outlines the following consumer rights:

1.  The right to basic goods and services, which guarantee survival.

2.  The right to be protected against the marketing of goods or the provision of services that are hazardous to health and life.

3.  The right to be protected against dishonest or misleading advertising or labelling.

4. The right to choose products and services at competitive prices with an assurance of satisfactory quality.

5. The right to express consumer interests in the making and execution of government policy.

6. The right to be compensated for misrepresentation, shoddy goods or unsatisfactory services.

7. The right to acquire the knowledge and skills to be an informed consumer.

8. The right to live and work in an environment which is neither threatening nor dangerous and which permits a life of dignity and well-being.

## The Advertising Standards Authority of Ireland (ASAI)

Why is a certain alcoholic drink 'probably' the best lager in the world?

The ASAI (www.asai.ie) was created to ensure that advertisements are fair, honest, in-offensive and legal. It acts as a watchdog ensuring fair play and listens to any complaints that are made by the public. Each complaint is judged individually and a ruling is made either way. If a judgment goes against an advertisement, at the very least the offending advertisement is withdrawn from circulation. The ASAI's criteria for acceptable advertising are as follows:

- An advertisement should be legal and honest.
- The advertisement should take into consideration its responsibility to the consumer and to society.
- The advertisement should conform to the generally accepted rules of fair trading and competition which are practised in business.

If someone feels they have been misled by a commercial advertisement, they can make a complaint to the ASAI. The onus is then placed on the advertisers to prove that their advertisement is fair, honest and responsible. If the advertisers fail to successfully defend their advertisement, the ASAI may take legal action or recommend that another more appropriate party take the action.

## The Consumer Protection Act 2007 and the Establishment of the National Consumer Agency

The Office of the Director of Consumer Affairs (ODCA) was created as a result of the Consumer Information Act 1978. In 2005 a report by the Consumer Strategy Group entitled *Make Consumers Count* identified important deficiencies in the protection and promotion of consumer rights in Ireland. In response to this the National Consumer Agency replaced the ODCA with the passing of the Consumer Protection Act 2007, which outlined the powers of the new agency. The National Consumer Agency was charged by the government to defend consumer interests and to foster a stronger consumer culture in

Ireland. The powers and role of the former Office of the Director of Consumer Affairs (ODCA) are now vested in the National Consumer Agency.

The stated purpose of the NCA is listed on their website (www.nca.ie) as follows.

---

The NCA:
- Represents the voice of the consumer
- Enforces consumer legislation
- Defends consumer interests at the highest levels of national and local decision-making

As a consumer advocate and a defender of consumer rights, the NCA has an important role in working with businesses, to help them to support compliance with regulatory obligations and to encourage best practice as regards consumer rights.

Designated officers of the NCA work alongside business and representative organisations to promote awareness of consumer issues and to enforce consumer law.

Our work is divided into five main functions:
- Research
- Information
- Enforcement
- Advocacy
- Education and awareness

**Main objectives of the National Consumer Agency**

Our aim is to provide strong and modern consumer protection, safeguarding consumers in Ireland and empowering them to understand and to exercise their rights.

To achieve our aim, we:
- Inform consumers of their rights through consumer information
- Promote a strong consumer culture in Ireland through consumer education and awareness
- Help businesses obey consumer law through our enforcement activities
- Represent consumer interests at all levels of local and national consumer policy development through targeted research and forceful advocacy
- Conduct investigations under a wide range of consumer protection legislation

**Courtesy and helpfulness**

Any person who contacts the NCA will be provided with a quality service that is helpful, courteous and effective:
- NCA staff will identify themselves to customers
- Deal with your query as soon as possible or arrange a call back to you if the information is not available
- Give you contact details for the relevant body or organisation if your query relates to a matter that is outside the remit of the NCA, and
- Respond promptly when voice or email messages are received

### Responding to customers

Queries will be dealt with quickly and efficiently. Letters will be acknowledged within 3 working days and we will endeavour to issue a substantive reply within 15 working days.

NCA will put customers in touch with appropriate members of staff without delay. If this is not immediately possible the customer will be informed and arrangements put in place to ensure that the matter is dealt with promptly at the appropriate level.

NCA will:

- Seek the views of its customers on the quality and relevance of the services it provides
- Welcome suggestions from its customers on how its services can be improved
- Keep its services and the operation of its Customer Charter under review

### Visits to businesses

When carrying out investigations our authorised officers will be courteous and helpful.

In the course of site visits they will show their identification card or authorisation and leave their contact details. They will also be prepared to give helpful advice and guidance.

### Information

Accurate and timely information will be provided in relation to any queries of our services.

Responses to queries will be appropriate, thorough and substantive, as circumstances allow.

To make informed choices, consumers need easy access to clear, concise, accurate information. Our consumer website, www.consumerconnect.ie, provides a broad range of consumer-related information, news, top tips and an email enquiry service. It also carries podcasts and other interactive features highlighting important consumer issues.

We update our website regularly. In the unlikely event that you can't find what you are looking for on our website, ring our friendly and helpful advisors on LoCall 1890 432 432.

We also:

- Publish information booklets, leaflets and brochures addressing consumer issues and topics
- Issue press releases
- Run media campaigns on television, radio and in the press to:
  - Ensure consumers are aware that the National Consumer Agency exists and can help them
  - Educate consumers about their rights and obligations

### Diversity and equality

We will respect the principles of equality and the diversity of our customers in the delivery of all services. We are committed to providing a service to our customers that upholds their rights to equal treatment established by the equality legislation.

We will aim to ensure that our services and facilities are accessible to all our customers including those with special needs.

### Confidentiality

It is the policy of the NCA to use its best endeavours to hold confidential any information provided in confidence to the agency, subject to any legal obligations such as the Freedom of Information Acts.

The information services currently provided by the NCA include:

- A consumer website: www.ConsumerConnect.ie, providing consumers with a range of information in relation to basic rights, updates on topical consumer issues and a channel to communicate with the NCA on issues of importance to them
- itsyourmoney.ie, a site providing price comparisons, guides and tools for consumer financial products and services
- A corporate website: www.nca.ie, providing those who supply products and services to consumers with information in relation to their obligations under consumer law and updates on topical consumer issues. This also offers access to the register of NCA-approved credit intermediaries and current media updates on consumer matters
- A consumer helpline on a national LoCall number 1890 432 432
- Publication of a Shoppers' Rights Card, available from participating retailers

*Source*: www.nca.ie.

The NCA also has an informative press release page that is a good source of information on aspects of consumer interests, from buyer protection tips to explanations and reflections on the latest consumer legislation.

## Credit and the consumer

### Introduction

The aim of this short guide is to tell consumers about their rights when shopping for credit.

Credit is the provision of money, to facilitate a purchase, which will have to be repaid at a later date, along with interest and other stated charges. Sources of credit include loans, overdrafts, credit cards, credit sales, charge cards, in-store cards, hire-purchase, leasing (consumer-hire), housing loans/mortgages, moneylending and pawnbroking.

The Consumer Credit Act 1995 is the legislation which covers credit provided to consumers only. A consumer is defined by the Act as 'a natural person acting outside his trade, business or profession'. Credit provided by a credit union is not covered by the Act.

## Calculating the cost of credit – the APR

APR stands for the annual percentage rate of charge – the interest rate which reflects the real cost of borrowing. The APR is defined as being the total cost of credit to the consumer, expressed as an annual percentage of the amount of credit granted. It is considered to be the best means of comparing the cost of different types of credit. In general, the lower the APR, the less the cost of a particular credit deal for you as a consumer.

The Consumer Credit Act 1995 requires that the APR be shown prominently in consumer credit advertisements and agreements.

## The advertising of credit

Advertisements of credit should contain the following details:

* the APR
* details of any charges additional to the payment of capital and interest
* a statement of any security which may be required
* a clear indication of any restrictions on the availability of credit
* where applicable:
    - the nature of the financial accommodation
    - the cash price of relevant goods/services
    - the total cost of the credit or hire-purchase price
    - particulars of the number, amount and timing of instalments
    - details of any deposit
    - the number of instalments which must be paid before delivery of the goods.

## Consumer credit agreements

If you enter a credit agreement the following details should be included:

* your credit agreement must be in writing, containing the names and addresses of and be signed by all parties to the agreement
* a copy of the agreement must be given to you on completion or within 10 days of that date
* the agreement must set out the costs of penalties which apply if you do not comply with the terms of the agreement.

You may withdraw from an agreement within 10 days of receiving a copy of it by giving written notice to the relevant creditor or owner that you are withdrawing from the agreement (this 10-day grace period is known as the cooling-off period).

You may forgo your right to a cooling-off period by signing a clearly worded statement to that effect separately from any other term of the agreement.

There may also be other specific details which should be included in an agreement depending on the type of credit involved, e.g. a credit card agreement must specify the credit limit involved. Details of the specific requirements are laid down in the Consumer Credit Act 1995 and are also available from the Office of the Director of Consumer Affairs.

In general, if the above requirements are not complied with, the agreement will be unenforceable by the creditor. In limited circumstances, however, a court may decide that the contract will be legally enforceable.

## Refusal of a credit application

If you are refused credit you are entitled to information on your credit references which may have influenced the refusal. You may also have information rectified or erased, or have a statement appended where the data is incomplete, incorrect or irrelevant to the purpose for which it is kept.

If the information is held on computer you are entitled to access under the Data Protection Act 1988. Where the information is not automated (not held on computer) you also have rights of access under the Consumer Credit Act 1995.

The main consumer credit reference bureau is the Irish Credit Bureau, tel. (01) 260 0388. Here the consumer can access credit reference material held on computer under the terms of the Data Protection Act 1988.

There is normally a charge of €6.35 for accessing any credit information. This must be paid when the necessary background information is being supplied with the application. It is not refunded if there is no information about you.

## Right to privacy

When you have entered into a credit agreement, the Consumer Credit Act 1995 prohibits visits or telephone calls about the agreement to you without your consent at any place between 9pm and 9am weekdays, or at any time on a Sunday or public holiday. Calls or visits to your place of employment are prohibited unless you reside there, or if reasonable efforts to contact you have failed.

Only the person(s) involved in the credit agreement may be contacted (unless other arrangements have been made).

These rules do not apply where the service of a document connected with legal proceedings is concerned.

## Complaints against banks and building societies

Complaints against a bank or building society should first of all be made to the institution involved. If the complaint is not solved at this stage then you, the consumer, have the right to complain to the Ombudsman for the Credit Institutions in writing. The Ombudsman will then advise you of the correct procedure.

The Ombudsman can deal with a wide variety of complaints, for example problems with accounts, direct debits, mortgages and other loans. You can complain about mistakes, bad administration, discourtesy, breaches of confidentiality, unfair treatment or discrimination.

The decision of the Ombudsman is binding on the bank or building society concerned, but you are free to accept or reject the decision.

## Problems with debt

Most people owe money to someone. Credit can be availed of through credit cards, overdrafts and loans. Some people can find themselves in serious debt. Borrowing should be carefully planned, taking into consideration ongoing expenses and income. If your expenses exceed your income it is extremely unwise to borrow further.

Consumers who find themselves in a difficult debt situation should act immediately by trying to cut back on expenses where possible. If a loan or credit repayment has not been met, you should arrange to meet the lender and explain why you failed to meet the repayments. They may be in a position to offer financial advice on an action plan to tackle the problem.

If they cannot help it may be useful to get in touch with your local Money Advice and Budgeting Service (MABS) for independent assistance with debt problems.

For information on general consumer matters you may also contact the following:

European Consumer Centre
13 Upper O'Connell Street
Dublin 1.
☎ (01) 809 0600

Consumers' Association of Ireland
43–44 Chelmsford Road, Ranelagh, Dublin 6.
☎ (01) 497 8600

The Consumers' Association is an independent and non-profit organisation working in the interests of Irish consumers.

Money Advice and Budgeting Service (MABS)
c/o Department of Social and Family Affairs
Áras Mhic Dhiarmada
Store Street, Dublin 1.
☎ (01) 874 8444

This service has 40 centres around the country to help consumers with money management advice.

## The Small Claims Procedure

The small claims procedure deals with claims that have so low a value that it would not be economically viable for them to be pursued through the normal channels of the Irish court system.

The small claims procedure is intended to offer consumers an effective and cheaper alternative to a solicitor for disputes involving amounts not exceeding €2,000. While this procedure was originally aimed at individuals, from 11 January 2010 businesses can also use the small claims procedure to make claims against other businesses.

The small claims procedure operates as part of the District Court. The District Court consists of a President and sixty-three ordinary judges. The country is divided into twenty-four districts with one or more judges permanently assigned to each district and the Dublin Metropolitan District. The applicant (the aggrieved party) need only go along to the local District Court and fill in a claim form, with the relevant fee (currently €18), to commence the procedure. The form is sent to the Registrar, who then sends a copy of it, along with a Notice of Claim, to the respondent (the party the applicant is in dispute with).

When the respondent receives the claim, they may choose to ignore it, admit, dispute it or counterclaim.

To counterclaim they follow the same procedure as the original applicant. If they admit, then they have to comply with submitting to judgement. If they ignore it, they are deemed to have admitted and will be treated in the same way. If they counterclaim or dispute it, they will most likely have to appear in court.

The procedure of hearings is as follows: the Registrar outlines the alleged facts to the court. The applicant is then classed on to give evidence and is questioned directly by the judge, there being no solicitors involved. The respondent is then given a chance to outline their version of events.  Both applicant and respondent will be able to bring witnesses, which can be questioned by both sides.  The applicant and respondent will also be allowed to question each other in their turn. The judge also questions them directly. If the judge decides in favour of the applicant, the respondent will be notified within a few days and will be granted approximately one month (28 calendar days) to pay the applicant. If the respondent fails to meet this requirement, the applicant can ask the Registrar to have the Order of Court executed by the Sheriff. Be aware that if you lose a claim, you will not have your fee refunded. Both claimant and respondent can appeal any decision if they do so within 14 calendar days.

### Courts Service

15–24 Phoenix Street North
Smithfield, Dublin 7
Ireland
Tel: 01-888 6000
www.courts.ie

For cross-border claims, a similar system is in place, namely the European Small Claims Procedure. Application forms for both procedures can be downloaded at www.courts.ie.

# The Ombudsman

An Ombudsman is an official appointed by the various associations to investigate complaints against its members. The process originated as a means by which citizens could get grievances against the government investigated, but it has expanded as a concept. For example, universities and various business and professional bodies have special ombudsmen to deal with complaints made against them by customers.

## The Government ombudsmen

The ombudsmen appointed by the Irish government examine complaints concerning administrative actions of government departments, the Health Service Executive and An Post. Their main website is www.ombudsman.gov.ie. The various ombudsmen have websites for their specialist area, such as www.pensionsombudsman.ie and www.financialombudsman.ie.

# The Financial Services Ombudsman

*(This information is taken from the 2005 Annual Report of the Financial Services Ombudsman.)*

The Financial Services Ombudsman offers a free and fair way of settling unresolved complaints.

The purpose of the office of Financial Services Ombudsman is to provide an impartial and independent service to public and financial services alike.

## Origins

The Ombudsman for Credit Institutions was an arbitrator of unresolved disputes between banks, building societies (and finance houses which were prescribed as Credit Institutions under Section 2 of the Consumer Credit Act 1995) and their individual customers. However, the office of Ombudsman for Credit Institutions ceased to exist on 1 April 2005 when it was absorbed into the office of Financial Services Ombudsman under the terms of the Central Bank and Financial Services Authority of Ireland Act 2004.

There have been voluntary ombudsman schemes in Ireland both for credit institutions and the insurance sector since the early 1990s. This was in recognition by these sectors that a complaints resolution process outside the Courts was necessary and appropriate. However, not all financial service providers were covered by these schemes.

While the voluntary schemes worked well, it was felt, by the McDowell Report on the Working Group on Financial Services 1999, that an Ombudsman scheme with enhanced statutory powers should be established for all providers of financial services. Such a scheme came into being on 1 April 2005 in accordance with the Central Bank and Financial Services Authority of Ireland Act 2004 and is known as the Financial Services Ombudsman's Bureau.

## Financial Services Ombudsman's Bureau

The Bureau consists of:

1.  Financial Services Ombudsman.

2.  A deputy ombudsman and staff for each of the various divisions of financial services under the Financial Services Ombudsman's current remit. These currently include such services as:

*   banks
*   building societies
*   insurance companies, both life and general
*   credit unions
*   mortgage, insurance and other credit intermediaries
*   stockbrokers
*   pawnbrokers
*   moneylenders
*   bureaux de change
*   leasing companies
*   credit sales companies
*   health insurance companies
*   hire purchase providers.

Twenty staff members were employed by the Bureau on a permanent basis in 2005 while four were employed on a contract or temporary basis.

The Financial Services Ombudsman is a statutory officer who deals independently with complaints from consumers about their individual dealings with all financial services providers that have not been resolved by the providers after they have been through the internal complaints resolution systems of the providers. The Ombudsman is therefore the arbiter of unresolved issues and is impartial. Broader issues of consumer protection are the responsibility of the Irish Financial Regulator.

All personal customers, limited companies with a turnover of €3,000,000 or less, unincorporated bodies, charities, clubs, partnerships, trusts, etc. can complain to the Ombudsman. The Ombudsman offers a free service to the complainant.

The Ombudsman may investigate any type of complaint by a customer who is dissatisfied about:

*   the provision of a financial service by the financial service provider
*   an offer by the provider to provide such a service
*   failure by the provider to provide a particular financial service that has been requested.

But a customer is not entitled to make a complaint if the matter complained of:

*   is or has been the subject of legal proceedings before a court or tribunal
*   occurred more than six years before the complaint is made
*   is within the jurisdiction of the Pensions Ombudsman.

A complaint may not be investigated by the Ombudsman if in his opinion:

- it is vexatious or frivolous, or not in good faith
- the subject matter is trivial
- the conduct complained of occurred at too remote a time to justify investigation
- other redress means were available
- the complainant has no interest or an insufficient interest in the conduct complained of.

## The Ombudsman's decisions

The Ombudsman, after an investigation, can direct the financial services provider to do one or more of the following:

- rectify or change the conduct complained of or its consequences
- provide reasons or explanation for that conduct
- change or modify a practice relating to that conduct
- pay compensation up to a maximum of €250,000 or €26,000 annuity
- take any other lawful action.

The Ombudsman has extensive legal powers to require the financial service provider to provide information, including the power to require employees to provide information under oath. If necessary the Ombudsman can enter the premises of providers and demand the production of documents, etc. In the event of non-compliance the Ombudsman may seek a Court Order. Anyone who obstructs the Ombudsman commits an offence and is liable to a fine of up to €2,000, imprisonment for up to three months or both.

## Co-operation with the Pensions Ombudsman, the Financial Regulator and EEA member schemes

A Memorandum of Understanding was agreed between the Financial Regulator, the Financial Services Ombudsman and the Pensions Ombudsman in October 2005 and finalised and signed by the three parties in February 2006. The three offices work closely together. Meetings between the three parties are held regularly and when deemed necessary. The aim is to ensure that no consumer will 'fall between two stools' and that matters appropriate to each body will be referred accordingly.

The Bureau, like the pre-existing voluntary schemes, is also a signatory to the Memorandum of Understanding on a cross-border, out-of-court complaints network for financial services in the European Econmoic Area (FIN-NET). The Bureau has an obligation under FIN-NET to ensure efficient exchange of information between European ombudsmen and other comparable schemes.

If the Ombudsman receives a complaint about a financial service provider regulated in the UK for investigation by a regulatory authority in another EEA member state, which is regulated by the Financial Services Authority in the UK, such a complaint may be referred to the Financial Ombudsman Service comparable to the Financial Regulator here. The Ombudsman may refer that complaint to the Ombudsman Scheme of the appropriate EEA member state to be dealt with there.

## Procedure for dealing with complaints

### 1. Initial contact

Upon initial contact the complainant's name and address are entered into the Case Management Complaint System and a reference number is generated.

### 2. Form issued

The complainant is sent a complaint form, guide for complainants and explanatory leaflet, as per the Bureau's website. The complaint form must contain a warning to the complainant that if the Bureau does not receive a completed complaint form within 28 days the complainant's case will be closed.

### 3. Complaint is assessed

Once the complaint form has been returned, the complaint is assessed to determine whether it falls within the remit of the Bureau, as delineated by the provisions of the Act. It may be necessary to request further information from the complainant at this point.

### 4. Procedural Letter

Once it has been determined that the complaint falls within the Bureau's remit, the Procedural Letter is sent to the complainant. The Procedural Letter contains a brief outline of the Bureau's procedures and a request to the complainant to write to a nominated member of Senior Management in the Financial Service Provider, outlining his complaint and requesting a response. The Financial Service Provider must respond, proposing a resolution to the complaint and stating that in the event that the complainant is not satisfied with the response, he may treat it as sufficient grounds to refer the complaint to the Bureau. If the complainant is satisfied with the Financial Service Provider's response, he must inform the Bureau and his case will be recorded as 'Settled'. If he is dissatisfied with the response, he must submit it to the Bureau as the Financial Service Provider's Final Response. The Procedural Letter must contain a warning to the complainant that the Financial Service Provider's Final Response must be submitted to the Bureau within 28 days.

*Each Financial Service Provider must nominate to the Bureau ONE designated person to issue the Financial Service Provider's Final Response. The Financial Service Provider's Final Response Letter may be signed by this person or on his behalf. Where it is signed on behalf of the nominated person, the author must stipulate this. The complainant will receive one prompt letter.*

### 5. Notification of complaint to Financial Service Provider

On the same date of issue as the Procedural Letter to the complainant, the Notification of Complaint Letter is sent to the Financial Service Provider, informing it that a complaint has been lodged with the Bureau. A copy of the completed complaint form is attached to this letter.

The Procedural Letter and its prompt, together with the Notification Letter, must contain the following warning:

If the Financial Service Provider fails to issue a Final Response to the complainant within 28 days, the Bureau may intervene at this point. If, however, the failure to submit a Final Response is by the complainant's own omission, the case will be closed.

The Bureau may take the Financial Service Provider's failure to respond to the complaint within the designated timeframe into consideration when adjudicating upon the complaint.

## 6. Determine whether Formal Investigation is warranted

Once the Bureau is in receipt of the Complaint Form from the complainant and the Final Response of the Financial Service Provider, they must be assessed to determine whether a Formal Investigation of the complaint is warranted.

If it is determined that the response of the Financial Service Provider was reasonable under the circumstances, the complaint will not proceed to investigation. At this point a View will be issued to both parties based ONLY on the information contained in the Complaint Form and the Final Response letter. This View will be subject to the Review and Appeal procedures of the Bureau.

If the View is appealed, it will be reviewed by the Deputy Ombudsman. If the Deputy Ombudsman decides that a Formal Investigation is warranted, the complaint will be assigned to an Investigator and both parties will be notified. If the Deputy Ombudsman decides that the View should stand, the View becomes the Deputy Ombudsman's Finding which is subject to the Review and Appeal procedures of the Bureau.

## 7. Formal Investigation

If it is determined that a Formal Investigation of the complaint is warranted, the complainant will be informed that his case is proceeding to investigation. The Financial Service Provider will be required to submit all papers on the complainant (relevant to the complaint) to enable the Bureau to investigate and adjudicate upon the complaint. (Should the Investigator feel it necessary, a Summary of Complaint will be forwarded to the Financial Service Provider.) The Financial Service Provider will be given a maximum of 30 working days within which to comply with this request. The complainant must be informed at this point that the investigation should, in general, take at most 60 working days. However, for certain cases supplementary information will be necessary, which may cause the 60 working days to be extended.

When the relevant papers are received by the Bureau, the case will be assigned to an Investigator.

## 8. Finding of the Deputy Ombudsman

The Bureau may attempt to negotiate a settlement between the parties at this point. Failing this, the Deputy Ombudsman issues a Finding on the matter. Each party is given 25 working days to accept or appeal the Finding.

Where the 25 working days have lapsed and either party has submitted no appeal, the Finding becomes a Final Decision and is binding on both parties.

## 9. Final Decision of the Ombudsman

Where either party submits an appeal, the Financial Services Ombudsman will review the Finding of the Deputy Ombudsman and the appeal submission, and then issue a Final Decision which is binding for both parties.

The Final Decision of the Ombudsman will, in general, be issued within 15 working days after the expiration of the appeal period.

Where no new issues are raised in an appeal submission, the Financial Services Ombudsman may deem that the Finding issued by the Deputy Ombudsman is the Financial Services Ombudsman's Final Decision. The Complainant is informed of this by way of letter from the Financial Services Ombudsman.

The Final Decision is binding on both parties, subject to further appeal by either party in the High Court.

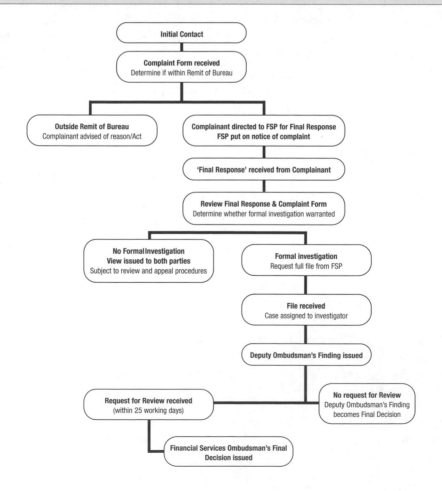

## Financial service providers subject to the Ombudsman's remit

The following financial service providers are subject to the Financial Services Ombudsman's remit:

1. Regulated by the Financial Regulator:
   - Credit institutions                              79
   - Life insurance companies                         53
   - Non life insurance companies                    135
   - Investment business firms                     1,100
   - Retail intermediaries                         2,400
   - Collective investment schemes                 3,000
   - Fund service providers                          230
   - Credit unions                                   435
   - Bureaux de change                                14
   - Moneylenders                                     50
   - Stock exchange and members                       14
   - Finex trading members                            38
   - Futures and options exchanges                     2
   - Money broker                                      6
   - Approved professional bodies                      3

2. Voluntary Health Insurance Board                   1

3. Consumer Credit Act regulated firms including pawnbrokers, hire purchase firms and others      200

TOTAL                                             7,760

## Major decisions published on the Bureau's website

Below is a summary of the major decisions made by the Bureau in the period from April to December 2005 and published on its website.

*Credit institutions*

- Elderly couple's unsuitable High Risk Investment – €56,000 compensation.
- Fall in investment value of 80-year-old person's joint investment – not upheld.
- Inappropriate investment advice – €20,000 compensation.
- Fee of €25,000 on transfer from fixed to variable rate of interest – not upheld.
- Endowment mortgage shortfall – not upheld.
- Direct debits and technical problems in bank – €750 awarded.
- ATM card withdrawals – not upheld.
- Building society had to repay €29,000 to a couple who switched their commercial mortgage to another provider. An early redemption fee of six months' interest was charged. The Ombudsman has directed the society to change its policy to the actual loss incurred.
- Nature of derivatives investment was not explained and €6,500 was awarded.

- Olympic Games – excessive hire of cars by credit card – not upheld.
- Complaint of €23,000 allegedly missing from a credit union account – not upheld.
- Credit union did not inform a member of his rights and €250 compensation was awarded.
- Credit card and anti-fraud measures are appropriate even when they cause inconvenience.
- Bank was wrong to withhold title deeds and €5,000 compensation was awarded.

### Insurance

- Life assurance – customer care issue – partly upheld and €1,000 compensation awarded.
- Travel insurance – replacement passport – €50 awarded.
- Income protection policy – policy voided for non-disclosure – not upheld.
- Mortgage protection policy – complaint partly upheld and Financial Regulator informed for industry-wide action.
- Travel insurance – definition of close relative – not upheld.
- Loan protection policy – trouble in settling case – €200 and apology.
- Medical expenses insurance policy – repudiation of claim on grounds of pre-existing condition – complaint not upheld.
- A complex total permanent disability and critical illness claim for €100,000 was initially rejected by the insurance company but a mediated statement of €33,000 was reached by the Ombudsman.
- Payment protection plan including disability benefit – benefit reinstated as complaint upheld.
- Medical expenses insurance – following a review by the Ombudsman the cost of surgery undertaken outside Ireland was met, without admission of liability, at an amount that would have been paid if it were carried out in Ireland.
- Medical insurance – a claim for the cost of a hip replacement was not upheld but the particular policy exclusion needs clarity.
- Stolen motor vehicle – Ombudsman increased valuation offer by €1,000 to €3,700.
- Household buildings policy – alleged storm damage of €80,000 not upheld.
- Life assurance – a 'with profits endowment policy' should not have been issued and accordingly the premiums paid had to be refunded.
- Whole of life policy allegation of misleading information – compromise settlement agreed.

### Contact details

Financial Services Ombudsman's Bureau
3rd Floor,
Lincoln House,
Lincoln Place,
Dublin 2

Locall: 1890 882 090
Tel: 01-662 0899
Fax: 01-662 0890
Email: enquiries@financialombudsman.ie
Website: www.financialombudsman.ie

## Examples

### Case example A

A customer sought advice from her bank as to how best to invest the sum of €30,000. She told the credit institution that she wanted a ten-year investment product in which the capital sum would be secure and on which she would have interest payments every six months. She was advised to invest in a particular bond and did so. She understood she was to receive €1,500 in interest every six months. When the first payment arrived accompanied by a statement, she noticed that the capital sum was reducing. When she brought this to the attention of the institution she was assured that the sum always reduced in the early years but would be more than made up in later years. Five years later she noticed that the value of the capital sum was now only €20,000 and she brought her complaint to the Ombudsman.

The Ombudsman acknowledged that while the product sold to her was somewhat complicated and difficult for the layman to understand, this was all the more reason for the institution to take great care in advising its customer. In this case the Ombudsman was not satisfied after his enquiries that the greatest care had indeed been taken. The Ombudsman's finding was that the institution had not made a thorough study of this lady's overall financial situation and he found it difficult to see therefore how any investment advisor could give sound investment advice in the absence of such knowledge. The Ombudsman accepted that maintenance of the capital sum intact was a prime consideration and he was not satisfied that the fact that a portion of the income was being taken from the capital sum in order to make up part of the six-monthly payments was ever properly explained to the complainant. The Ombudsman ruled that inadequate advice was given in this particular case and that the product which was sold was unsuited to the customer's particular circumstances. He awarded €6,500 in compensation.

### Case example B

A couple with a mortgage complained that their mortgage was the subject of mistakes by the credit institution concerned over a period of years. The errors were not discovered by the mortgage provider, but by the complainants themselves. On investigation it was discovered that the account was correct until 1997 but that then mistakes had started which were not corrected until eighteen months later.

The problem arose when the account was changed from a fixed rate to a variable rate of interest. The Ombudsman found that there were nineteen separate mistakes during the eighteen-month period resulting in the balance outstanding being overstated by several thousand euro. Charges for late payments were overstated on a number of occasions resulting in arrears notices being triggered along with threats of legal action. Even when the institution wrote to the customers eventually acknowledging that mistakes had been made and showing the correct balance, it totally failed to explain to the customers what exactly had been happening and what the consequences for future payments would be. The mortgage provider concerned pleaded that it had 'spent many man hours' trying to solve the problem which was due to a systems failure. However, the Ombudsman noted that while these 'man hours' were being spent, the customers' account was left to meander along to a point where the institution ought to have known that this would cause great difficulties for the customers. Nobody contacted the customers about this and all the customers got were arrears notices of increasing severity of tone. The Ombudsman's finding was that there was gross maladministration of the account which caused great distress, anxiety and inconvenience to the complainants. He awarded €5,000 in compensation.

### Case example C

A couple who fell into arrears on a loan account had a judgment registered against them by the loan provider. The fact of this judgment was duly recorded on the Irish Credit Bureau records. The complainants subsequently satisfied the amount in full but the record on the Bureau had never been amended to reflect this, and as a result the credit rating of the customers was adversely affected during a period of two and a half years. When the complainants contacted the lender they found that they were as they put it 'sent from Billy to Jack' in their efforts to have the matter sorted out.

The Ombudsman on investigation found that the loan provider had been negligent in that it allowed a period of two years to elapse after the customers had discharged the judgment in full before lodging the Satisfaction Piece in the High Court and was also negligent in not providing a competent person to deal with the complainants' file once the problem was raised.

The Ombudsman made a finding that the complainants' credit rating had been adversely affected during the two-and-a-half-year period in question due to the dilatory action of the lender. The Ombudsman awarded €2,000 compensation.

### Case example D

A customer with a loan account alleged that he was overcharged on interest over a period of three years. The customer brought this to the attention of the loan provider. After investigation the loan provider admitted the error. The complainant brought his case to the Ombudsman for compensation. The lender pointed out to the Ombudsman that the excessive rate of interest was shown clearly on the statement at all times and the customer should have drawn the lender's attention to it earlier and the matter would have been corrected at once. However the Ombudsman, stating the complainant had no obligation to spot mistakes on the loan provider's statements, found that all the responsibility for the overcharging over a three-year period must lie with the loan provider.

The Ombudsman awarded €7,500 in this case, half of which was restoration of excessive interest which had been charged, and the other half was compensation for the distress and inconvenience caused by the loan provider's failure to charge the proper rate of interest.

## Case example E

A small business had agreed a temporary increase in its overdraft from €5,000 to €10,000. However, due to an oversight at the branch, the new limit was not marked up. As a result of this failure to mark up the new limit, three cheques drawn by the company were dishonoured. There was a conflict of evidence as to what happened next. The complainants stated that the credit institution offered to write to the payees of the cheques explaining that the cheques were dishonoured wrongfully due to the institution's own mistake. The institution says it offered to do this but the company declined the offer. At all events it was not done. The Ombudsman made a finding that it was incumbent on the branch to do all it could to mitigate the damage and should have pressed the matter until it was quite clear that the company involved (the institution's customers) had expressed clearly that it did not want this to be done.

The three cheques which had been dishonoured had been issued by the company in the course of its business and the Ombudsman held therefore that it must be presumed to have suffered damage to its reputation. The Ombudsman awarded €7,000 in compensation.

## Chartered Accountants Regulatory Board

This board was established by the Institute of Chartered Accountants in Ireland to 'regulate its members, in accordance with the provisions of the Institute's Bye-laws, independently, openly and in the public interest'.

'The Chartered Accountants Regulatory Board is responsible for developing standards of professional conduct and supervising the compliance of members, member firms, affiliates and students' ( www.carb.ie).

## Current employment legislation

### 1994

*Terms of Employment (Information) Act 1994*
This Act updates previous legislation relating to the provision by employers to employees of information on such matters as job description, rates of pay and hours of work.

### 1996

*Protection of Young Persons (Employment) Act 1996*
This updates previous (1977) legislation and regulates the working conditions and employment of children and young persons.

### 1997

*Organisation of Working Time Act 1997*
This Act relates to the regulation of a variety of working conditions such as maximum working hours, night work and annual and public holiday leave.

### 2000

*National Minimum Wage Act 2000*
This Act introduces a national minimum wage.

### 2001

*Organisation of Working Time (Records) (Prescribed Form and Exemptions) Regulations 2001*
This EU Regulation requires that employers keep a record of the number of hours worked by employees on a daily and weekly basis, to keep records of leave granted to employees in each week as annual leave or as public holidays and details of the payments in respect of this leave. Employers must also keep weekly records of starting and finishing times of employees.

*Protection of Employees (Part-time Work) Act 2001*
This Act replaced the Worker Protection (Regular Part-time Employees) Act 1991. It provides for the removal of discrimination against part-time employees where such discrimination exists. It aims to improve the quality of part-time work to facilitate the development of part-time work on a voluntary basis and to contribute to the flexible organisation of working time in a manner that takes account of the needs of employers and workers. It guarantees that part-time workers may not be treated less favourably than full-time employees.

## Carers' Leave Act 2001

This entitles employees to avail of temporary unpaid carer's leave to enable them to care personally for persons who require full-time care and attention.

## 2003

### Protection of Employees on Transfer to Undertakings Regulations 2003

This legislation applies to any transfer of an undertaking, business or part of a business from one employer to another employer as a result of a legal transfer (including the assignment or forfeiture of a lease) or merger. Employees' rights and entitlements are protected during the transfer.

### Protection of Employees (Fixed Term Work) Act 2003

This Act protects fixed-term employees by ensuring that they cannot be treated less favourably than comparable permanent workers and that employers cannot continually renew fixed-term contracts. Under this legislation employees can only work on one or more fixed-term contracts for a continuous period of four years. After this the employee is considered to have a contract of indefinite duration.

## 2004

### Maternity Protection Act 2004

This replaced previous legislation and covers matters such as maternity leave, the right to return to work after such leave and health/safety during and immediately after pregnancy.

### Maternity Protection (Amendment) Act 2004

This legislation made significant improvements to previous maternity protection legislation including new provisions relating to ante-natal classes, additional maternity leave, breastfeeding, reduction in compulsory period of pre-birth confinement, etc.

### Equality Act 2004

This legislation makes significant amendments to the Employment Equality Act 1998, such as providing for extension of the age provisions of that Act to people under the school-leaving age (from 16 years) and those over 65 years. It also amends the Equal Status Act 2000 to extend the definition of sexual harassment and shift the burden of proof from the complainant to the respondent.

### Employment Equality Act 2004

This prohibits discrimination in a variety of employment-related areas. Discrimination is prohibited in relation to gender, sexual orientation, marital status, family status, race, age, religious belief, disability and membership of the Traveller community. The Act also regulates against sexual and other harassment.

## 2005

### Safety, Health and Welfare at Work Act 2005

This legislation replaced the provisions of the Safety, Health and Welfare Act 1989. It consolidates and updates the existing health and safety law. Changes include the provision for higher fines for breaches of safety legislation.

### Adoptive Leave Act 2005

Provides for adoptive leave from employment, principally by the adoptive mother and for her right to return to work following such leave.

## 2006

### Parental Leave Act 2006

This Act allows for a period of unpaid parental leave for qualifying employees to care for their children and for a limited right to paid leave in circumstances of serious family illness (*force majeure*).

## 2007

### Unfair Dismissals Act 2007

This updates the unfair dismissals law from 1977.

## The Safety, Health and Welfare at Work Act 2005

This Act replaces the Safety, Health and Welfare at Work Act 1989. It lists the legal requirements for the control of health and safety at work.

Its intention is to secure the safety of all workers, all workplaces and all visitors and passers-by.

**It emphasises the responsibility of all employers and stakeholders to ensure that they provide a safe work environment for all those employed by them directly or indirectly.**

It is the responsibility of all employers to provide a safe working environment for their employees. This includes designing a safe workspace and eliminating any potential hazards, for example in the construction industry, making sure that all scaffolding is securely built and enclosed in a safety mesh to prevent workers falling from a great height. It also involves ensuring that workers are not exposed to any chemicals or other hazards that could damage their health. Employers must also ensure that workers' behaviour does not put other workers at risk. This includes bullying from other workers or management, horseplay, dares or any work culture that discourages employees from complying with standard safety practices.

## It outlines the responsibilities of workers themselves in the protection of their own health.

Workers must attend all health and safety training provided by their employer. They must follow the correct health and safety procedures for their job including using all tools and machinery in the recommended way. They must point out any defects at work that might prove a health and safety risk. They must not endanger themselves or other workers through horseplay or bullying. They must not present themselves for work while intoxicated, which may put themselves or others in danger.

## It outlines the systems needed within companies, etc. to work to meet those health and safety requirements. In this way the Act takes a preventative approach rather than a purely punitive one.

The Act highlights the need for all employers, including the self-employed, to manage health and safety to prevent workplace injuries and ill health. All hazards and risks should be identified and assessed and then a written safety statement should be prepared. Once completed, the statement should be reviewed at least once a year and updated when necessary.

Employers must consult their employees on health and safety matters at work. They should nominate at least one competent member of staff to keep them updated on all health and safety matters. They must also provide employees with all relevant information on the health and safety issues specific to their work environment.

## It describes how the Act will be enforced.

Safety representatives have a right to inspect the place of work. The Health and Safety Authority provide these inspectors, who will offer advice and information as they carry out the inspection. If necessary an inspector will serve a direction for an improvement plan. This will require the employers to submit an improvement plan for dealing with an existing specific risk. The employers have one month to do this.

Inspectors have other enforcement powers at their disposal:

1. *Improvement Notice.* This sets the time limit for when a health and safety violation must be eliminated.

2. *Enforcement Notice.* This will be served when an employer has failed to comply with the law.

3. *Prohibition Notice.* This requires the immediate halt of whatever activity is causing or bearing the health and safety risk. The Health and Safety Authority may also apply to the High Court prohibiting or restricting the use of a place of work.

Those who fail to comply with the law can expect to pay 'on-the-spot' fines of up to €1,000 for certain offences.

If prosecuted, the courts may impose fines and/or prison sentences. Directors and senior managers can be convicted as individuals if it can be shown that a health and safety violation was committed by their organisation through their own neglect, consent, connivance or authorisation.

## The Health and Safety Authority (HSA)

The Health and Safety Authority (HSA) is a state-sponsored body that was established as a result of the Safety, Health and Welfare of Work Act 1989 and reports to the Minister for Enterprise, Trade and Employment.

The HSA is responsible for the administration and enforcement of health and safety at work in Ireland. It inspects places of work to ensure that both workers and employers are complying with the law. It investigates accidents and causes of ill health in the workplace. Where necessary it will act against non-compliance, serving notices, directions, on-the-spot fines or taking offending parties to court where they may have a fine and/or a prison sentence imposed on them.

The HSA also offers advice to employers, employees and the self-employed on all aspects of workplace health and safety.

The HSA encourages research and education into the whole area of health and safety. It provides a number of DVDs and publications on health and safety.

The HSA has a very useful website at www.hsa.ie and can also be contacted at 1890 289 389.

## The National Irish Safety Organisation (NISO)

The NISO was established in 1963 to assist the manufacturing and construction industry in matters of safety. It is a voluntary limited company that now complements the work of the Health and Safety Authority which was established in 1989.

The NISO is funded by an annual grant from the Irish Insurance Federation, the state, the sale of safety literature and membership subscriptions.

It aims to promote health, safety and welfare in the workplace through conferences, seminars, its free regular *Health and Safety* magazine and training in occupational safety, health and welfare.

It provides safety representative training courses and competitions in farm and school safety. There is also an Occupational Safety Award scheme and an all-Ireland Occupational Health and Safety Quiz.

The NISO is a really useful organisation for companies to join because it offers relevant advice on how best to comply with the 2005 Safety, Health and Welfare at Work Act. It can be contacted at:

NISO
A11 Calmount Park
Calmount Avenue
Ballymount

Dublin 12
Tel: (01) 465 9760
www.niso.ie

## Fire, Water and Road Safety

Employers should contact the Department of the Environment at 01 888 2000 or at their own website if they have queries regarding fire safety. The Irish Water Safety Association is at www.iws.ie and the Road Safety Authority can be reached at the old National Safety Council address, www.nsc.ie

## The European Union

As Ireland is a member of the European Union it must bring into effect the minimum level of consumer protection legislation required by EU rules. These rules are brought into effect by Irish legislation. A great deal of consumer protection has been legislated for in Ireland in this way. However, Ireland can introduce consumer protection legislation that exceeds the EU minimum requirement if it so wishes. Therefore there are some laws in Ireland that protect consumers that are not derived from EU requirements because they exceed the minimum requirements. All countries within the EU are in similar situations and so some degree of variation in consumer legislation can be expected from one country to another. It is useful to look at another EU country, for example Germany, to see the differences and similarities with Ireland. While early consumer protection was distinctive, we can see that later legislation is similar to our own. Visit www.beuc.eu, the website of BEUC, the European Consumers' Organisation.

### Consumer protection in Germany

The following extract is taken from *Facts about Germany*.

> Products made in Germany compete with goods made from all over the world. Consumers have a greater choice than ever before. But such a wide variety is a problem for them too since it has become increasingly difficult to judge quality and value for money. In addition, there are dangers to health and dishonest sales methods. As a result, consumer protection now plays an important role in the life of the community.
>
> In 1964 the Federal Government, together with the Association of Consumers' Unions, set up a foundation in Berlin known as 'Stiftung Warentest', which tests goods of all kinds, from the ballpoint pen to the personal computer, as to quality, value for money and compatibility with the environment. Services, too, are tested. This organisation meanwhile screens about 1,700 articles in roughly 100 comparative testings each year.

Stiftung Warentest only calls upon independent experts and institutes and has earned a good reputation from consumers and manufacturers alike. The latter are glad to advertise the fact that their products have been deemed 'good' or 'very good' by Stiftung Warentest.

The foundation's main publications are the magazine *Test*, which appears monthly and has a circulation of about 1 million, and the magazine *FINANZ-Test*. Test results are also regularly publicised in some 160 newspapers and periodicals as well as on the radio and television.

The public can also seek advice from roughly 350 regional consumer centres, which provide information on the quality and prices of goods and services and receive financial support from the government. Before parliament introduces new consumer protection legislation, it consults the consumers' unions.

The Association of Consumers' Unions (AgV) is the national organisation of consumer organisations and social-policy-orientated member associations. These above all include the consumer centres in the federal states. The function of the Association of Consumers' Unions is to promote consumer interests and support the consumer information activities of its member organisations. In order to improve consumer protection, the Association of Consumers' Unions is actively involved in many political and economic-sector bodies at the national and international level, cultivates close relations with parliaments and drafts proposals and position papers for legislative initiatives.

Consumer protection has been considerably improved by legislation. The Act on General Terms and Conditions of Contract protects customers from the pitfalls contained in small print; the Consumer Credit Act enables the borrower to cancel a loan and requires information to be provided by the lender; the Foodstuffs Act protects customers from damaging substances in food; the Travel Contract Act forces operators to fulfil their promises; the Product Liability Act makes manufacturers liable for flawed products. There are also many other laws to protect consumers. They concern such matters as the labelling of foodstuffs, strict criteria for pharmaceutical products, the tolerability of detergents and price tags on goods in shop windows. The Association of Consumers' Unions and the consumer centres jointly publish brochures, leaflets and other advisory material on all subjects of relevance to consumers.

As the countries of the European Union grow closer together, legislative initiative in the area of consumer protection is also increasingly shifting to the European Union. The Union issues directives which must be converted into national law in the member states.

## Protection of workers' rights in the EU

*Q. How is the EU involved in protecting workers' rights?*

**A.** There are a number of directives and regulations which deal with workers' rights – particularly in relation to equality and health and safety. These directives and regulations are brought into force in Ireland. Some of the workers' rights legislation which we have in Ireland at present is derived from EU rules. The laws on redundancy payments and unfair dismissals do not, in general, arise from EU rules.

*Q. What is the Social Charter?*

**A.** The Social Charter is basically a charter of workers' rights which was agreed in 1989 by 11 member states of the EC. The UK did not sign. The member states who subsequently joined have all agreed to the charter. The Social Charter itself is a declaratory document. It is a statement of aims and intentions without legal force. From a practical point of view, the more important document is the Social Charter Action Programme. This contains the proposals which are designed to implement the general aims of the charter.

There were 47 separate proposals for action in the Commission's Action Programme on the Social Charter. Some of these involve legislation while others involve recommendations. Still others provide for programmes for specific groups, for example the disabled and older people. Many, but not all, of these proposals have now been implemented.

The Social Charter must be distinguished from the social policy provisions of the Maastricht Treaty. The Treaty contains a Protocol on Social Policy. This Protocol includes an Agreement on Social Policy by 11 of the 12 member states (and subsequently agreed to by the new member states). It is sometimes referred to as the 'Social Chapter'.

*Q. Is there EU legislation on the rights of part-time workers?*

**A.** Yes. In EU language, part-time workers are described as 'atypical' workers. There is one directive and two proposed directives on atypical work. The directive on health and safety for atypical workers came into effect at the end of 1992. Broadly it provides for the same health and safety rights for part-time and temporary workers as full-time and permanent workers enjoy.

The two proposed directives deal with social insurance and protective labour legislation for atypical workers. They provide that atypical workers should have the same access to social assistance, to workers' representative bodies and to vocational training. In employments where there is a workforce of more than 1,000, employers would have to specifically justify using atypical workers. Atypical workers should also have social protection, holidays and dismissal allowances in broadly the same way as full-time and permanent workers. There has been no progress on these proposed directives for some time. In Ireland, part-time workers who work at least 8 hours a week already have broadly the same rights as full-time workers.

*Q. What is the EU position on equality?*

**A.** The Treaty of Rome has a provision that men and women should get equal pay. To date the EU has issued a number of directives to implement the principle of equal treatment:

*   a directive on equal pay
*   a directive on equal treatment as regards access to employment, vocational training and working conditions
*   three directives on equal treatment in matters of social security.

*Equal pay.* Considerable progress has been made in the implementation of equal pay in all member states. All have legal provisions incorporating Community law on the equal pay principle. At this stage there is very little, if any, direct discrimination but there are problems with questions such as indirect discrimination, definition of equal value and payment for part-time work. The European Court of Justice has, in a number of cases, interpreted the Equal Pay Directive broadly.

*Equal treatment.* The directive on equal treatment requires the member states to implement the principle of equal treatment between men and women as regards access to employment, vocational training and promotion and working conditions. Equal treatment means the absence of any discrimination on the grounds of sex, particularly as related directly or indirectly to matrimonial or family status. Like equal pay, the principle of equal treatment is expressed in the laws of all member states but there are problems in implementation, particularly regarding indirect discrimination and access to education and vocational training.

*Social security.* The first EC directive on the implementation of equal treatment in social security schemes has been implemented. In Ireland the main effects have been that women qualify for the same rates of unemployment and disability benefit as men and that they may qualify for unemployment assistance. The directive on equal treatment in occupational social security schemes has also been implemented. These directives all allow for major exceptions to the principle of equality – notably survivors' benefits, family benefits and retirement age. There is a proposal to provide for equal treatment in these areas but it has not made progress.

*General equality activities.* The EC has set up a number of bodies with responsibility for promoting equal opportunities. Among other things, these bodies monitor the application of existing directives and try to ensure that the equal treatment principle is taken into account in the formation of other policies, for example in education, training, etc. It promotes positive action in firms and organises or supports a variety of activities in the field of women's rights.

*Positive action.* The EU recognises that legal provisions for equal treatment are not in themselves enough to remove existing inequalities affecting women in working life. Action needs to be taken by governments, both sides of industry and other bodies to counteract the prejudicial effects on women in employment arising from social attitudes, behaviour and structures. The Council of Ministers adopted a recommendation on positive action in 1984. Since then the EU has encouraged and supported positive action in various sectors and has published a guide to assist those involved in positive action.

*Equal opportunities programmes.* There have been four equal opportunities programmes since 2000, though the 2003 and 2006 directives on Equal Treatment in Employment and Occupation have yet to be implemented in some EU countries, such as the UK.

## Q. What EU legislation is there on health and safety?

**A.** Health and safety issues were given specific prominence by the Single European Act. The Social Charter provides that, 'Every worker must enjoy satisfactory health and safety conditions in his working environment. Appropriate measures must be taken in order to achieve further harmonisation of conditions in this area while maintaining the improvements made.'

The Framework Directive was agreed in July 1989. It provides for a general obligation on employers to ensure the health and safety of workers. Among its detailed provisions is a requirement that particularly sensitive risk groups must be protected against the dangers which specifically affect them. Subsequent directives build on this Framework Directive – these include directives on safety on construction sites, on VDUs, etc.

*Pregnancy directive.* Under the health and safety measures there is a directive on measures to encourage improvements in the health and safety of pregnant workers, women workers who have recently given birth and those who are breastfeeding. It came into effect in October 1994.

This directive provides that employers must assess in advance any risks which may occur and working conditions or working hours must be changed accordingly or the women must be moved to other work or given time off. This must not result in any loss of employment rights and there must be compensation for any loss of pay.

Pregnant workers are entitled to paid time off to undergo ante-natal medical examinations and they may not be dismissed because of the pregnancy.

There must be two weeks of obligatory maternity leave; a right to a minimum of 14 weeks' leave and the employment rights of women on maternity leave must be maintained. Maternity benefits may not be less than those payable to people out of work because of illness.

## Q. What about paternity leave?

**A.** A directive on paternity leave was agreed and came into effect in 1998. It gave the right to 14 weeks unpaid leave to parents. This leave may be taken any time until the child reaches eight.

## Q. Does the EU have a policy on child-care facilities?

**A.** The Child Care Recommendation recommends that member states should take or encourage initiatives to enable women and men to reconcile their occupational, family and upbringing responsibilities arising from the care of children. It encourages initiatives in providing child-care facilities while parents are working, seeking work or in training; in providing special leave for employed parents with flexibility; in examining the environment, structure and organisation of work to make them more responsive to the needs of workers with children; and in encouraging the sharing of occupational, family and upbringing responsibilities between men and women, i.e. increased participation by men. This is a recommendation and has no legal force.

### Q. Does the EU regulate hours of work?

**A.** There is a directive on working conditions which has been agreed and will be brought into effect over the next few years. It deals with hours of work, shift work conditions, holidays, etc. It provides for:

* a minimum daily rest period of 11 hours in 24
* at least one rest day in every seven days
* the average weekly working time would not be more than 48 hours (including overtime) in a week
* a minimum of four weeks' paid holidays (the legal minimum in Ireland at present is three weeks) and a worker would not be allowed to accept financial compensation in lieu of holidays
* no overtime by night workers and a maximum of eight hours' work in 24 for night workers; special health and safety precautions for night and shift workers
* derogations are allowed for specific circumstances and specific kinds of workers.

The directive should come into effect three years after its adoption but some provisions may be deferred for longer. The 48-hour rule may be deferred for seven years provided certain other health and safety measures are put in place. The new holidays entitlement need not be implemented for six years.

If the current proposals were to be agreed their effects in Ireland depend on whether or not the government chooses to derogate. There is no general legislation on night work in Ireland at present. The holiday entitlement would be greater than the current statutory minimum but probably not much greater than the current practice.

### Q. Are there rules governing young people at work?

**A.** Yes. There is a directive on the protection of young people at work that has been in place since June 1996. It is part of the overall health and safety legislation.

### Children aged 14–16

The directive provides that children under 14 may not be employed. Those over 14 may be employed in light work outside the school term provided it is for not more than seven hours a day or 35 hours a week. Those over 15 may be employed during the school term but not for more than eight hours a week. They may not be employed between 8pm and 8am; they must have minimum rest periods and minimum breaks.

There are provisions for making certain exceptions to these general rules.

### Young people aged 16–18

Young people may work up to eight hours a day and 40 hours a week. In general, they may not work between 10pm and 6am and they must have minimum rest periods and breaks. Again, there are provisions for exceptions for certain circumstances.

### Q. What other areas are covered by EU laws?

**A.** There are a number of other directives, of which the following are probably the most important.

*European Works Council*
There is a directive that came into effect in September 1996 on the establishment of a European Works Council in Community-scale undertakings. It applies to undertakings with at least 1,000 employees within the EC and at least 100 employees in each of two member states. The objective of these councils is to provide a forum for informing and consulting employees.

*Directive on an employer's obligation to inform employees of the conditions applicable to the contract of employment relationship*
This directive came into force on 30 June 1993. It was implemented in Ireland by the Employment (Information) Act 1994. It applies to every paid employee except those in employment of less than 1 month or of less than 8 hours a week. The employer must notify the employee of the essential aspects of the employment relationship. These include the amount of paid leave, notice period, pay, length of working week and, where appropriate, the collective agreements governing the conditions of work. This must be given to employees not later than two months after they start work. If the employee is being posted abroad he/she must receive similar information about the conditions that will apply as well as information relating to expenses, currency, etc. When employment conditions are changed other than by statute or collective agreement then the new conditions must also be given in writing not later than a month after they come into effect.

*Directive concerning the posting of workers*
This directive deals with the employment conditions of workers who are sent abroad to perform contracts or sent to another establishment of the company abroad for periods of more than three months. The directive applies regardless of the country from which the worker was sent. The objective is to ensure that, whatever country's law governs the contract, the worker is not deprived of certain basic protective legislation in force in the host country – the laws in relation to working time, minimum rates of pay, holidays, health and safety, equality of treatment, non-discrimination on grounds of race, sexual orientation, etc. It does not affect the question of the social security contribution payable.

*Directive on Collective Redundancies*
The Protection of Employment Act 1977 implemented this directive, which sets out a system of notification and consultation in the event of collective redundancies. The directive was amended – with effect from June 1994 – in order to make it applicable to proposed collective redundancies affecting workers within the territorial scope of the treaty no matter where the controlling undertaking is located.

The amended directive also provides for some small changes in the information and consultation requirements – the scope of the consultations is widened to include proposed social measures geared to helping the rehabilitation, redeployment and social and vocational reintegration of redundant workers.

*Transfer of Undertakings Regulations (1980)*
These regulations provide for the protection of employees' rights when there is a change of employer.

*Regulatory affairs*
This is a profession within regulated industries that ensures that the company they are employed by complies with all of the rules, regulations and laws pertaining to their business.

## Exercises

1.  What does the Data Protection Act 1988 protect people against?

2.  Does the Data Protection Act 1988 cover written records?

3.  Outline the main terms of the Sale of Goods and Supply of Services Act 1980.

4.  What Act will protect you if you are badly electrocuted by a faulty shower?

5.  Outline the main terms of the Consumer Credit Act 1995.

6.  What is the ASAI?

7.  What is the purpose of the ASAI?

8.  What is the function of the National Consumer Agency?

9.  How do I make a claim under the small claims procedure?

10. What is an ombudsman?

11. Name one ombudsman that protects consumers in Ireland.

12. How do you contact an ombudsman?

13. How does Irish consumer protection differ from that of other countries within the EU?

## Useful websites for consumers

Advertising Standards Authority of Ireland
www.asai.ie

Chartered Institute of Arbitration
www.arbitration.ie

Citizens Information
www.citizensinformation.ie

Commission for Aviation Regulation
www.aviationreg.ie

Commission for Communications Regulation
www.comreg.ie

Commission for Energy Regulation (CER)
www.energycustomers.ie

Commission for Taxi Regulation
www.taxireg.ie

Competition Authority
www.tca.ie

European Consumer Centre Ireland
www.eccireland.ie

European Consumers' Organisation
www.beuc.ie

Financial Regulator
www.financialregulator.ie

Financial Services Ombudsman
www.financialombudsman.ie

Food Safety Authority of Ireland
www.fsai.ie

Health Insurance Authority
www.hia.ie

Injuries Board
www.injuriesbaord.ie

Irish Business and Employers Confederations (IBEC)
www.ibec.ie

Irish Payment Services Organisation Ltd
www.ipso.ie

Law Society of Ireland
www.lawsociety.ie

Money Advice and Budgeting Service (MABS)
www.mabs.ie

National Consumer Agency
www.consumerconnect.ie

National Irish Safety Organisation
www.niso.ie

Pensions Board
www.pensionsboard.ie

Register of Electrical Contractors of Ireland (RECI)
www.reci.ie

Society of the Irish Motor Industry (SIMI)
www.simi.ie

# 10

# PREPARING A CUSTOMER CARE PROGRAMME

**Topics covered in this chapter:**

- How to prepare a customer care programme
- Making a presentation
- Audio-visual aids

The most important people in your organisation are your customers. You want to ensure that your customers are happy with every aspect of their consumer transaction. But are you sure you are doing that to the best of your ability? Even if you are a paragon of customer service virtue, can you be sure that every member of staff values your customers as much as you do, especially when you are not personally attending to a situation?

Such questions trouble many companies that have come to realise the value of their customers. The answer is to treat customer care as seriously as any other part of the operation. For example, in the kitchen of a restaurant, there are policies and procedures in place to ensure certain standards of hygiene and safety, and even in the presentation of food, are met. The same attention to detail should be applied to customer service. Staff should be shown how you wish each customer-related situation to be handled. This will result in the consistent treatment of customers by staff throughout the company. In order to achieve this in practical terms, each organisation needs to develop a customer care programme tailored to their own particular needs.

In order to produce a satisfactory customer care programme for staff you will have to do careful research. You need to know all you can about the company, its origins, its products and goals. Discover what its greatest successes and failures have been and how they have shaped the way the company is today. Compile a hierarchical chart of all the staff that are employed by the company. Include any biographical information that might be useful. Try and figure out how these people relate to each other. This will help you see if a breakdown in communication in some area might be affecting staff morale in general.

If possible, see if any people have left the company to take up jobs elsewhere. If you can, try and find out why they decided to leave the company. A company with a high level of staff turnover usually has poor staff care and is forced to spend large amounts of money on recruitment. Research has shown that while money is often a consideration in why people change jobs, poor management is also a contributory factor. Most people will not readily change from a job they are happy in. Progressive employers recognise this and are putting greater effort into developing more pleasant work environments. Similarly, if staff have recently changed jobs to join your firm, find out why and ask them if they are still happy with their decision. Examine the work environments of all employees from offices to despatch. Find out if they are clean, safe, fully equipped and warm. Then interview the staff, guaranteeing them confidentiality. Find out what they like about working for your company and also what they dislike about it. Note any suggestions they make.

Interview customers and get as much feedback as possible from them using as many of the methods mentioned in this book as you consider helpful. If the company has lost customers recently, try and find out why.

Be sure to use secondary sources. A lot of research has been done into how to improve staff morale in order to increase productivity and reduce staff turnover. Look at other companies that have successfully applied customer care programmes and see if your customer care programme can benefit from their experiences. Talk to staff from other companies and find out what they like about where they work. Now you should have the raw material from which to design your customer care programme.

A customer care programme is only useful when it is implemented. Many companies have invested a great deal of time, energy and money into such programmes and then leave them unused at the back of a shelf. In order to prevent that happening to your customer care programme, you have to first identify why expensively produced programmes end up gathering dust.

One of the key reasons for failure is commitment. Some managers who commission such programmes don't really understand their significance or they expect that the mere act of obtaining a customer care programme will do the trick. Many of the staff feel the same way and the programme fails to work because no one is really committed to making it work.

Another reason is hostility. Some managers erroneously see customer care as an opportunity to put more pressure on their 'lazy' staff and make them more accountable. But the managers are often shocked when they discover they have a role to play in customer care too and that they might also need to become more accountable for their actions. The customer care programme is quickly forgotten. Staff may be hostile to the programme because they see customer care of any sort as unnecessary or they may be suspicious of management's motives.

Finally, many customer care programmes fail because they are too complicated, waste too much time and can interfere with the company's work.

So when you begin to design your customer care programme, keep it simple, impartial and open.

From the following customers' and employees' comments, identify the basic values of the company:

'They are a bit expensive, but everything they produce is of the highest standard.'

'They have a great after-sales service.'

'They are really friendly and nothing is too much trouble.'

## Once you know what the company's strengths are, you can make a virtue of them.

With the aid of management and staff ascertain what the company would most like to be remembered for. They may wish to be remembered as the fastest, the best value or the most luxurious. Such values can be developed into a mission statement. Take the ideas and work them into a short paragraph or two that briefly outlines the company's own personal approach to customer care and its commitment to it. Then go a step further and summarise it into a one-line motto. For example: 'Cheapest in Europe or your money back.'

Now ask management what attitude they would ideally like their employees to have when talking about what it is like to work for the company. From that, develop another mission statement which relates management's commitment to their employees.

Both statements should be made available for staff to read and should help lessen any anxieties that staff might have about the programme. It is important to get the staff on your side. The attitude of front-line staff must be positive because, ultimately, it is the customers who are affected by it.

Now hold a series of brainstorming meetings with management and staff to develop strategies for implementing the company's mission statement. Get all members of staff involved. If they all see the problem and all develop the solution, they will support it in practice. This has been identified as one of the key strengths of Japanese companies. In the past, when, say, a businessman was dealing with an American company, he could expect a fast decision, but when dealing with a Japanese company, he would have to wait much longer for a reply. The difference was that in the Japanese company many people would be consulted before a decision was reached, but once the decision was made, it was fully backed by all concerned. By contrast, decisions could be made in the American company without such elaborate consultation but they would meet with serious obstacles when they were being implemented.

When you have reached some decisions together about how to enhance the quality of customer service in the company, compile a guidebook that can help staff implement the new programme. Then prepare a presentation where you outline the new programme to the staff.

## Presentations

Presentations have grown in importance in recent years. They are seen as an important business tool because you can impart information to a target group and then receive instant feedback. They can be used to sell products, report on current projects or problems and educate staff about new policies and procedures. A manual or pamphlet on the same subject could go unread for months or could just go straight in the bin. By bringing people to a presentation you can at least ensure that they have some awareness of what you are trying to do. You can also gauge their reactions to it. There are benefits to be had from their questions and suggestions. You would never get as much feedback from circulating a pamphlet as people will not bother to write to you or seek you out and may assume that, as you have already produced a pamphlet, the subject is closed. As companies find presentations so useful, more and more people are being asked to make them.

## Preparing for a presentation

Once you have collected your information together, you have to decide how to organise it and how to express it in presentation form. There is no point writing a speech or an essay. Those structures are too restrictive for a presentation.

Organise your information into separate points, and write out the main points on cards. Write two or three points on each A5 size card with a black felt pen. Make sure your writing is relatively large. If you write as normal on the cards, you will find yourself squinting and getting lost. If you write down too much information on each point then you will find that you are reading it out as if it was an essay and will not be giving an effective presentation. Number your cards in the top left-hand corner in case you drop them, and only write on one side of the cards to avoid confusion. If you are accompanying your presentation with visual aids, add prompts on your cards telling you when to change slides or turn on the DVD, etc.

An overhead projector, VDU or chart can be used instead of cards. You can put your main points up on the screen and go through each one. On television you will see politicians and TV presenters using teleprompters which scroll the information out on the screen before them. These can be tricky to use so practise beforehand, otherwise your audience will see your eyes following the words across the screen. Before the presentation be sure that you have practised using all the equipment you will need to avoid embarrassment later. Just before the presentation, check that all your equipment is there and in working order.

### Posture

As we saw in Chapter 2, body language is a huge part of how we communicate. If we want our presentation to have a positive effect on the audience we must use positive body language. Stand up straight with your feet slightly apart. This imparts a strong, confident and alert image to the audience. Do not stand rigid like a statue, however, as this gives the impression that you are absolutely terrified. Have your hands by your sides or holding your notecards but make sure that you use your hands for gesturing and emphasis throughout the presentation. Do not keep them in your pockets as this looks very sloppy.

Avoid repeating the same gesture. When I was at university one lecturer would take off, wipe and replace his glasses every 40 seconds or so during each lecture, which lasted an hour. I can't remember the subject he lectured in, I only remember being distracted by this repetitive gesture. Such displacement activities – gestures from which we subconsciously take comfort in times of stress, like giving a lecture – ruin the impact of a presentation. Find out if you have a particular displacement activity. If you have, it could be very distracting for your audience, so try to minimise your reliance on it and in time try to eliminate it entirely. Unfortunately, though, human nature being what it is, we have a tendency to replace one displacement activity with another. Take heart from a well-known film clip of two seasoned politicians, Tony Blair and John Prescott, taken at a conference just before the 2001 British General Election, where both of them are furiously twiddling their silver pens.

Lean slightly towards the audience. People lean towards each other when they wish to become more intimate. This could be to block out others or to impart a secret. It is a conspiratorial act between the people involved and can be very bonding. If you lean towards your audience they will unconsciously pick up on your positive gesture and will respond accordingly.

In order to understand the importance of good posture and appropriate gesturing, try and imagine the opposite. Imagine that you are at a presentation where the speaker is slumped in a chair or standing with a slouch. These positions make the speaker look lazy or indifferent to the presentation they are about to give. A speaker who folds their arms looks defensive and cannot use their hands for gesturing. Clearly, nail biting, scratching, hair-twirling and other similar habits must be avoided. Practise in front of a mirror or record yourself if you can beforehand. You might be very surprised at what you see!

## Voice projection

Most people are not accustomed to speaking to large groups of people. You may be surrounded by friends and colleagues at lunch, in the pub or at a party but you are not speaking to them all at once. In order to speak to a large group we have to modify the way we talk so that we are clearly heard and understood. A lot of people speaking to an audience for the first time either speak as they normally do or start shouting. Neither method is fully effective. Normal speaking will be too low and too rapid to follow and shouting will get you heard but it is not something that the human voice or your audience's ears can endure for long.

What you need to do is project your voice. Instead of increasing the volume of your voice, as in shouting, you increase its strength. Imagine your voice coming from deep down within you, from your diaphragm. Now practise by aiming your voice at a person or spot about three-quarters of the way down the room that you are to give your presentation in. Normally you would be used to aiming your voice at someone much nearer you or at a distance away in an empty space. This is the same thing except that there will be people in the room, which affects the acoustics. Our voice is our means of projecting sound waves, which usually bounce easily off the floors and walls of rooms. That's why people sound particularly good when they sing in the bathroom – great acoustics. But things like carpets and people in the room can make it harder for sound waves to bounce back and so you will have to practise projecting your voice with greater intensity.

Protect your voice by taking your time and by having a glass of water nearby. Our mouths tend to dry up when we are nervous and that is no help when you are speaking to a large group of people. It is also a handy displacement activity if you have a memory lapse or need a quick break during the presentation. Now you know why some politicians seem thirsty. Though shouting is generally wrong as it hurts your voice and makes you seem hysterical, don't be afraid to raise your voice when you want to emphasise a point.

### Delivery and tone

People who simply read their notes often have a dull monotonous tone because they fail to vary their delivery. If your presentation is well prepared, you can deliver it in a more relaxed and confident tone. Listen to how politicians vary their tone when they speak. For important points their delivery becomes more intense and they hold eye contact with their audience. They may also use body language to hit their point home. A well-timed pause can also be effective, particularly after a rhetorical question. For example:

> 'Do you think the environment is going to clean itself up? Do you think the industrialists are going to do it?'
>
> *Pause for effect*
>
> 'No. It's up to you and me ...'

Note also the use of repetition 'Do you think ...?' Repetition is used all the time by public speakers to great effect.

Finally, make sure you are understood. Do not speak too fast or mumble. Be careful to avoid words that you are not confident about or those you cannot pronounce correctly or easily.

### Contact with the audience

A presentation is not a speech. A presentation should be natural and interactive. Try and establish a rapport with the audience. Your selection of presentation aids will play an important part in this. Choose presentation aids that will not break the contact you make with your audience.

Begin your presentation by introducing yourself and by acknowledging your audience in some personal way. Note how at rock concerts bands often make a big effort to show the audience they can distinguish this concert venue in their minds from others. They will mention the town's name and perhaps local nightspots or tourist attractions they have visited. They may also employ a local star as their support act. They might have learned a few phrases of the local language. This is always greatly appreciated by the audience.

In order to maintain contact with your audience, you must look at them. Eye contact is very important when bonding with your audience. There is something very remote about a speaker who picks a spot on the wall and talks to it, particularly if it is the fire exit sign. But don't spend all your time looking at one person. Your eyes should slowly move about the room and by the end of the presentation you should have made eye contact with most of the audience on several occasions. Merely reading from your notes without looking at your audience is not giving a presentation. You will seem distant and detached because you are not making eye contact. Good public speakers are constantly reading the body language of their audience. They learn whether the audience is following the presentation or not. They can see if the pace is too fast or too slow. They can adjust their delivery to suit the audience.

If you are restricted to a stage or platform, use it as much as you can. Try not to stay stuck to one spot. If you have room to walk around, then do so. It adds variety to your presentation and keeps those further back in your audience involved.

In some presentations, a measure of audience participation is included. When this is well managed it can be a very positive thing. It can keep the audience alert and revive flagging concentration and enthusiasm. One simple method of doing this is by asking the audience questions or asking them to come with suggestions or examples. You can also give them exercises to perform either individually or in groups. With groups you can introduce a competitive element to make the procedure more productive and interesting or fun. Use role-play. For customer service presentations this can be very effective. For example, you could ask members of the audience to role-play a situation where a customer returns a faulty product. Instruct the customer to be apologetic, reasonable, irate or unreasonable in a succession of role-plays. Get the volunteers to switch roles to give the performers and the rest of the audience an insight into both sides of customer relations. They will be able to empathise with both customer and staff as both individuals have been plucked from their audience.

## Pacing

You want the presentation to move at an acceptable pace for your audience. If the pace is too slow they will lose interest. If the pace is too fast the presentation will seem fragmented and the audience will find it impossible to keep up. Vary the pace of your presentation to keep it interesting. Start off slowly and put your audience at ease. Then alternate between a reasonably fast pace and a more relaxed one. Use visual aids to add variety and interest. If you are new at giving presentations, practise first. Use a recorder and a stopwatch. Place the microphone at the back of a room as similar in size as possible to the room that you will be doing your presentation in. This will help you assess the pace of your presentation as well as the strength of your voice projection. The stopwatch will help ensure your presentation is of the correct duration. It can be very hard to estimate the amount of material needed for a presentation of any duration unless you run through it a few times.

## Visual aids

There are many different audio-visual aids available. Used correctly they can enhance and add interest to a presentation. However, using too many visual aids and relying on them too much can ruin your presentation as it will lack substance. Here are some examples of some aids that you can use in your presentation. Whichever you choose be sure to incorporate prompts into your presentation so that you remember to use them at the correct time.

- *Wallcharts.* These are a very basic visual aid. They are portable, reusable and very cheap to make. Make sure the script is clear and large so that it can be read by everyone. Try not to make it look cluttered with too much information or it will be too hard to follow. We can usually remember between five and nine unconnected things at a time so limit yourself to that many points in your chart.

  Colour is important for enhancing your chart. It will make the more important points stick out and will brighten up illustrations. But for both script and chart, try to use no more than three colours. Too many colours will make your chart look too 'busy'. Try to limit the variety of script styles and sizes that you use. Too much variety will lessen the impact of what you have written.

  Hand-made charts have their place in schools and small companies but if you are trying to impress business colleagues you should use a more professional chart-production method. Do not rely too heavily on charts during a sophisticated presentation.

- *Blackboards.* A blackboard is useful for jotting down information during the course of a presentation. However, if the information you wish to impart is too lengthy it can cause a break in the flow of your presentation because you will lose contact with your audience when you turn your back.

  You can prepare information in advance but you are limited to only as much as can cover the board once. Also, the audience can be distracted from what you are saying by reading the information before it is needed. Cloth or paper can be draped over the board if you wish to reveal what is written on it at a specific time.

  Be careful that your handwriting is straight, legible and large enough to be read by the entire audience. If you are using a computer as part of your presentation it is a bad idea to use a blackboard as the chalk dust particles can damage the machine.

- *Whiteboards.* A whiteboard has the same strengths and weaknesses as a blackboard except that a whiteboard can be safely used next to computer equipment. If you are using a whiteboard during your presentation, make sure you have plenty of markers with you as they quickly run dry. Make sure they are not permanent markers or you could spend most of your presentation trying to clean the board. If the worst does happen, white spirit will clean off permanent marker.

- *Flipcharts.* A flipchart is a great presentation aid. You can write out your main points on the chart. You can attach charts and diagrams to pages of the chart. Then you can flip over the pages as your presentation progresses. You can have your note cards cross-referenced to the pages of a flipchart so you can flip back again to important pages. You can also use a flipchart in the same way as a whiteboard, to write out points as they occur in the presentation. Make sure that you have plenty of fresh markers handy.

Flipcharts are also safe to use near computers and great for groups of about 30 or under. More than that and it can be difficult for people furthest away to see what is going on.

- *Slides.* This form of presentation is becoming outdated. It can be costly as it involves compiling relevant slides. You have to be careful to load the slides into the carousel correctly or they might be upside down or in the wrong sequence. Whatever you do, do not drop them.

  You need a darkened or semi-darkened room to show the slides in. This can cut you off from your audience especially if you are at the back of the room with the projector. You cannot easily flit from slides to talk and back. In addition it will be hard for your audience to take notes in the dark.

- *Videos/DVDs.* These can be a very impressive way to begin or end a presentation. However, they can be expensive to make and despite that can still sometimes look cheap.

  Another disadvantage is that you can become redundant and cut off from the audience, reduced to simply flicking a switch. But if you are trying to reach a very large group of people in different locations, they can be very useful.

- *Overhead projectors.* Overhead projectors have the advantage of allowing you to prepare acetate sheets in advance or you can write on them during the course of your presentation. Either way it is relatively easy to write legibly. However, they do have disadvantages. If writing during the presentation, you will be cut off from your audience to some extent and the lights may have to be dimmed so that the audience can read the overheads. If the room is too dark, they won't be able to take notes.

  Do not overload your sheets with information or the audience will be too busy writing to listen to you. Make sure that the room you are using has an overhead projector in it or else all your acetate preparation will be in vain. Check in advance that the bulb hasn't blown. Bulbs can be expensive and are easily damaged if the projector is moved from room to room. You will need special heat-resistant acetate sheets if you want to photocopy material for overhead projection and these are expensive.

- *Actors.* It can be very expensive to use actors to demonstrate new customer care procedures so you might try volunteers from the workplace. However, this can be time-consuming and requires a lot of organisation, especially if your presentation is off-site.

- *Audio.* You can use audio on its own or as an accompaniment to slides or other images. You can also use it as sound effects for your actors. If you do use it as an accompaniment make sure that it is properly synchronised with whatever visual aids you are using.

- *Presentation software.* Nowadays computers can do marvellous things to brighten up presentations. You can use presentation software such as PowerPoint to print up beautifully illustrated handouts which can also be used on the overhead projector. You can also use PowerPoint to display directly from the VDU. You simply use the package to organise your notes and add graphics. Many sophisticated graphics techniques are available where information can be blended or moved in and out or revealed gradually for effect. You have a huge choice of images, movement styles, font sizes and styles, and colours.

These packages can be very easy to use and with a little practice anyone can become quite competent. You can control the speed of presentation with the mouse so you can tailor everything to suit yourself and your audience.

• *Brochures.* These are a very expensive visual aid but extremely impressive. They are often used by companies who are trying to impress audiences with their wealth and prestige. They look good and you can be sure that each member of your audience is going home with a complete, correct and detailed record of the presentation. They can also be reused at other presentations and even allow those who did not have an opportunity to attend the presentation to have a fair idea of the presentation's content. Make sure, however, that the brochure is always up to date and remember that a good percentage of your brochures may never be read.

## Exercises

1. What, in your opinion, is the purpose of a customer care programme?

2. Why is it important for a company to adopt a uniform approach to customer care?

3. Discuss this view: If you don't deal directly with the public, there is no need for a customer care programme.

4. Write an essay on a customer care programme that you have first-hand experience of, either as a customer or as a member of staff.

5. Compare and contrast the customer care policies of two organisations that you have studied.

6. Outline the customer care policy of one organisation that you have studied.

7. Outline what you think might be the most important aspects of a customer care programme for a fast-food restaurant.

8. Outline what you think might be the most important aspects of a customer care programme for a medical practice.

9. 'Customer care programmes only mean more work for the already overworked and undervalued staff.' Discuss.

10. Why do you think business presentations have become so popular?

11. Do you think that business presentations are a valuable use of company time? Justify your answer.

12. What advice would you give to someone about to make their first presentation?

13. What advantages does a flipchart have over a blackboard?

14. What advantage(s) does a blackboard have over a flipchart?

15. What are the advantages and disadvantages of using PowerPoint?

16. Give a presentation to your class on 'Customers are our business'.

# 11

# CUSTOMER CARE PROGRAMME CASE STUDY – DX IRELAND

D X Ireland is an excellent example from which to study customer service, as that is the entire basis of its operation. In Chapter 1 we looked at how customer service must evolve in order to maintain its edge. DX Ireland is a case in point. Ireland already had a postal service, but it could not meet all its potential customers' needs. By providing that extra service, DX Ireland created and maintains its niche in the market.

DX Ireland focuses on the very particular needs of businesses and the public sector. Here are just a few examples:

- delicate items such as optical lenses, surgical and pharmaceutical equipment
- valuable items such as emergency stock and samples for the retail trade
- urgent items for medical procedures, legal transactions, etc.
- confidential items such as prototypes, legal documents and reports for the legal profession, public sector, retail trade, etc.

As you can appreciate from the examples above, there are many items that need to be delivered that one cannot simply put in the local letterbox for delivery tomorrow or the day after. If a business has a very urgent and precious item to deliver, it is going to choose its courier carefully. The challenge for DX Ireland was to become that courier, the delivery service that could reliably and consistently provide the extra service it promised. In the following pages you will see DX Ireland's comprehensive customer care programme. It deals with all the services available, but just as importantly, it illustrates the experience the company has with preventing and resolving errors and accidents. As we have seen before, the true worth of customer service is best seen when things go wrong.

Businesses can apply for membership to avail of DX Ireland's DX Exchange services. They will then be able to send their mail in any of the 250 document exchanges throughout Ireland. Mail for delivery can be dropped at the customer's local document exchange and inbound mail is collected by the customer from their DX box in the same exchange. The services are provided at extremely competitive rates. These document exchanges operate for longer than the traditional business day and the delivery system has more flexibility to deal with tight deadlines and unusual items than more generic postal methods.

## Introduction

Customer service is the provision of service to customers before, during and after a purchase. It is also a series of activities designed to enhance the level of customer satisfaction – that is, the feeling that a product or service has met the customers' expectations.

In the current economic climate, customer service is extremely important as more and more people are looking for lower costs and value for money. In order to grow our business steadily over the next three years, we need to provide the highest standard of customer service to our existing customers along with winning new business. It is a proven fact that it is cheaper to keep existing customers than to try and win new ones, so in that spirit, DX Ireland has created a Customer Care Programme that outlines the steps we plan to take in order to make our customers feel that we appreciate their business and look forward to continuing to provide quality service to them in the future.

This report will begin with a look at the service commitment provided by DX Ireland, which outlines the various different services we provide to our customers. Details on 'New Customers' and the 'Value for Money' aspects of our offering will follow, showing how easy it is to become a DX member and the various different payment options. 'Dealing with Complaints' outlines the process our customers can follow when logging issues that have affected their service.

The 'Customer Satisfaction Measurement' section will show how we measure our service in the form of surveys, measuring the customer service experience and making regular contact with our customers, old and new. Our Service Measurement is based on a Quality Mail Survey that takes place every week and the findings are reported back to management.

It is our belief that by providing the best customer service in the mail delivery industry, we will become the company of choice for existing and future DX customers nationwide.

## Our service commitment

DX is Ireland and the UK's leading independent mail and courier company. Founded amidst the postal strikes of the 1970s, DX was the first and only alternative to An Post and Royal Mail.

DX continues to be the preferred choice today for businesses who:

- depend on getting their mail on time
- want peace of mind with a secure and reliable mail service
- enjoy our highly competitive prices.

DX offers an unrivalled level of reliability and security. Details of our services are outlined below.

## DX Exchange

All regular mail posted before 17:00 with the correct address and DX number will be delivered before 09:00 the next day.

## DX Tracked Mail Service

All tracked mail posted before 17:00 with the correct address and DX number will be delivered before 09:00 the next day. Tracked mail can be traced throughout its journey and the delivery manifest is signed off by the driver upon delivery to the exchange.

## DX Courier

All consigned items and untracked items posted before 17:00 with the correct address will be delivered the next day. Consigned items can be traced throughout its journey and signed for by the recipient upon delivery.

## DX Tracked Specimens

All DX Tracked Specimens will be collected daily and delivered the next business day within Ireland and within two business days in Great Britain. DX Tracked Specimens will be traced throughout their journey and are signed for upon delivery.

## New customers

Becoming a DX customer is a quick and easy process. Potential customers can contact DX via the telephone or website and obtain an application form. Upon receipt of a completed application form (with original signature), subject to conditions, the customer will be a fully functioning member of the DX network within five working days and is assigned their own DX number.

A Starter Pack is sent to the new customer with box keys and instructions on how to use the DX service. Information on the DX Directory is also provided so that customers can easily access addresses for every other DX customer within Ireland and the UK. New customers are also given details of how to use their local exchange when posting mail. All outgoing mail for areas outside the local exchange is placed in a clearly labelled Onwards Box. Any outgoing mail for customers within the same exchange can be posted directly into the DX box of that particular member. Outgoing mail is collected from the Onwards box post at 17:00 and incoming mail is delivered before 09:00 the next day.

## Value for money

DX provides a next-day postal delivery service that is up to 30 per cent less expensive than the competition. Customers do not have to frank or weigh items that they are sending out, which saves time and money.

Coming up to the annual renewal date, the customer receives a letter approximately two weeks before the annual fee is due, advising them of their upcoming annual subscription. Customers pay for the service in advance and the standard payment frequency is yearly. A customer may pay by direct debit, cheque, credit card, laser, electronic transfer or bank draft.

## Customer complaints procedure

We welcome all comments from our customers, as we are committed to providing the best service possible to our customers. We may be in contact with customers from time to time in relation to testing the quality of the service. If customers want to let us know how we're doing, they can log on to www.thedx.ie and leave their comments in the 'Contact Us' section.

- If the service provided has not met our customers' expectations, they can contact us at the following:
  1. Log on to www.thedx.ie and access the Customer Service Section.
  2. Call us at 01 879 1700, Monday to Friday, from 08:30 to 18:00.
  3. Fax us at 01 842 1056.
  4. Or write to us at:
     The Customer Service Department
     DX Ireland
     DX 1
     Dublin
  Written responses are provided within three working days of receiving letters.

- In order to process complaints efficiently, we require the following information from our customers:
  1. Name and original address of the receiver.
  2. Sender's name and address.
  3. Reference and/or tracking number.
  4. Contact details, e.g. mobile number, work telephone number, email, etc.
  5. DX service used, e.g. DX Exchange, DX Courier, etc.
  6. Date item was sent and/or collected.
  7. Detailed description of the contents and packaging (for loss and damage).

- If a complaint is received about a member of staff, we will follow the process below:
  1. The customer is required to fill in a form detailing the nature of the complaint.
  2. The complaint is managed by an investigation committee and the person involved is interviewed.
  3. The committee will then decide if any further action needs to be taken and the customer is updated accordingly.

## Customer satisfaction measurement

In order for DX Ireland to improve our overall Customer Service Department, we have incorporated a number of Customer Satisfaction Measurement Functions into our everyday processes. It is our belief that with regular communication, we will be able to improve our business and the relationships that we have with our existing and new customers. Feedback is communicated into the various business groups so that the service is continuously improving.

### Online survey

Previous surveys that were sent to our customers yielded a 14 per cent response rate and gave us a good indication of what we were doing right but also where we could improve. The DX Ireland website at www.thedx.ie incorporates an online Satisfaction Survey. Through the website, the user can download the DX Directory, order consumables, check the status of tracked items and contact the team here at DX Ireland.

As customers navigate their way around the website, they will be greeted with a pop-up asking them if they would like to take part in the online survey. The timeframe for completing this would be a maximum of 5 minutes, therefore encouraging more customers to participate, as it would not infringe too much on their valuable work time. Results can then be reported and analysed and improvements made to our overall operation.

### Measuring customer service experience

When customers contact DX Ireland, what impression do they have of us after they put the phone down? Were they happy with how their query or issue was dealt with? Was the phone answered within two rings? Was the person courteous and friendly? Did they solve the issue straight away? If not, did they provide regular updates as to the status of the issue? Was the issue resolved in a timely and efficient manner? The answer to these questions should all be a resounding YES!

We will contact every customer who has had a query or issue in the last two weeks to find out how they felt they were treated by the staff at DX Ireland. This type of contact provides valuable information regarding how we deal with our customers, how seriously we take their problems and what steps we take to rectify various different situations. It also gives us a chance to check if they have had any other issues or queries since they logged the last query. All review calls are recorded on the database and followed up again two weeks later to determine if there had been any other service issues. Any comments are also recorded and dealt with straight away and any ongoing issues are followed up to resolution.

DX will randomly contact customers at different times of the year. Customers could receive a call every six months to determine if the DX service is satisfactory for the customer and this gives the customer a chance to voice any concerns or express opinions.

## Regular customer contact

### New customer contact

At DX Ireland, our contact doesn't end when a new customer is set up. After the customer has been using the service for one month, they receive a phone call from the Customer Service Department to determine how they have been getting on and if they have encountered any problems since they joined up. It is also a chance to check that all concerning details about the customer are correct on our system. All calls are logged on the Members Database in the comments section with the date and name of the person who rang, and if any issues are reported they are assigned to a member of staff who will take ownership of the issue until its resolution

After the customer has been with us for six months, we contact them again and follow the same procedure as before. All information is logged and any comments noted for future reference. As the customer is now familiar with the DX Exchange service, we will introduce them to other services that may be of benefit to them.

### Anniversary cards

When a DX customer has been using the DX Exchange service for five years, the DX Managing Director sends out a card with a note of thanks and a small present for their continued support. This shows loyalty to our most valued customers and lets them know that we are grateful for their business and that we want to continue to provide the best service possible to them for many years to come.

## Service measurement

Ongoing service measurement is a key element in determining if we are maintaining our promised service standards. DX Ireland undertakes Weekly Quality Mail Surveys. The purpose of the survey is to covertly monitor the efficiency of the DX postal service. The aim of the survey is to determine the percentage of test letters that arrive the next day before 09:00.

# Appendix 1: DX Ireland customer service charter

## Your rights

- That if you join DX Ireland you will have immediate access to thousands of fellow customers within Ireland and the UK.
- That if you choose to join the DX Network you will be a fully functioning customer within five working days of us receiving your completed application.
- That we will provide a choice of delivery services to cater for your various needs.
- That your mail will be delivered securely and efficiently in accordance with the chosen delivery service product criteria.
- That we will remain committed to being the most competitively priced overnight delivery network in Ireland.
- That all queries will be dealt with promptly within a 24-hour timeframe.
- That any complaints will be resolved as quickly and completely as possible.

## Your responsibilities

- It is the responsibility of customers to provide accurate and up-to-date information on their completed application forms.
- Be aware that different service levels of security and traceability exist for different DX products to ensure delivery of your critical/sensitive items.
- Customers should make themselves aware of the contents of the DX Directory in order to get the best service possible. This is available online at www.thedx.ie.
- It is vital that customers address and label their mail correctly. Incorrectly addressed mail may result in a delay in delivery.
- Ensure mail is delivered to DX before 17:00 to guarantee next day delivery.
- It is important that customers follow the correct procedures when using the exchanges. When posting mail to members within the same exchange, post directly into their DX boxes. Outgoing mail for all other destinations should be placed in the Onwards Box, which is clearly labelled. Any oversized items may be left in front of or on top of the Onwards Box for collection.
- For added peace of mind, customers should include their own details on any item that they want delivered by DX Ireland. In this way, any misaddressed mail or other discrepancies can be quickly resolved.
- DX Ireland will ensure that your item will arrive safely at the point of delivery. However, DX Ireland's responsibility towards the item ceases after delivery.
- Customers should not send prohibited items through the DX. Please contact Customer Service for a list of prohibited items.

## Customer feedback

• We welcome all comments from our customers, as we are committed to providing the best service possible to our customers.

• We may be in contact with customers from time to time in relation to testing the quality of the service.

• If you want to let us know how we're doing, you can log on to www.thedx.ie and leave your comments in the 'Contact Us' section.

• If you have a query or feedback you can:

1.  Log on to www.thedx.ie and access the Customer Service Section.
2.  Call us at 01 879 1700, Monday to Friday, from 08:30 to 18:00.
3.  Fax us at 01 842 1056.
4.  Or write to us at:
    The Customer Service Department
    DX Ireland
    DX 1
    Dublin

• In order to process your query efficiently, we require the following information from you:

1. Name and original address of the receiver.

2. Sender's name and address.

3. Reference and/or tracking number.

4. Contact details, e.g. mobile number, work telephone number, email, etc.

5. DX service used, e.g. DX Exchange, DX Courier, etc.

6. Date item was sent and/or collected.

7. Detailed description of the contents and packaging (for loss and damage).

# DX Document Exchange

## when important documents can't be late

The DX Document Exchange is a unique, pre 09h00 mail network dedicated exclusively to delivering business documents, parcels and pouches. Established over 30 years ago, we now deliver approximately 40,000 items every day, using a secure network of collection and delivery points known as 'Exchanges'.

The service is particularly suitable for companies with a branch network where it is used as an internal post system, as well as for businesses who communicate with the legal and financial communities, government or professional services companies.

Our customers include Solicitors in the Republic of Ireland, most major banks as well as government agencies and professional services companies.

www.thedx.ie **01 879 1700**

# Business mail that maximises productivity and profitability

trusted · reliable · secure

## DX DOCUMENT EXCHANGE

### The benefits of DX Membership

Thousands of organisations already depend on DX to provide reliable, overnight pre 09h00 delivery and exceptional value for money. Joining the DX means you become part of a long-standing community of business professionals, with access to a range of dedicated services, all provided through a secure, closed loop network.

The annual DX Member renewal rate of over 97% is testament to DX's high quality service and proven mail handling ability.

- Collection after 17h00 and overnight delivery pre 09h00 as standard
- Reduced administration – no need to weigh, frank or stamp
- Significant cost-savings on your mail budget
- Secure, efficient network, dedicated to business mail
- Simple addressing system
- Access to 5,000 members
- Tracked service for important or urgent items

### Secure, fast and reliable

When a business joins the Document Exchange, they become a DX Member, and are given a secure mailbox at their local Exchange. Our couriers collect your outgoing mail from the Exchange after 17h00, and deliver your inbound DX mail into your mailbox by 09h00 the next day as standard. So you can make the most of every working day. For Members within your own Exchange, you can simply deliver mail directly to their post-boxes at any time you desire. And once you've become a DX Member, you can make use of a range of additional services, all designed to save time and money for your business.

### How the Document Exchange works

Member posts Document Exchange mail into Onwards Mail Box at local Exchange.

DX courier collects mail after 17h00.

Mail is processed for next day delivery pre 09h00.

Mail posted into Member's mailbox by 09h00.

---

TRUSTED DX SERVICES :

DX is Ireland & the UK's leading independent mail and courier company providing a range of products and services delivering approximately 40,000 items per day in the B2B market.

DX
36-37 North Park
North Road
Finglas, Dublin 11

TEL    01 879 1700
FAX    01 842 1056
DX     DX 1 Dublin
EMAIL  info@thedx.ie

DX/IRE/GB/DOCEXCHANGE-DATASHEET/V1

**01 879 1700**
www.thedx.ie

# 12

# CUSTOMER SERVICE AND TECHNOLOGY

Topics covered in this chapter:

- **Customer service on the Internet**
- **The principles of good online customer service**
- **Assessing websites**
- **Using technology to improve customer service**
- **Using Twitter and Facebook for customer service**
- **Customer service technology glossary**

## Introduction

Customer service has gone technical and this has had enormous benefits for companies and for customers. Technology has empowered customers. Firstly, they are informed about the choices they make. A customer can go online and ask 'what is the best car for towing a caravan?' and get answers from people who have been in the same position. They can research purchases before they make them and do not have to rely on the salesperson's patter. Secondly, they can tailor a lot of their trading to suit their situation. A customer who is in a hurry can go to a self-checkout line in a supermarket. They can be in total control of their purchasing experience and if they check something in twice, they will see it immediately and can get it rectified. Likewise, they can go online at midnight and book cinema tickets for two days hence if they want to. Bills can be paid online and even appointments can be made this way, saving time and money for the customers.

The business benefits by cutting costs and generating greater profit. A self-checkout system means that fewer people need to be employed operating the tills. Online services have processes that are mainly automated, which cuts down on the number of staff required. In addition, it turns your business from a 9 to 5 operation to a 24/7 one. Customers will shop more when no effort is required. You might not fly to London to buy a fancy stapler, but it is very easy to order it from a London supplier in the comfort of your own home.

## Customer service on the Internet

In 1969, the United States Department of Defense connected three computers in California to one in Utah with the idea of protecting data in the event that any one of these computers was attacked by an enemy. From this little acorn came the Internet. These four computers quickly multiplied and the MILNET was formed to link computers on many US military sites, while the ARPANET began to link non-military sites, mainly universities, because in those days people did not have computers at home and many businesses had yet to be computerised. Computers were incredibly expensive, of limited capacity and agonisingly slow. The word 'Internet' was used for the first time in 1982, but it was nothing like the system we have today. It wasn't full of film clips and social networking sites. The amount of information was limited and there was little point advertising on it. It would be another 10 to 12 years before it would be of use or interest to the general public, and even then it was rather slow.

In November 1998, Katie Donovan wrote an article for the *Irish Times* in which she explored the phenomenal success of Kenny's Bookshop in Galway. Des Kenny had shown amazing foresight by becoming only the second bookshop to go on the Internet in 1992. By 1998 he had developed his website into an online bookshop and formed a virtual book club that was despatching books to over 1,400 customers in 45 countries – figures that any earthbound bookshop could only dream of.

In a relatively short period, the Internet has grown to become an essential aspect of any successful business. For most organisations it now forms a large part of how they actually do business, and for others, like the hugely successful Amazon, which has become the largest online retailer in the US since its foundation in Seattle in 1994, it is the entire basis of their existence.

The early days of the Internet had a Wild West feel. It was new, lawless territory, and if a business ripped a customer off there was very little the customer could do to get redress. Some may have thought that online businesses did not need to worry about customer service. It was hardly likely that you would ever be banging down the door of a website demanding your money back, and though you might have complained to nine of your friends, that was hardly going to put a customer from Korea on the alert. However, a lot has changed since then. Legislation has been put in place to protect us from some of the dangers of the Internet, customers have become a lot savvier and businesses have come to realise that on the Internet, customer service is more important than ever. As the Internet does not offer the opportunity of redress in the manner of an actual business with premises you can see and visit, trust becomes even more crucial. Would you confidently deposit your money in a bank operating from the back of a minibus? In addition, because you are paying by credit card, most customers are wary of handing over such sensitive information to a blinking screen. As a result, many online businesses that did not inspire customer trust and loyalty failed while those that grasped the importance of providing good customer service to online customers have gone from strength to strength.

## What good online customer service should be

### 1. User friendly

The customer should not need a degree in computer science or some sort of digital data treasure map in order to find information on a website. The website should be so well designed that a potential customer can easily follow his or her way around it.

### 2. Transparent

Make sure that your address, telephone and fax number are clearly visible on the home page of your website. Customers should have absolutely no difficulty finding it. This reassures customers that somewhere there is a door that can be banged upon if needs be.

### 3. Informative

Offer as much help and information as you can on the website. This will both help potential customers but will also diminish your workload because it saves you time answering the most common questions.

If you create a FAQ page, most people will go there first before contacting you directly. Then there are potential customers who would never contact you, so this is the only chance you will have to win their trust. To compile your Frequently Asked Questions page, monitor all questions that you have been asked and also get people from outside your business to look at your website and list what they would like to know. You are likely to be too well versed and too close to your business to realise the kind of concerns that the customer may have. If your type of business allows it, display a price list, highlight delivery and other sundry charges and include a currency convertor.

Be visual. Include photographs of stock that will help people make an informed purchase.

### 4. Interactive

Create a facility on the website where customers can contact you directly by email.

Offer live support. Add VoIP to your website's technology. This allows the customer to click on an icon and get through to an actual human being.

Write a blog. This adds a human dimension to your site and if you are entertaining, customers may just drop in to read what you have to say and may buy something while doing so.

### 5. Automated

There are some websites that tell you a lot but won't allow you to purchase without ringing or going through some other process. You will sell a lot more if you automate. It allows people to buy at 2 a.m. Sunday morning, on Christmas Eve or whenever they get the impulse. It means that rather than having lots of people taking orders and not being able to keep up, the customer is presented with an efficient system and knows there is someone they can contact if there is a glitch. As it is automated, people can make their purchase immediately. The 24/7 nature of the service prevents people being confined to shopping online 9 to 5. This reduces staff being overwhelmed by gluts of orders at certain times of the day/week while having fallow periods on other occasions.

## 6. Secure

Customers want to feel that when they part with their credit card details, their information won't end up funding someone else's lifestyle. Nowadays many trusted websites use PayPal, though it is not without its critics and in 2002 it was sued for alleged violations against the Electronic Funds Transfer Act, but that need not concern the regular customer unduly. As well as using PayPal or some other trusted funds transfer business, you could instantaneously send a receipt and reference number to their email address, which also allows them to easily print it.

## 7. Up to date

Don't just create a website and leave it. A good online website should be constantly updated and modernised. A customer who comes across a dated website may assume that the company behind it is no longer in business or they might wonder if your business is as behind the times as your site. In addition, constant updating shows the customer that there is a human behind the site and that is reassuring, even if they never contact you directly. You could also include a 'What's new' feature.

## 8. Reliable

As with all customer service, there is no point promising the moon and then not delivering. Be reliable, consistent and solve problems quickly.

## 9. Prompt

There was a time when you wrote to a business and did not quibble if it took a week to get a reply. In truth, the post office often got the blame for delays on things that had yet to land in any letterbox. 'It's in the post' has been said so often that now it is generally meant ironically. However, email has put paid to that time-honoured excuse and if people email you and do not get a reply by the close of business the next day, they feel that they are considered unimportant or that the email has been ignored or forgotten. So remember to try to tackle all those emails as soon as you can. The more quickly you reply, the more valued the customer will feel and this will build loyalty and trust.

## 10. Supportive

If we buy something in a shop and can't figure out how to work it or it breaks down, we can return to the shop. If your online business wants to compete with that kind of service, it needs to offer support. Begin by having a trouble-shooting page on your website. A well-researched one should have the answers to most of the basic problems. If that can't help the customer, then there should be an option for them to contact someone local, either on the phone or online, to help them.

It is not a bad idea to use Web 2.0 technology to create a forum where customers and staff can chat together to resolve issues.

## 11. Open to feedback

Create a facility on your website where customers can give feedback. Also, float the occasional online customer satisfaction survey. If you have an online forum you can also learn a lot about what makes your customers happy. Respond to this feedback and let your customers know that they are being listened to.

Some companies also have pages where customers can review products they have bought. These can be brutally honest, but customers trust them more because they know if something actually gets a positive review, it must be good.

## 12. Restrained

Do not preach to the converted and vex the faithful. Do not constantly clog up your loyal customers' screens with special offers, newsletters and recommendations. This can be a real turn-off. I know of customers who left businesses because they felt that the company constantly harassed them. While CRM is a valuable tool, it must be used sparingly. If I buy a guidebook to Italy for my holidays online, I'm very annoyed if the next day the site is recommending guidebooks to Tunisia, China and Peru.

## 13. Personal

Though you may never meet these customers, you can still build up a relationship with them. You can create an online community for regular customers and communicate with them through message boards. Over time you can get to know their likes and dislikes and develop little deals and treats for them. Simple things like posting a birthday greeting can make the customer feel valued. You can also keep a record of previous transactions. For example, you can use it to avoid recommending a book they have already bought from you or to look up exactly what colour hair dye or make-up a customer prefers.

## Assessing websites

- Have a look at the following sites and see how well they apply the above principles. Be sure to visit different pages on the sites. Also look at online forums where people may praise or criticise these websites to get an idea of their track record.
- Ask yourself which sites inspire the most trust in you and why.
- Use this grid to help you. Give each website a score from 0 to 10 based on the 13 points listed above. Zero should mean non-existent, 1= very poor and 10 = excellent.
- Write a brief note on each individual score, saying why you gave the marks that you did for each point.
- Now compare your marks and your notes with your colleagues/classmates. Did you come up with similar marks or was there a wide disparity? If so, why?
- What does this tell us about customer perceptions in customer service?

| Website | 1 | 2 | 3 | 4 | 5 | 6 | 7 | 8 | 9 | 10 | 11 | 12 | 13 | Total |
|---|---|---|---|---|---|---|---|---|---|---|---|---|---|---|
| www.amazon.co.uk | | | | | | | | | | | | | | |
| www.bookshop.kennys.ie | | | | | | | | | | | | | | |
| www.fetac.ie | | | | | | | | | | | | | | |
| www.apple.ie | | | | | | | | | | | | | | |
| www.debenhams.ie | | | | | | | | | | | | | | |
| www.ford.ie | | | | | | | | | | | | | | |
| www.eddiestobart.com | | | | | | | | | | | | | | |
| www.ryanair.ie | | | | | | | | | | | | | | |
| www.aerlingus.ie | | | | | | | | | | | | | | |
| www.tesco.ie | | | | | | | | | | | | | | |
| www.waterstones.ie | | | | | | | | | | | | | | |
| www.itunes.ie | | | | | | | | | | | | | | |
| www.ebookers.com | | | | | | | | | | | | | | |
| www.moviejunction.ie | | | | | | | | | | | | | | |
| www.eddieizzard.com | | | | | | | | | | | | | | |
| www.gaeitytheatre.ie | | | | | | | | | | | | | | |
| www.hairybaby.com | | | | | | | | | | | | | | |
| www.ebay.ie | | | | | | | | | | | | | | |
| www.daft.ie | | | | | | | | | | | | | | |

Why not repeat this exercise with some websites that are of relevance to your areas of interest?

| Website | 1 | 2 | 3 | 4 | 5 | 6 | 7 | 8 | 9 | 10 | 11 | 12 | 13 | Total |
|---|---|---|---|---|---|---|---|---|---|---|---|---|---|---|
| www. | | | | | | | | | | | | | | |
| www. | | | | | | | | | | | | | | |
| www. | | | | | | | | | | | | | | |
| www. | | | | | | | | | | | | | | |
| www. | | | | | | | | | | | | | | |
| www. | | | | | | | | | | | | | | |
| www. | | | | | | | | | | | | | | |
| www. | | | | | | | | | | | | | | |
| www. | | | | | | | | | | | | | | |
| www. | | | | | | | | | | | | | | |
| www. | | | | | | | | | | | | | | |
| www. | | | | | | | | | | | | | | |
| www. | | | | | | | | | | | | | | |
| www. | | | | | | | | | | | | | | |
| www. | | | | | | | | | | | | | | |
| www. | | | | | | | | | | | | | | |
| www. | | | | | | | | | | | | | | |
| www. | | | | | | | | | | | | | | |
| www. | | | | | | | | | | | | | | |

# How can I use technology to improve customer service?

## 1. Use it to improve organisational effectiveness

Streamline ordering, delivery and billing. Use technology to make your business as efficient as possible.

## 2. Use it to save money

Technology can save you a fortune on storage and labour and extend your trading hours. Pass some of these savings on to your customers.

## 3. Set up a website and make it informative and interactive

This is a great marketing and trust-building tool.

## 4. Use it to survey your customers

This is a cheap and efficient way of getting feedback. It is also relatively non-intrusive and because it is anonymous, people feel they can be more honest than if you are standing hopefully in front of them with a clipboard or if you have posted a survey to their address.

## 5. Set up a Twitter account and a Facebook page

On Twitter you can set up an account and send updates to all who choose to follow you. These updates are called tweets and are 140 characters long. People can choose to follow you and can @ reply to you on Twitter. This allows your customers or potential customers to have a voice and helps the company with its customers. You can also upload photos, which people can view by visiting your account.

**Examples:**
- www.twitter.com/avocaireland: Stores and cafés
- www.twitter.com/concern: Worldwide charity organisation
- www.twitter.com/debenhams: Department store
- www.twitter.com/dell: Computer manufacturer
- www.twitter.com/merrionstreet: Irish government news service
- www.twitter.com/rtefrontline: Current affairs programme
- www.twitter.com/starbucks: Chain of coffee shops
- www.twitter.com/toyota_europe: Car manufacturer

Facebook is a social networking site where you can set up a personal or company page. People can 'like' your company or they can also like an update on your page. You can upload albums of photos onto your page and you can update these photos whenever you want so people can look up what you are selling, making or doing. You can also include links to your website, links to sites where your products are mentioned and you can also upload videos. People can comment on all of these features. Every Facebook user has friends who can view their comments, so the page has the potential to continually increase its exposure to potential customers. The more friends your page has, the more it can make.

**Examples:**
* Ace Coaches Party Coach (coach hire)
* Acer (computers)
* Alexander Wang (men's clothing)
* Ben & Jerry's Ireland
* Coca Cola (this Facebook page has links to Twitter, YouTube and Flickr)
* Dell
* Disneyland
* Dunrovin Cakes
* Galway Guide (Arts and Entertainment)
* Greenes Restaurant Cork
* Guinness
* Guinness Hurling Supporters Group Cork
* Harrods
* Marks Models Cork (model cars, aeroplanes, etc.)
* Pendrix display (retail display solutions)

See below for further hints on how to use Twitter and Facebook.

## 6. Use it as part of CRM

Use it to learn about your customers' likes and dislikes by visiting forums. Also use it to track the histories of your current customers with a view to cross-selling and to keeping them happy in the future.

## 7. Use it to research the competition

See how your competition organises their site. See how people feel about their products and service. Go on a forum and ask a few questions yourself.

## 8. Use it to source the latest developments in customer service

Look at online business sites and visit online bookshops. Learn the latest ideas that can help improve your customer satisfaction rating.

## How to use Twitter for customer service

* Set up your account. This is a fairly simple procedure where you will have to choose a username and set up a profile. As this is a business account, you want the username to be the name of your company or product. Hopefully these haven't been taken already.
* The next thing you do is create a profile that best reflects your business. Don't

exaggerate, or within 10 minutes a tweet will come in from a customer that will bring you back to earth.

- Be sure to feature your website on your Twitter profile. Set up a link from your website to your Twitter page.
- Include a photo. A photo of your premises is reassuring; a photo of you is personal.
- Do a Twitter search. Use keywords like your company name, your products or even your location. For example, if you own a hotel in Letterkenny, why not search for things to do in Letterkenny and offer your hotel as a suggestion. Then do a Twitter search of the competition and see how they are faring.
- Offer tips and advice and link to appropriate sites. For example, if you sell running shoes, why not offer links to sites that are recruiting for athletic events.
- Answer tweets promptly. Make it clear that you are listening. Be helpful.
- Ask questions yourself. If you are running a promotion or ad campaign, why not ask people what they think? Get people to engage and invest in your company by offering advice. Thank them for it even if they have cut you to the quick.
- Retweet. If someone tweets something good, tell the world. It is very flattering for the initial tweeter.
- Keep it relevant. A business account may be managed by one person, but it still isn't a personal account. Be pleasant and informative about the products and if you want to tell the world your girlfriend left you or you hate U2, leave that for another account.
- Keep it interesting. People will get bored if your tweets are always about a product, service or how fantastic you are. Throw in a little personality. Maybe a staff member is training for a marathon using your running shoes. You could have occasional tweets from them about how they are faring without always mentioning how comfy those shoes are. If more than one person tweets, it can add variety.
- Know when it is best to say nothing at all. Whatever you do, do not get sucked into debates about the two greatest argument starters: politics and religion.

## How to use Facebook for customer service

- You can link your Twitter account to your Facebook account. This will allow your tweets to be posted on your Facebook page simultaneously.
- You can include many more photos and videos on your Facebook page and they will be there for people to peruse at their leisure.
- People can use this site to ask questions, answer questions and begin threads. Though information is moved down your wall pretty quickly when there is a lot of posting coming in, once a person posts on a thread they will be alerted every time someone adds to that thread.
- Follow threads relating to your products and company. Also follow threads relating to the competition.
- Update your page regularly with attractive pictures, links and posts.

## Some customer service technology terms

### Avatar

Avatar is taken from Hinduism, where it loosely means the incarnation of a divine being on earth. On the Internet it means an online image that represents you in chat rooms, forums and online games.

### Blog

The word 'blog' is a contraction of 'web log'. This is a site or a page on a site, usually maintained by one individual, for all the world like a digital diary or newspaper column.

### Chat room

These are instant message boards or forums where you can join in an ongoing discussion and chat to many other people who are also online.

### Cloud computing

This is a remote application storage system. Before, if you had a computer and you uploaded an application, then you could use that application on the device. Cloud computing means that you can acquire an application and not upload it anywhere. It is stored by a cloud server and you can access that application with whatever device you desire, be it your PC, laptop, netbook or smartphone. Cloud computing is in its infancy but offers exciting future possibilities for CRM.

### CRM (customer relationship management)

CRM is a system that seeks to use technology to co-ordinate customer data and manage customer interaction. (See Chapter 5.)

### E-commerce (electronic commerce)

This is the buying and selling of goods on the Internet.

### Flickr

This is a website that hosts and shares photographic and video imagery. Users can use a free or subscription account to upload their images. It is also available as an application on some mobile phones.

### Forum

An internet forum is an online message board where people can converse. You can view postings without registering as a member but cannot post. If you decide to become a member, you usually choose a unique username and then log in. You can start a conversation or join in on another conversation. These conversations are known as threads.

You can also upload an image next to your username, often called an avatar, and you can include a signature. Forums differ from chat rooms in that threads are generally archived, at least for awhile anyway. You can converse with people who are not online at the same time as you.

There are a plethora of forums on the Internet. Many of them are for specific interest groups, be it politics, sports, fitness, relationship advice, help for a particular illness or disability, technical support, stamp collecting, etc. If your rabbit has a cough, there's probably a forum that has already discussed it.

Forums can be a useful resource for customer service. Some forums discuss the various merits of certain products and by reading these sites you can learn an awful lot about how your current customers are getting on. Examples:

- www.bookgrouponline.com
- www.clri.net
- www.cosmeticsforum.net
- www.esato.com
- www.prescriptiondrug-info.com
- www.wineloverspage.com/forum/village/

## SFA (sales force automation)
This is a type of sales force management system that uses digital information systems as part of CRM. It tracks all interaction between the customer and the company and helps predict future customer behaviour as well as streamlining customer interaction with the company.

## SMS (short message service)
This is text messaging, and with almost 2.5 billion people texting regularly, it is the most widely used data application in the world.

## SurveyMonkey
This is an American company that provides online survey services. Any user can avail of it to create their own surveys. This is a useful way of creating online customer satisfaction surveys. It is also used a lot in academic research.

## VoIP (voice over Internet protocol)
This term covers technologies that transmit voice digitally. Common examples of VoIP are Skype and Viber. It can be used for one-to-one talking or for groups, as in video conferencing.

## Web 2.0
This is a web application that allows users to interact on the Internet on an expanded scale. Social networking, forums, wiki and blogging sites use this technology.

## Wiki
Wiki means 'fast' in Hawaiian. It is a technology that can be used for the creation of sites

that can be uploaded and then edited on a continual basis. The most famous site of this type is Wikipedia, which is a combination of the words 'wiki' and 'encyclopaedia'. Its charm and its flaw is that it is self- editing. There have been a few hoaxes in its past, such as fabricated quotes and biographies, not to mention unintended errors. Wikileaks is another controversial site. It has been deliberately leaking secret and sensitive documents from various countries onto the very public Internet to the horror, embarrassment and anger of those states.

### YouTube

This is a video-sharing website. Users can upload their own videos for viewing by millions. Uploading other people's work can get users into difficulty with copyright.

## Exercises

1.  How do you think technology has raised customers' expectations?
2.  Name three applications that can help a business with customer service and justify your choices.
3.  Explain the following terms: (a) VoIP (b) tweet (c) forum.
4.  What advice would you give to a business intending to set up a Twitter account?
5.  How would you assess the customer service value of a company's or institution's website?
6.  Briefly assess the following websites.
    a.  www.ticketmaster.ie
    b.  www.thetraveldepartment.ie
    c.  www.irishtimes.com
    d.  www.crokepark.ie
    e.  www.thereelpicture.com

# APPENDIX ONE

## BUSINESS GLOSSARY

### Types of businesses and organisations

### What is an organisation?

An organisation is when a group of people come together and organise themselves in order to achieve certain goals. This is a very general definition for a very general concept. The goals of an organisation may be to generate profit, as with most companies, or they may be to look after the needy, to spread information about hygiene or the prevention of dangerous diseases. There are also religious organisations who seek to spread their faith throughout the world or organisations that seek to increase awareness of a certain language, skill, sport or culture.

### What is a private sector organisation?

These are organisations established by private individuals with the aim of generating profit through the buying and selling of goods or services.

### What is a public sector organisation?

A public sector organisation is one that is financed by local or central government taxes and in return is responsible for providing a wide range of services to the community. Public sector organisations can be responsible for water supply, road maintenance, education, prisons, libraries, hospitals or tax collecting, for example.

### What is a business?

A business is when one or more people come together to provide a service or to sell a product in return for money or some other benefit. There are as many different types and sizes of businesses as there are businesses. The vast majority of businesses are attempting to make a profit and to expand. Some businesses have been set up to provide funds for charity, for example Oxfam.

### What types of businesses are there?

#### Sole traders

A sole trader is a business that is owned by only one person. It is therefore often a small business, for example a local corner shop or a hairdresser's. It is also one of the easiest to set up as you can choose to trade under your own name without having to register a trading name and incurring a registration fee. It means that you can begin your business immediately. However, it also means that you are classed as self-employed by the Revenue Commissioners and are therefore taxed at a higher rate than if you qualified for corporation tax. A sole trader must also register for VAT.

A sole trader has unlimited liability. This means that you would not be obliged to publish your business accounts, but it also means that in the event of the business failing, you would be personally liable for all the debts your company has. This could include losing your own private property, such as your house or car, which can be seized and used to pay off the debt.

From a customer care point of view sole traders have the advantage of getting to know their customers personally and being able to deal quickly and authoritatively with any customer complaints that may arise. The downside of being a sole trader is that you have to master all the jobs that are done by specialised staff in larger companies. You have to buy stock, manage accounts, deal with customers, complete VAT and tax returns and be personally liable for any mistakes you make.

### Partnerships

A partnership must consist of at least two people responsible for a business. The maximum number of partners allowed is 20. Forming a partnership requires more paperwork than starting in business as a sole trader. Everything has to be agreed in advance and the agreements are recorded in a document called the Deed of Partnership. This can be used to stipulate particular details that could become contentious later. For example, one partner might contribute a great deal of capital to a business, another a modest amount and a third may bring specific expertise. This would affect the partners' decision on what a fair division of the profits might be. The partners might not all be able to contribute the same amount of time to the business and this may also influence how the salaries are calculated.

A partnership has unlimited liability, each partner being personally liable for any debts incurred by the partnership. However, a partnership means that, unlike the sole trader, one person is not solely responsible and liable for everything, as the partners can consult and rely on each other. The individual talents within the group should complement the strengths and weaknesses. However, this means it is very important to choose the right partners as an unsuitable partner can cause a lot of problems.

### Co-operatives

The story of the co-operative movement begins with Robert Owen (1771–1858). He had made his fortune in the cotton manufacturing industry of Manchester. In 1799 he bought New Lanark Mills in Scotland. There he put his own enlightened views into practice. He provided good housing and sanitation for his workers. Rather than have children working in the mill, he declared that they must attend the school he provided for them free of charge. This concern for his workers was unprecedented. In 1813 he articulated his ideas in his *New View of Society*. He believed that people were to a large extent the product of their environment and that they should work together to improve their lives rather than simply compete with each other.

From 1799 until 1815 England was at war with Napoleon Bonaparte. Napoleon had attempted to defeat England with a continental blockade that prevented England from trading with the numerous countries under his rule. This plus the cost of war put a strain on England's resources. In 1815 there was widespread unrest when Parliament passed the Corn Law which prevented people from importing wheat until the price of English wheat had reached 80 shillings a quarter. The government argued that this would encourage native wheat production, thus producing more wheat and preventing famine. Many saw this move by the government, which in those days consisted only of landowners who had enough money and influence to get into Parliament, as passing an act to ensure the safety of their own incomes.

By 1817 England was plunged into a severe depression. Robert Owen suggested that 'villages of co-operation' be formed for the poor where they could work together and share the profit. This is the first instance of an attempt being made to form a co-operative. Unfortunately for Owen, his ideas were not applied widely until some time later. The first successful co-operative movement was founded in the cotton-producing town of Rochdale, Lancashire, in 1844. The ideas of the Rochdale pioneers, known as the Rochdale principles, were quickly seized upon and by 1864, when the Co-operative Wholesale Society was founded, there were co-operatives (co-ops) all over England, Scotland and Wales.

Sir Horace Plunkett is remembered as the great champion of the Co-operative Society in Ireland. At the age of 25 he travelled to America for health reasons and remained on a ranch in Wyoming for 10 years, returning to Ireland in 1889. He was appalled by the poor standards of farming that he encountered in Ireland. He saw that farmers lacked money and resources and the knowledge of up-to-date, efficient farming methods. He appealed to the government for help and when he saw that none was forthcoming he decided to help the farmers to help themselves. He had seen how co-operative societies had worked well in America and correctly calculated that they would have the same positive effect here. The first Irish Co-operative Society was founded in Doneraile in 1889. By 1894 there were between 30 and 40 co-ops in Ireland. Plunkett then brought them together to form the Irish Agricultural Organisation Society. By 1900 there were approximately 900 co-ops in Ireland.

The Rochdale principles still guide the co-operative societies today. They have open membership, which means that anyone can join. Money invested in the co-operative yields a low return as a co-operative is interested in equipping and educating its members, and profits are often diverted for that purpose. If there is any profit left for members, it is distributed in a manner that reflects the amount of trade the individual members do with the co-op. A co-op works on the democratic principle of one member, one vote. Management is elected by the members during the annual general meeting and co-operatives co-ordinate activities with other co-operatives.

## Companies

A company is an organisation formed for the purpose of generating profit. In order for a business to be classed as a company it must have shareholders: a private limited company must have at least one shareholder and a maximum of 50, while a public limited company must have at least seven, with no maximum limit.

Shareholders have shares in a company. A private company cannot sell shares publicly on the stock exchange but a public company can. A company can acquire money through selling shares and this is called share capital. The company then uses share capital to make more money. If the company makes a profit, this money is distributed to the shareholders and this is called a dividend. The size of the dividend depends on the number of shares a shareholder holds.

If the company fails, the shareholders lose any money they had invested in the company as share capital. The shareholder, however, has limited liability. This means that if the company folds with debts that it cannot pay then the creditors are not entitled to seize company members' or shareholders' private property. The only exception to this would be if the director of the company acted improperly or was shown to be aware of improper activity within the company. In return for limited liability, the accounts of the company must be published. 'Ltd' after a company name tells you that it is a private company and that is has limited liability; 'plc' after a company name tells you that it is a public company with limited liability. The company must be registered as such with the Companies Registration Office, which is located in Parnell Square, Dublin.

## Franchises

A franchise is a company selling a particular brand or giving a particular type of service. To illustrate what a franchise is, we could take, for example, a restaurant, a beautician, a chemist, a cinema or a hairdresser's. Say, then, a particular hairdresser has built up a business and has salons in a couple of locations. The premises have been given a uniform look; therefore customers of one of the premises can instantly recognise the others owned by the same hairdresser. The staff all dress the same, the decor and pricing is also the same. Then the hairdresser develops a range of products bearing the company name and logo. As these products become more famous, the hairdresser might consider making more money by developing a franchise. The hairdresser would become a franchiser.

Staying with our example, another hairdresser might then consider setting up their own salon. They have the option of trading under their own name or they could become a franchisee, which means they would be allowed to trade under the name of the franchiser. To become a franchisee, they pay for a licence from the franchiser to trade under the franchiser's company name. Then the franchisee has to decorate their own premises and dress their staff in the same way as in the other salons within the franchise. The franchisee buys products from the franchiser to ensure that the range and quality match those of the rest of the franchise. A percentage of the sales are paid as royalties by the franchiser to the franchisee. If the franchisee wishes to sell their business, they have to consult the franchiser.

Despite the constraints there are sound reasons for taking the franchise option. Large franchises, for example McDonald's, spend enormous amounts of money on advertising, which the franchisee immediately benefits from. A well-known brand name means that potential customers know what to expect. Going back to our hairdresser example, a person in a new town might be worried about finding a good hairdresser. When they recognise a well-known franchise name they can be sure they will be treated in a manner that is already familiar to them. If the franchisee was trading under their own name, the franchiser could open up new shops with other franchisees nearby and threaten their success. By buying into the franchise themselves, the franchisee is protected from such competition. Franchisers do not generally authorise too many franchises close to each other because the shops could fail through oversupply. Trade would be discouraged and other potential franchisees might lose confidence in the franchise.

## Business alliances

A business alliance is where one company helps another in order to create more profit, both for itself and for the other company.

A good example is where a company that manufactures washing machines forms an alliance with a company that makes washing powder. These two industries are not in competition; rather, they complement each other. The washing machine company recommends the washing powder to its customers and the washing powder endorses the washing machine brand. A free box of the powder is often included with every machine while the powder might run a competition on its boxes with the washing machines as prizes. As well as potentially increasing the profits of both companies, they can also save money by commissioning advertisements where both products are featured.

## Multinational companies

A multinational company is a company that has business interests in many countries. For example, Coca-Cola has its headquarters in Atlanta, Georgia, in the US but it has many bottling plants throughout the world. It also has majority shares in other companies.

## Semi-state bodies

These are businesses that are owned by and answerable to the government. They are usually companies that are essential to the development and running of the country but are expensive to establish and maintain. The ESB is a good example of this. Electricity is necessary to improve living conditions and promote industry. However, in the mid-1920s no company would undertake the expense of improving Ireland's hopelessly inadequate electricity supply network as there was no possibility of getting an early or even mid-term return on their investment. Consequently, the government undertook in 1924 to build a hydroelectric generation plant at Ardnacrusha near Limerick. In 1927 the government set up the Electricity Supply Board to manage the supply of electricity in Ireland.

## Some basic business terms

*Ad hoc* – means 'for this'. Anything formed on an ad hoc basis is formed for one particular purpose only. For example, you could form an ad hoc committee for the purpose of installing disabled toilets on the third floor of your building. Once that had been achieved, your ad hoc committee would disband.

*Agenda* – a document which lists the topics to be discussed at a meeting. It is circulated in advance before a meeting so that people can prepare their contribution. It is used during the meeting as a guide. People attending the meeting should stick to the agenda.

*Agenda paper* – supplementary information that may accompany an agenda. For example, if one of the items on an agenda is to discuss the purchase of one of two properties, an agenda paper might include maps and photographs of the properties so that members attending the meeting can make an informed decision.

*Ballot* – when voting is carried out in secret, for example by filling in a voting paper and casting it into a covered box, as opposed to a show of hands.

*Casting vote* – when the chairperson of a meeting (who has a vote like everyone else at the meeting and casts it in the same manner) is allowed, in the event of a tie, to cast a second vote in order to break the deadlock.

*Caveat emptor* – means 'let the buyer beware'.

*Committee* – a group within an organisation that is delegated specific tasks, for example a health and safety committee.

*Loan* – an arrangement where property is given by one party to another on the understanding that it will be returned or where money is given by one party to another on the understanding that it will be repaid. In most cases, conditions are attached to loans. For example: the property may be used for an agreed purpose only; the property must be returned in the same condition it was in at the time it was loaned; the lender must be compensated for wear and tear.

*Minutes* – a record of a meeting.

*Motion* – a proposal put forward for discussion at a meeting.

*Nem. con.* – means 'without dissent', that is, no one voted against the motion but some abstained.

*Open voting* – voting where there is no secrecy, for example a show of hands or an oral vote.

*Poll* – to count and record votes.

*Quorum* – the minimum number of people that must be present at a meeting to allow the meeting to be considered valid. If not enough members attend, a meeting is said to be not *quorate*, which means that any decision reached in such a meeting is invalid.

*Resolution* – a motion that has been accepted by a meeting.

*Standing committee* – a permanent committee dealing with long-term and enduring issues such as health and safety.

*Ultra vires* – relates to issues and decisions that are beyond the powers of the organisation.

*Unanimous* – when everyone present at a meeting votes for the motion, without exception.

# APPENDIX TWO

## SPELLING

The standard of spelling that people acquire nowadays seems to be dropping. There are many reasons for this, the most significant being that many students are encouraged to attach little importance to good spelling. In some exams the ability to spell often has no bearing on the marks received and in others the marks deductible as a result of bad spelling are negligible. In business, however, spelling is very important and companies are always complaining that they are unable to recruit secretarial staff who can spell properly and that graduate entry-level staff are just as bad, if not worse. Most general entrance exams for banks, government bodies and large companies include a spelling test. Good spelling therefore remains a valuable skill that could improve your job prospects and help you create a better impression of your company for your customers.

There is no denying that English spelling can be complicated. The only way to improve your spelling is through practice. People who read a lot tend to spell well. You can also work on your spelling by memorising lists of the most frequently misspelled words. Use a dictionary and look up words that you are unsure about or have misspelled, learn the correct spelling by heart and apply it. Never guess a spelling when writing a business letter. Also, if in doubt sound it out. Often breaking up a word into its different syllables can make spelling easier. Here are some basic spelling rules that will help improve your spelling if you apply them. Unfortunately there are exceptions to many of these rules but they still are a useful guide.

The *vowels* in English are a, e, i, o, u.

All the other letters are called *consonants*.

Every vowel has two basic sounds: the narrow (short) vowel sound, so called because it is the sound made when the vowel is pronounced when the mouth is narrow; and the wide (long) vowel sound. To make the wide vowel sound, you simply widen your mouth as you pronounce it. The 'a' in 'cat' is a narrow vowel sound, while 'a' in 'hate' is a wide vowel sound. Here are some other examples:

| Vowel | Narrow | Wide |
|---|---|---|
| a | tap | tape |
| e | net | need |
| i | kit | kite |
| o | not | note |
| u | cut | cute |

In many other languages the change from narrow to wide vowel sounds is made with the aid of an accent, fada or umlaut. In English, we move from narrow to wide by simply placing another vowel after the vowel that we wish to widen. The second vowel remains silent. It is there only to tell us to pronounce the first vowel wide. For example:

| | |
|---|---|
| cot | coat |
| run | ruin |
| bet | beat or beet |
| red | reed or read (exception: 'read' as in 'I have read') |

We can achieve the same effect if the second vowel is separated from the original vowel by one and only one consonant. For example:

| | |
|---|---|
| kit | kite |
| hat | hate |

In each case the first vowel goes from narrow to wide and the second vowel remains silent. If we want the first vowel to remain a narrow sound we can protect it with a second consonant. For example:

| | | | |
|---|---|---|---|
| can | caned | canned | |
| hop | hope | hopping | hoping |

If we take the example immediately above, we see that the 'o' retains its narrow vowel sound in 'hopping' because the 'i' is now too far away to affect it. Now take out the second 'p' and the 'i' can again change the 'o' to a wide vowel sound as in 'hoping'. Now we can see why the words listed below have double consonants:

| | |
|---|---|
| following | running |
| swimming | beginning |
| sitting | embarrass |
| committee | belligerent |
| matter | barrister |
| accommodation | |

and why the following words have single consonants:

| | |
|---|---|
| binary | rising |
| excitable | probation |
| fatal | |

There are always exceptions to rules. One of the reasons there are so many exceptions to spelling in English is because English borrows words from other languages, for example:

| | |
|---|---|
| canal | manifesto |
| ridiculous | petal |
| brevity | frenetic |

## When to use 'ei' and when to use 'ie'

The rule 'i' before 'e', except after 'c' only applies to the wide vowel sound.

### 'i' before 'e'

| | |
|---|---|
| achieve | believe |
| relief | fierce |
| field | fiend |

The 'i' before 'e' rule also applies sometimes when the 'ie' makes an 'eh' sound as in 'friend'. It also sometimes applies to the 'eye' sound, as in applies, died, dried, hierarchy and implies.

### except after 'c'

After 'c' use 'ei', as in the following examples:

| | |
|---|---|
| ceiling | perceive |
| deceit | conceit |
| receive | |

There are many exceptions to this rule. This is because 'ie' and 'ei' can have many different pronunciations. In many cases the pronunciation can be your guide to correct spelling. For example:

| | |
|---|---|
| 'ay' sound | beige, weigh, rein, heir |
| narrow 'i' sound | foreign, forfeiture |
| wide 'i' sound | height, eiderdown |
| 'eh' sound | leisure |
| narrow 'u' sound | ancient, omniscient, patient |
| 'oo' sound | lieutenant, view |

## Double or single 'l'?

The only word that ends with 'full' is the word 'full'. Otherwise use a single 'l' at the end, '...ful'. For example:

| | |
|---|---|
| wonderful | thankful |
| bountiful | grateful |
| pitiful | shameful |
| doleful | |

But, back to 'll' when not at the end of the word:

| | |
|---|---|
| wonderfully | thankfully |

| | |
|---|---|
| bountifully | gratefully |
| pitifully | shamefully |
| dolefully | |

## 'C' and 'g'

'C' and 'g' can differ from other consonants in that they can be affected by the vowels 'i' and 'e'. If 'c' or 'g' are immediately followed by 'i' or 'e' in a word it alters their pronunciation: 'c' goes from the hard 'k' sound to a soft 's' sound while 'g' becomes a soft 'j' sound. For example:

| | |
|---|---|
| car | city |
| cloak | centre |
| goal | giant |
| great | gentle |

Now you can understand the spelling of the following words:

| | |
|---|---|
| management | species |
| cement | accessible |
| accent | panic |
| panicked | iced |
| mimic | mimicked |

Can you see why there are two 'c's in 'accessible' and 'ck' in 'mimicked'? How would these words be pronounced otherwise?

## Forming plurals

The most common way of forming a plural in English is to add 's', particularly if the word ends in 'e' in the singular. For example:

| | |
|---|---|
| horse | horses |
| race | races |
| dog | dogs |
| widow | widows |

If a word ends in the letter 'y' and there is a vowel immediately before it, the same rule applies. For example:

| | |
|---|---|
| monkey | monkeys |
| day | days |

If, however, there is a consonant immediately before the 'y' in the singular the 'y' becomes 'ies' in the plural. For example:

| | |
|---|---|
| lady | ladies |
| frequency | frequencies |

The exceptions are proper nouns. For example:

Mr Barry
The Barrys are moving to Manchester

Words ending in 'ch', 's', 'sh', 'tch', 'ss', 'x' or 'z' generally take 'es' in the plural. For example:

| | |
|---|---|
| lunch | lunches |
| bus | buses |
| wish | wishes |
| clutch | clutches |
| boss | bosses |
| fox | foxes |

Words ending in 'f' or 'fe' change to 'ves'. For example:

| | |
|---|---|
| life | lives |
| half | halves |

There are some exceptions:

| | |
|---|---|
| cliff | cliffs |
| scarf | scarfs or scarves |
| chief | chiefs |

Words ending in 'o' can be 'os' or 'oes' in the plural. There is no rule to follow here other than to learn by heart the following list:

| | |
|---|---|
| tomatoes | volcanoes |
| cargoes | heroes |
| vetoes | haloes |

Some words change their vowels to form plurals. The main ones are:

| | |
|---|---|
| foot | feet |
| tooth | teeth |
| man | men |
| woman | women |
| goose | geese |

Some nouns are the same in the plural as they are in the singular:

fish
salmon
mackerel
hake
sheep
deer
series
species

Some words are always in the plural:

cattle
scissors
pants

Some words may seem plural to us but should be treated as singular (for example, use 'is', not 'are', as in politics is interesting):

family
economics
politics
athletics

## How to form the plural of a hyphenated word

Mother-in-laws, or mothers-in-law? Answer: mothers-in-law.

The plural 's' goes to the noun being counted. In the above example we are counting the mothers, not the laws.

Other examples are:

| | |
|---|---|
| lady-in-waiting | ladies-in-waiting |
| man-of-war | men-of-war |
| passer-by | passers-by |

## Words that are commonly misspelled

Try and learn the following words:

| | | |
|---|---|---|
| absence | accentuate | accommodation |
| accumulate | acquaintance | agitator |
| altogether | apostrophe | archaeology |
| architecture | auxiliary | beneficial |
| benevolent | bureaucracy | business |
| complement | compliment | conscientious |
| convenience | criticism | disappear |

| | | |
|---|---|---|
| disappoint | efficient | eighth |
| embarrassment | encyclopaedia | exaggerate |
| fascist | February | haemorrhage |
| harass | humorous | idiosyncrasy |
| knowledge | laboratory | liquor |
| marriage | medieval | mischievous |
| necessary | noticeable | paediatric |
| parallel | psychology | questionnaire |
| queue | recommend | restaurant |
| schedule | schizophrenia | singeing |
| skiing | tenant | visor |
| Wednesday | | |

# APPENDIX THREE

## OFFICE ADMINISTRATION

### Incoming mail

Dealing with incoming mail can require a lot of organisation. Even in a small company the volume of incoming mail can be extremely high. It is important to get it sorted and distributed to the right people as soon as possible, preferably before they begin their working day.

### Collecting the mail from the letterbox or mail drop site

*   *Registered mail* will only be delivered if there is someone there to sign for it. Otherwise a note is left and the registered mail can be collected at the local sorting office. Remittances, that is, money and other forms of payment, are often sent by registered mail. Before signing for registered mail, check that you are being given the letter(s) you are signing for.

    Keep registered mail separate from other post. If someone has gone to the trouble and expense of having a letter registered, it must be important. Open the letter promptly, making a note that it was registered and whether any remittances were included.
*   *Recorded mail* is not the same as registered mail but it is mail for which the sender has paid extra for a record of postage. You will need to sign for it, but again, check that you are receiving the letter you are signing for.
*   *Parcels* should be checked if you are signing for them. Make sure they have not been damaged in transit.

    If a package is suspicious, do not touch it unless you absolutely have to, for example to move it onto a flat surface to prevent it from falling or to take it to an area of the office or building where it will cause the least damage. But touch it only if you absolutely must and do not allow anyone else to touch it either. Call the building's security, immediately outlining the situation. Evacuate the office and building as quickly as you can, securing the building after you. Make sure that passers-by, building and office staff do not congregate outside the building, blocking entrances and exits and putting themselves in danger.

Take the mail back to your desk and sort it in the order:

*   Mail marked URGENT – open and deliver immediately.
*   Registered mail – see above.
*   Mail addressed to the organisation – this will be the bulk of your mail – open and deliver it.

• Mail marked PRIVATE; PERSONAL; CONFIDENTIAL; ADDRESSEE ONLY. Deliver unopened.

Return any misdirected mail to the post office unopened if possible.

## Opening the mail

Open the envelope and empty it of its contents. Keep the contents together, pin or paperclip it, and do not mix it up with the contents of previously opened envelopes. There may be photos, receipts, cheques and all kinds of miscellaneous items in the envelope.

Stamp the letter with the date and, if company policy, the time.

### Receiving and recording remittances

If remittances are included, make sure that the amount on the remittance corresponds with the amount stated in the accompanying document. If it doesn't, make a note of it and pass the information on to the relevant person.

Make sure that all cheques received contain valid dates. Banks' rules can vary, but normally you are given three months from the date on the cheque in which to cash it. After that the cheque is out of date and cannot be cashed. Check that the amounts written in words match those written in figures. Ensure that the payee's name is correct. All cheques should have been signed and any alterations made to cheques should also have a signature. Report any discrepancies to the relevant person in your office. Make sure that all payments are recorded and credited to the customer's account.

Write the amount remitted, the method of payment (cheque, postal order (po), bank draft (bd) or cash) on the corner of the document.

Initial the document.

Record all details of remittances received. Most organisations have a remittance book or a cash receipts journal for this purpose. Collect up all the remittances received and enter the details in the remittance book. When you are satisfied that everything is correct, pass the remittances on to the relevant person. They will sign for the remittances that they have received from you.

## Sorting the mail

Depending on the size of the organisation you work for, you could be dividing up the mail between departments, offices or individuals. Use separate trays to stay organised. If you are sorting mail into departments, keep mail for the individuals in that department sorted.

Deliver the mail to the departments, offices and individuals.

Before you dispose of envelopes, make sure that they are completely empty. Check your desk or work area to ensure that nothing has been overlooked.

## Outgoing mail

Letters at work are often dictated and then typed up, or they are simply typed up, then sent to the relevant person for signature. It is important to check before posting that every letter has a signature.

Check also that any items to be included, such as receipts or remittances, are attached and ready to go in the envelope.

Make sure all the letters have the correct envelope. Then check the details on the envelope against the address in the letter. If they do not match, find out which one is incorrect and ensure that it is retyped correctly.

Carefully fold the letter and place it in the envelope. A4-size letters are usually folded in three. The bottom third of the letter is folded over the middle third with the top third folded over them both. This means that when the letter is opened you just lift up the top flap, pull back the bottom flap and the letter is the right way up and ready to read.

Each envelope then has stamps attached or is franked by machine. Details relating to the letters – the address, date and cost – are recorded in the postage book.

The envelopes are tied in bundles with all the addresses facing the same way.

Instead of sticking stamps on the envelopes in the office many organisations choose to have all their mail processed at the post office.

Items such as registered mail, airmail, parcels, recorded delivery and anything else that requires special forms or labelling all have to be handed in at the post office for processing. They should therefore be kept separate from the ordinary mail in the outgoing post.

Make sure that all outgoing mail is sent or taken to the post office. Get a receipt for all mail charges. This may be entered in the postage account book or petty cash depending on the practice of the organisation.

## Making appointments

In your appointments diary, record the name of the person with whom you have made an appointment, along with the name of the organisation or interest they represent and the date and location of the appointment. Include any other useful information, such as the telephone numbers of the contact person, and the location and directions if needed.

If you made the appointment by telephone, confirm it by letter.

If you made the appointment well in advance, confirm it again by letter about a week beforehand.

Make sure you know how to get to your destination. Allow sufficient time to get there. Make sure you don't cram your diary with too many appointments.

If you are unable to honour an appointment due to unforeseen circumstances inform the other party as quickly as possible, apologise and arrange another appointment if it is feasible.

## Orders

The purpose of an order is to record a request made by a buyer to a seller to supply goods.

Each order form is allocated a serial number which is usually already printed on the form. Several copies of each order are needed so the form will have duplicate copies attached and these are filled in either manually, electronically or by using carbon paper. One copy is sent to the supplier of the goods so that they can make up the order. Another copy is sent to the accounts department, where it is retained and checked against the invoice. The invoice will normally be sent in from the supplier on delivery of the goods. They will expect payment within 30 days of delivery of goods. Another copy of the order is sent to the stores section, so that they can prepare for the arrival of the goods and check that the goods supplied correspond exactly with what was ordered.

The order form should be filled in correctly by the buyer. The following information will be requested:

- The name and address of the buyer.
- The date in which the order form is being filled in.
- The items requested. Specify the serial number or catalogue code of the items requested exactly. Give a brief description if necessary. Make sure you state the exact quantity requested. List the price of each item so that if there is a discrepancy between the price listed and the price charged, it can be spotted. Where necessary specify the method of delivery. Specify where you want the goods delivered and give directions if need be. Also state which delivery bay you want the goods to be delivered at if it is important.

Before signing the form, the buyer should check that it is correct in every detail.

## Invoices

An invoice is prepared by the supplier to obtain payment for goods supplied. It contains the following information:

- The name and address of the supplier.
- The name and address of the buyer.
- The name and catalogue or serial number of the goods purchased.
- The number of the relevant order form.
- The quantity and description of goods purchased.
- The length of time allowed before payment is due, usually within one month of delivery.

Several copies are made of the invoice. The first copy is sent to the buyer. One copy is sent to the accounts department where it is used for cross-checking against the remittance eventually received. A copy of the invoice is sent to the delivery section where it will be presented to the customer upon delivery of goods. A copy is also sent to the store section. This helps stock control to balance goods dispatched with goods received and invoiced.

# Email in the office

- Email is like all other business communication: it should be polite, accurate and concise. People receive more and more of their work communication by email. They may have hundreds to read every day so they will not appreciate unnecessarily long or vague emails. In addition, people hate getting irrelevant emails that clutter up their inbox and waste their time. So use the 'reply to all' function sparingly.
- Title
  Make sure that your title is concise and relevant. This will ensure that it is read and also that it can be retrieved from archives easily later on. Always store a copy of important emails that you send in either your sent folder or your archive.
- Address
  There are three ways you can address an email: 'To', 'Cc' and 'Bcc'.
  - 'To' should be used for people you are directly addressing.
  - 'Cc' should be used for people who might find the information you are sending useful to know but are not directly involved with this particular communication.
  - 'Bcc' is not used very often. The people whose addresses are listed in 'To' and 'Cc' do not know that the people who are addressed in 'Bcc' are also receiving these emails.
- Opening and closing salutations
  'Dear Sir', 'Dear Mr Browne', 'Dear John' are all acceptable ways to begin an email. It is very similar to a letter. Your closing salutations can also be similar to a letter and you can vary them depending on your level of intimacy with the recipient, i.e. 'Regards, Suzanne', 'Regards, Suzanne Twomey', 'Yours sincerely, Suzanne Twomey'. If you haven't addressed your opening salutation directly to a person (e.g. 'Dear John') but have used a title instead (e.g. 'Dear Sir'), you can use the closing salutation 'Yours faithfully, Suzanne Twomey'.
- Please avoid the following:
  - Too much punctuation; it looks unprofessional. Punctuate as you would any other business communication.
  - Emoticons. Even less professional than excessive punctuation.
  - Abbreviations, such as BTW (by the way). Not everyone knows what the abbreviations mean and this can lead to confusion.
  - Formatting. Do not format messages to have fancy fonts. If the recipient does not have a similar server your message might appear as incomprehensible code.

**Remember, email is a very insecure method of communicating; never send anything that you would be ashamed to see splashed on the front page of *The Examiner*.**

# APPENDIX FOUR

## EXERCISES AND ASSIGNMENTS

### 1. FETAC Level 5 exercises

### Sample exam papers NCVA Level 2/FETAC Level 5

### The written exam

The written exam is worth 30 per cent of the final mark. It is structured as follows:

* *Section A.* There is a choice of twelve short questions. Ten must be attempted at two marks per question. Maximum marks: 20.

* *Section B.* There is a choice of three structured questions. Two must be attempted at 40 marks per question. Maximum marks: 80.

Therefore 100 marks in total = 30 per cent.

### Sample exam paper 1

*Customer service written exam*

Duration: 1 hour and 30 minutes
Weighting: 30 per cent

*Section A*

Answer any ten of the following twelve short questions:

1. List two elements of good customer practice.

2. Identify any two needs and wants of customers.

3. Define the term 'customer service'.

4. Give two examples of features of organisational presentation that affect customer perception.

5. Name two things that you should never do when answering the telephone.

6. What is an 'internal customer'?

7. Explain the term 'quality service'.

8. List two advantages of a mobile phone over a fax machine.

9. What is a 'customer charter'?

10. Explain the following terms:

    a. CE
    b. ISO

11. Name one Act that protects customers in Ireland.

12. What is the ASAI?

## Section B
Answer any two of the following three structured questions:

### Question 1
   a.  What is a customer care policy?
   b.  Outline the customer care policy of an organisation you have studied.
   c.  Outline a suitable system for dealing with customer complaints.
   d.  How best can we deal with compliments?

### Question 2
   a.  What is body language?
   b.  Outline four examples of positive body language.
   c.  Outline four examples of negative body language.
   d.  Discuss ways in which awareness of body language can help us improve our customer services?

### Question 3
   a.  Define discrimination.
   b.  Specify groups that may be discriminated against.
   c.  Outline what legislation is in place to prevent discrimination on the basis of gender.

## Sample exam paper 2

### Customer service written exam
Duration: 1 hour and 30 minutes
Weighting: 30 per cent

## Section A
Answer any ten of the following twelve questions:

1. Give two examples of modern technology which facilitates the rapid transmission of information.
2. List two organisations that follow good customer practice.
3. What is the role of customer contact staff in an organisation?
4. Give an example of two active listening skills.
5. Define the term 'external customer'.

6. What is 'non-verbal communication'?
7. Define the term 'discrimination'.
8. Give an example of three ways in which customers may be discriminated against.
9. What is an 'ombudsman'?
10. What is the function of Fáilte Ireland?
11. What is the function of the Director of Consumer Affairs?
12. What is a customer care policy?

## Section B

Answer any two of the following three structured questions:

### Question 1

  a.  Explain what is meant by customer perceptions.
  b.  Give four examples of ways in which customer perceptions can be influenced. Justify your choices.
  c.  Outline the potential consequences of good and bad first impressions on customers.

### Question 2

  a.  Distinguish between internal and external customers.
  b.  Outline how you would deal with incoming mail.
  c.  What would you do if you discovered a suspicious parcel?
  d.  Outline how you would prepare outgoing mail for postage.

### Question 3

  a.  Why is it so important to practise good telephone techniques in business?
  b.  Outline a system of good practice for staff when answering the phone.
  c.  What must staff never do when answering the phone?
  d.  How would you respond to complaints made over the telephone?

## Sample exam paper 3

*Customer service written exam*
Duration: 1 hour and 30 minutes
Weighting: 30 per cent

## Section A

Answer any ten of the following twelve questions:

1. Name two guides that assess quality in the catering trade.
2. What does HSA stand for?

3. Define the term 'primary data'.

4. What organisation ensures that advertisers are regulated in Ireland?

5. What are standards of excellence?

6. Name the four tangible elements of good customer practice.

7. What is the social charter?

8. What is the function of ELCOM?

9. What is a closed question?

10. What is a sole trader?

11. What is CRM?

12. Define market segmentation.

*Section B*

Answer any two of the following three structured questions:

**Question 1**

   a. Name the stages in a team's life.

   b. Name four personality types that would be useful to include in a team and say how they would contribute to the team's success.

   c. Name the three qualities that you think are most important in a team leader and justify your choice.

   d. What is the benefit of teamwork?

**Question 2**

   a. What is the function of the Financial Regulator?

   b. Who can use the services of the Financial Regulator?

   c. How does the Financial Regulator process a complaint?

**Question 3**

   a. What is discrimination?

   b. Name four groups that have experienced discrimination.

   c. What advice would you give to clothing retail staff about helping customers with a visual impairment?

## 2. Customer services presentations

Working as part of a team, prepare a class presentation on one of the following topics. Upon completion, reflect on what the experience has taught you. Use the self-assessment form on pages 283–4 to guide you.

## Suggested topics

- Select two organisations and outline their customer care policies. Include their customer charters in your presentation. Explain and evaluate their customer charters.
- Describe the customer care policy of a company that you have studied.
- How to deal with a difficult customer.
- Profile the means by which quality services are measured. Include the Q Mark, ISO ratings, hotel ratings, the Michelin guide and the Egon Ronay guide in your presentation.
- The Sale of Goods and Supply of Services Act 1980.
- The Consumer Information Act 1978.
- Compare England's Data Protection Act 1984 with similar legislation in Ireland.
- Investigate the existence of comparable legislation or regulations in Ireland and at least one other country.
- Explain what an ombudsman is and outline their duties and powers. Include examples from at least two ombudsmen that you have studied.
- The Advertising Standards Authority.
- The small claims procedure.
- Equal status legislation.
- Discrimination.

## Customer care session

Deliver a short customer care session, based on the customer care programme you developed. The programme should reflect:

- the company's customer care policy
- the specialist nature of the industry
- meeting different needs
- codes of practice, standards of excellence
- specific legalities within the industry nationally and internationally
- customer contact skills
- criteria for measuring quality service
- other relevant issues within the specialist industry
- demonstrate appropriate presentation skills, for example voice projection, contact with audience, pacing, tone, delivery, etc.
- customer care.

# 3. Observe and comment on customer and service provider behaviour

## Introduction

This forms part of the practical skills test for NCVA Level 2/FETAC Level 5. Weighting: 20 per cent.

A blank form follows on pages 281–2.

### Format

An observation of customer and service provider behaviour in an organisation is made over the period of one hour. Log the time at 5–10-minute intervals.

Make a list of the customers and state what their purposes were in visiting your establishment. Provide a narrative of what occurs in the work environment. Note and comment on customers' and service providers' actions and reactions in various situations. You should clearly identify customer needs and wants and be aware of the actions required to meet those needs. Compile in advance a checklist of the activities you expected to see and then mark them off as they happen over the course of the hour. Finally, write a personal reflection on the experience.

### Customer behaviour

'Log the customer behaviour over a period of one hour.'

Candidates will be expected to note and comment on the items in the following list:

*   Log the time every ten minutes.
*   Note the number and type of customer contacts, for example telephone, face to face, computer, internal customer, etc.
*   Describe the nature of customer contacts, for example enquiry, complaint, appointment, delivery, etc.
*   Note the customer's behaviour, for example assertive, aggressive, submissive.
*   Note any non-verbal communication – pitch, posture, expression, eye contact, gestures, etc.
*   Note the customer's needs and wants.

### Service provider behaviour

'Log the provider's behaviour over a period of one hour.'

This observation should occur during the same hour as the customer observation, with the same time intervals clearly noted. Candidates will be expected to note and comment on the items in the following list:

*   Note the provider's behaviour, for example assertive, aggressive, submissive.
*   Note any non-verbal communication – pitch, posture, expression, eye contact, gestures, etc.

- How does the provider present themselves?
- Note the customer contact skills that were employed during the observation, for example active listening, watching for clues, alertness, confidence, loyalty to the organisation, etc.
- Log the response to the needs of customers.
- Log the outcome of each contact.
- Suggest creative solutions or accommodations to meet customer needs based on what you have learned.

### Personal comment

Candidates are required to give a personal reflection on the organisation's customer care policy, stating what they felt was good or bad about it and making suggestions as to how the customer care policy could be improved.

## Sample customer and service provider observation form – completed (candidate's answers are shown in italics)

### Customer care vocational observation

Weighting: 20 per cent

Name of candidate: *Mary Smith*
Class code: *Bus 1.1*
Date of observation: *22.10.2012*
Time of observation: *2.30pm–3.30pm*
Name of company/organisation where observation is to be undertaken: *John Murphy, Chartered Accountant*
Address of above: *26 Main Street, Ennis, Co. Clare*

Write a brief note, outlining your position and duties during your work experience: *While on work experience, my position was that of secretary. During my time there, I did a variety of secretarial work, I updated files, photocopied documents and filed them, I sorted the incoming mail and filled in the appointment book. I also did a lot of word-processing.*

Give a description of the layout of the office/room, etc. where the observation is to be undertaken. What is the area's function? List the equipment that is available there and in adjoining rooms that is relevant to the work of this room. Note the type of customer contact that this room is used for. Mention any special circumstances peculiar to your vocational area. *The office I work in is for one accountant. You walk in the front door and you are immediately in the secretarial/reception area. There are low seats and a coffee table provided for people who are waiting. There are also some magazines and a water cooler.*

*Behind the reception counter, there are three workstations. Mr Murphy employs two full-time secretaries and he or the part-time staff occasionally use the third station. He also regularly has an apprentice accountant. The workstations each have a computer, printer and telephone. There are two fax machines and a photocopier in this office. There are three filing cabinets in the corner. The shredder is in the back hall, to keep the noise down. Mr Murphy's office is also through this hall. He has his own workstation, phone and filing cabinets. He can contact us through the intercom. He has an office table and five chairs, for consultation purposes.*

List the names and occupations of those who will work in the room during the period of the observation, including yourself in the list:

*Mary Smith, on work experience*
*Patrick Donnelly, secretary to Mr Murphy*
*Anne Thompson, general secretary*

### Customer behaviour

Log the customer behaviour over a period of one hour.

Date of observation: *22.10.2012*
Time of observation: *2.30pm–3.30pm*
Name of candidate: *Mary Smith*
Class code: *Bus 1.1*

*2.30–2.40: Patrick rang a client to query him about missing documents. The client was confused, so Patrick explained what was missing in detail.*

*2.40–2.50: A customer visited the office looking for a Mr Albert Murphy. Anne sent her to the solicitor up the street, who is Mr John Murphy's cousin.*

*2.50–3.00: There was no customer contact during this period.*

*3.00–3.10: A very impatient customer called in looking to see Mr Murphy immediately. I told him that that was not possible as Mr Murphy was busy and this man had no appointment. The customer became a bit aggressive, so Anne took over. She told him to wait while she asked Mr Murphy if he could see him. Mr Murphy was on the phone. She invited the customer to wait. Meanwhile another customer rang Patrick with a query.*

*3.10–3.20: The impatient customer was still waiting. Patrick decided to distract him by asking him about Clare's chances in the Munster final. Anne received a fax from Dublin.*

*3.20–3.30: As Mr Murphy was still on the phone, Patrick asked the customer if he would prefer to make an appointment for another day. The customer agreed to this and I found a cancellation in the appointments diary for the day after.*

## Service provider behaviour

Log the provider's behaviour over a period of one hour.

Date of observation: *22.10.2012*
Time of observation: *2.30pm–3.30pm*
Name of candidate: *Mary Smith*
Class code: *Bus 1.1*

*2.30–2.40: Patrick rang a client and was very diplomatic towards him as some important documents were missing. He then carefully explained the situation to the customer, who was unsure as to what documents Patrick was searching for.*

*2.40–2.50: Anne was very friendly to a customer who thought she was in the offices of Mr A. Murphy, the solicitor. This happens quite a lot. Anne pointed her up the street to the correct address.*

*2.50–3.00: There were no customers in the office or on the phone, so Patrick decided to give the customer waiting area a quick tidy. He was very annoyed when he found some chewing gum stuck to a magazine and complained to Anne about children destroying the waiting area.*

*3.00–3.10: I was a bit intimidated by a very impatient and assertive customer. Anne saw my discomfort and came to my rescue. I was a bit embarrassed, but Patrick gave me a sympathetic smile. Anne was polite but firm with the customer. Meanwhile, Patrick fielded a phone query very efficiently as he had all the relevant information nearby.*

*3.10–3.20: Patrick dealt really well with the difficult customer. He started talking about the Clare hurling team with him. Soon he had the customer laughing.*

*3.20–3.30: As Mr Murphy was still busy, we could not ask him to see this impatient customer. Patrick asked him if he would like to make an appointment for the following day (I had found a cancellation). The customer was now happy to do that.*

## Sample customer and service provider observation form

Use additional sheets, as necessary, attaching these together once your observations are complete.

### *Customer care vocational observation*

Weighting: 20 per cent

Name of candidate: ————————————————————————————————

Class code: ——————————————————————————————————————

Date of observation: ————————————————————————————————

Time of observation: ————————————————————————————————

Name of company/organisation where observation is to be undertaken:

————————————————————————————————————————————

Address of above: ——————————————————————————————————

Write a brief note, outlining your position and duties during your work experience:

————————————————————————————————————————————

————————————————————————————————————————————

————————————————————————————————————————————

————————————————————————————————————————————

Give a description of the layout of the office/room, etc. where the observation is to be undertaken. What is the area's function? List the equipment that is available there and in adjoining rooms that is relevant to the work of this room. Note the type of customer contact that this room is used for. Mention any special circumstances peculiar to your vocational area.

————————————————————————————————————————————

————————————————————————————————————————————

List the names and occupations of those who will work in the room during the period of the observation, including yourself in the list:

————————————————————————————————————————————

————————————————————————————————————————————

————————————————————————————————————————————

————————————————————————————————————————————

————————————————————————————————————————————

## Customer behaviour

Log the customer behaviour over a period of one hour.

Date of observation: ————————————————————————————————

Time of observation: ————————————————————————————————

Name of candidate: ————————————————————————————————

Class code: ——————————————————————————————————————

- Log the time every ten minutes.
- Note the number and type of customer contacts, for example telephone, face to face, computer, internal customer, etc.
- Describe the nature of customer contacts, for example enquiry, complaint, appointment, delivery, etc.
- Note the customer's behaviour, for example assertive, aggressive, submissive.
- Note any non-verbal communication – pitch, posture, expression, eye contact, gestures, etc.
- Note the customer's needs and wants.

### Service provider behaviour

This observation should occur during the same hour as the customer observation. Log the provider's behaviour over a period of one hour.

Date of observation: ————————————————————————

Time of observation: ————————————————————————

Name of candidate: ————————————————————————

Class code: ————————————————————————————

- Note the provider's behaviour, for example assertive, aggressive, submissive.
- Note any non-verbal communication – pitch, posture, expression, eye contact, gestures, etc.
- How does the provider present themselves?
- Note the customer contact skills that were employed during the observation, for example active listening, watching for clues, alertness, confidence, loyalty to the organisation, etc.
- Log the response to the needs of customers.
- Log the outcome of each contact.
- Critically assess the customer care provided.
- Suggest creative solutions or accommodations to meet customer needs, based on what you have learned.

### Personal comment

Give a personal reflection on the organisation's customer care policy. State what you felt was good or bad about it and make suggestions as to how their customer care policy could be improved.

## Class presentation self-assessment form

Name of candidate: ——————————————————————

Class name: ——————————————————————————

Name of group: —————————————————————————

Names of other members of your group: ——————————————

Subject of class presentation: ————————————————————

Answer the following questions. Use a separate sheet for your answers to the general questions at the end. Submit the completed form to your facilitator, attaching the additional page(s).

What was my role in the team? ————————————————————

———————————————————————————————————

———————————————————————————————————

Did I think that I was suited to the role? ———————————————

———————————————————————————————————

———————————————————————————————————

Did I complete this role to the best of my ability? ————————————

———————————————————————————————————

———————————————————————————————————

Did I make a satisfactory contribution to the team? —————————

———————————————————————————————————

———————————————————————————————————

Do I feel that other members of the team would agree with my own assessment of my performance? (Justify your answer.) ——————————————

———————————————————————————————————

———————————————————————————————————

What was my greatest strength as a team member? (Explain why.) ——————

———————————————————————————————————

———————————————————————————————————

What was my greatest weakness as a team member? (Explain why.) ——————

———————————————————————————————————

———————————————————————————————————

Rate yourself on the following qualities and attributes. Here 1 means you feel you have very little of this quality and 10 means you feel you have an excessive amount of this quality.

Assertiveness: _____

Organisational ability: _____

Ability to handle stress: _____

Ability to accept responsibility for my actions: _____

Ability to delegate: _____

Ability to take orders: _____

Ability to take instruction: _____

Ability to accept criticism: _____

Ability to work on my own initiative: _____

Passivity: _____

Complacency: _____

Ability to work to deadlines: _____

Ability to deal with problems within the team: _____

Ability to criticise other team members positively: _____

Ability to maintain team morale: _____

Ability to make suggestions: _____

Ability to take suggestions: _____

General questions, to be answered on a separate sheet.

1. Did you feel that the team worked well together?
2. Specify the particular strengths and weaknesses of the team as a whole.
3. Was there any team member who you felt did not do their fair share? Justify your answer.
4. Was there any team member who you felt did more than their fair share? Say why you think this happened.
5. Was there any team member who dominated the team to an excessive extent?
6. What did the team do individually or as a group to rectify any imbalances or any other problems within the group?
7. What did you learn about teamwork from this experience?
8. What will you be more aware of when involved in future teamwork assignments?
9. How important is it, in your opinion, to have a good team leader?
10. Add any other comments or observations.

# 4. Analysing the staff dynamic in a small restaurant

Identify when each member of staff is an internal customer.

• Look at the following flowchart carefully.

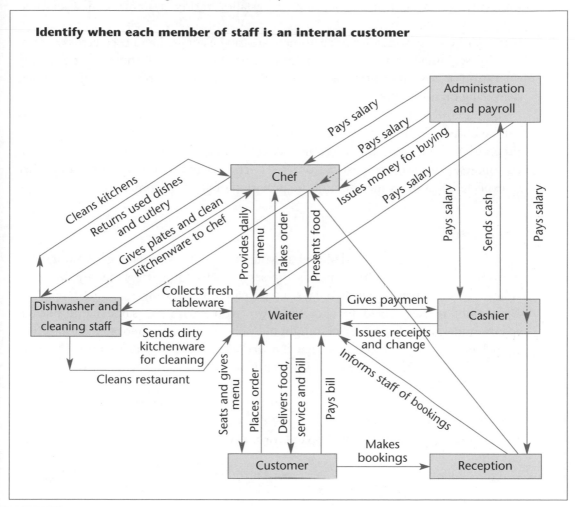

**Identify when each member of staff is an internal customer**

• List the title and function of each staff member.
• Identify each occasion when a member of staff must serve another member of staff, i.e. perform some task for another staff member so that member can do their job.
• Identify each occasion when a member of staff is an internal customer.
• List ways in which each member of staff could damage the external customers' (the person eating at the restaurant) opinion of the restaurant if they failed to play their role.
• Discuss the importance of front-line staff in creating a good customer experience.
• Discuss the importance of supporting front-line staff.
• Develop a similar flowchart for the company/institution that you work in and analyse in the same manner as above.

## 5. Assignments

1. Identify the methods of consumer protection operating in your vocational area, to include relevant consumer legislation, quality rating systems and associated regulatory organisations.
2. Consider how the principles of customer care can be adapted and used across a range of diverse business and service environments. Pick at least three examples, e.g. operating a leisure centre, working as an independent professional plumber, delivering oil nationally.
3. Prepare a PowerPoint presentation on the following topic: 'How customer perceptions can be influenced'. Be sure to include as many variables as you can.
4. Prepare guidelines for staff in your vocational area, covering general contact with customers, providing the best customer services, dealing with complaints and other unexpected challenges that disrupt the provision of good customer service.

## 6. Scenarios

1. Your boutique has been flooded and all your stock has water damage. Amongst the items damaged are three bridesmaids' dresses and a wedding dress that are due to be collected by the customer in two days, a day before the wedding.
2. A member of staff failed to spot that two people with the same name booked accommodation with your hotel tonight but only one has been allocated a room. The error has only been noticed now that the second customer has turned up. There are no more rooms left in the hotel. How can you sort this out now and how can you prevent it from happening again?
3. A customer has rung up to complain that the contents of the parcel that you posted him have been destroyed.
4. Your hairdressing salon is fully booked for today when suddenly the water supply is cut off.
5. You have spent two days icing a very special birthday cake but extreme weather means that the customer cannot collect it.
6. You are working for a public service that has recently experienced cutbacks when a member of the public accuses you of incompetence for making him wait so long.
7. You are leading a tour group when your flight has to make an unscheduled stop in a small airport due to bad weather at the original destination. It is late at night and the group was due to being a scheduled excursion early the next morning from their hotel.

# APPENDIX FIVE

## ASSOCIATIONS PROMOTING EQUALITY, UNDERSTANDING AND INTEGRATION IN IRELAND

*AGE ACTION IRELAND*
www.ageaction.ie

*AGE AND OPPORTUNITY*
www.olderinirelnd.ie

*AHEAD*
www.ahead.ie

*ALZHEIMER SOCIETY OF IRELAND*
www.alzheimer.ie

*AWARE*
www.aware.ie

*CARERS ASSOCIATION*
www.carersireland.com

*CENTRAL REMEDIAL CLINIC*
www.crc.ie

*CENTRE FOR INDEPENDENT LIVING*
www.dublincil.org

*CHILDREN'S RIGHTS ALLIANCE*
www.childrensrights.ie

*CITIZENS INFORMATION*
www.citizensinformationboard.ie

*DISABILITY FEDERATION OF IRELAND*
www.disability-federation.ie

*DISABLED DRIVERS ASSOCIATION OF IRELAND*
www.iol.ie/~ability

*DOWN SYNDROME IRELAND*
www.downsyndrome.ie

*DYSPRAXIA ASSOCIATION*
www.dyspraxiaireland.com

*ENABLE IRELAND*
www.enableireland.ie

*EQUALITY AUTHORITY*
www.equality.ie

*EQUALITY TRIBUNAL*
www.equalitytribunal.ie

*EUROPEAN MIGRATION NETWORK*
www.european-migration-network.org

*FEDERATION OF ACTIVE RETIREMENT*
www.fara.ie

*HEADWAY IRELAND*
www.headwayireland.ie

*IMMIGRATION COUNCIL OF IRELAND*
www.immigrationcouncil.ie

*INCLUSION IRELAND*
www.inclusionireland.ie

*IRISH CONGRESS OF TRADE UNIONS*
www.ictu.ie

*IRISH COUNCIL FOR CIVIL LIBERTIES*
www.iccl.ie

*IRISH DEAF SOCIETY*
www.irishdeafsociety.org

*IRISH SENIOR CITIZENS PARLIAMENT*
www.seniors.ie

*IRISH TRAVELLER MOVEMENT*
www.itmtrav.com

*IRISH WHEELCHAIR ASSOCIATION*
www.iwa.ie

*MENTAL HEALTH IRELAND*
www.mentalhealthireland.ie

*NATIONAL ASSOCIATION FOR DEAF PEOPLE*
www.nadi.ie

*NATIONAL CONSULTATIVE COMMITTEE ON RACISM AND INTERCULTURALISM*
www.nccri.ie

*NATIONAL COUNCIL FOR THE BLIND IN IRELAND*
  www.ncbi.ie

*NATIONAL DISABILITY AUTHORITY*
  www.nda.ie

*NATIONAL FEDERATION OF VOLUNTARY BODIES*
  www.fedvol.ie

*NATIONAL TRAVELLER MABS*
  www.nattravellermabs.org

*NATIONAL TRAVELLER WOMEN'S FORUM*
  www.ntwf.net

*NATIONAL WOMEN'S COUNCIL*
  www.nwci.ie

*PAVEE POINT TRAVELLERS CENTRE*
  www.paveepoint.ie

*PEOPLE WITH DISABILITIES IN IRELAND*
  www.pwdi.ie

*POST POLIO SUPPORT GROUP*
  www.ppsg.ie

*PWDI*
  www.pwdi.ie

*REHAB*
  www.rehab.ie

*SCHIZOPHRENIA IRELAND*
  www.schizophreniaireland.ie

# APPENDIX SIX

## TIPS FOR STUDENTS

### Preparing a bibliography

One of the easiest ways to keep track of your sources while working on a research paper is to list each source on separate index cards. Be sure to make a complete bibliography card for every source you examine. Using cards makes it easy to put your sources in alphabetical order and to add and delete sources. Once you have all of your cards in order, you have a preliminary bibliography for your assignment.

If you used a book in your research, you should record the following pieces of information on your card.

1. The book's ISBN number.
2. The book's title, underlined, followed by a period.
3. Author's name, last name first, followed by a period.
4. Place of publication, followed by a colon.
5. Publisher, followed by a comma.
6. Year of publication.

### Taking class notes

*Before class*

Do the assigned reading beforehand.
Review notes from the last class.

*During class*

Watch for the main topic, key points and organisation of ideas. Clues from the teacher that help you pick up these ideas include tone of voice, use of repetition, points made on board or instructions to underline, as well as phrasing, e.g. 'first', 'second', etc.

Make notes that highlight the main idea. Don't wait to be told to note something. If you think it's relevant then underline it.

Keep your notes in a ring binder. Write the name of the teacher, the date, the subject and the topic at the top of each page. Number each page of notes. Later you will be so glad that you did.

*After class*

Go back over your notes, filling in anything that you might not have had time to fill in fully in class. This will make your notes more useful later. Otherwise your abbreviations and half sentences will be like the Da Vinci Code when you come to prepare for your exam! Underline important points.

Review within 24 hours of writing your notes. Review again on a weekly basis. It will make life a lot easier by exam time.

It can be a good idea to record your notes and play them back when you are travelling, working or going to sleep. It will really boost your memory.

## Time management

Take some time at the start of each week to plan your time for the week. Prioritise your tasks. Make sure you spend the most time tackling the most pressing issues, making deadlines, etc. Don't just do the tasks you like. Study the subjects you dislike and you will get better at them and start to like them. When you study, study; when you relax, relax. Don't waste study time paring pencils, staring out the window or daydreaming. Likewise don't spend your down time worrying about studying.

## Evaluating websites

The Internet is an invaluable source of information for students and general research, there's no denying that.

However it's a cyber jungle out there. Sites can be created by anyone, no questions asked. So is that site on eczema by Dr John Murphy actually accurate? Does Dr Murphy know what he's talking about, is he really a doctor and is that really his/her name? Is it a site just trying to peddle quack medicine?

Does that historical site have certain political affiliations that might render its information at best biased and at worst blatant lies?

How do you tell a good website from a bad website? Which sites will give you proven facts and clearly argued theories and which sites will peddle you a flashy philosophy? Here are some guidelines:

### Who?

Look at who compiled the website. Is it by a famous, well-respected organisation like BBC online, the Irish government or Scoilnet?

Websites that have good authors don't try to hide this fact. Beware of websites that don't let you know who has written them or what their qualifications are. Look at the URL (address) to get more information about who compiled the website. Websites from Ireland often end with .ie, Germany, .de, etc. Personal websites or company websites usually end in .com. Organisations often end in .org.

### When?

Look at the date of your website.

When was the website created?
When was it last updated?
Is the information current?
Are there links to other sites?
Are those links still working? Chances are if the links aren't working then the site is probably not being updated.
Do you need to have up-to-date information for the topic that you are researching?

## What?

What is the objective of the website?
Is it trying to inform?
Is it trying to sell?
Is it trying to persuade?
Is it doing this openly or subtly?
Is it information or propaganda?

## Where?

Where does the information come from? Most authors of good websites will tell you where they got their information.
Did they do their own research?
Do they give you a bibliography of their sources? The less information they give you on sources, the more cautious you have to be.

## Why?

Why are you on this site?
Is it useful to your research?

# BIBLIOGRAPHY

Advertising Standards Authority for Ireland, *Code of Advertising Standards for Ireland*, 4th edition, Dublin: ASAI 1995.

Cooke, Sarah, *Customer Care*, 2nd edition, London: Kogan Page 1992.

*Collins Paperback English Dictionary*, Glasgow: HarperCollins 1991.

Dooney, Sean and O'Toole, John, *Irish Government Today*, Dublin: Gill & Macmillan 1992.

Evans, Desmond W., *People, Communication and Organisations*, 2nd edition, London: Pitman Publishing 1990, reprinted 1991.

Freemantle, David, *Incredible Customer Service*, Berkshire: McGraw-Hill 1992.

Harrison, John, *Office Procedures*, 3rd edition, London: Pitman Publishing 1994.

Leland, Karen and Bailey, Keith, *Customer Service for Dummies*, 2nd edition, Foster City, CA: IDG Books Worldwide, Inc. 1999.

Martin, William B., *Quality Customer Service for Front Line Staff*, 1st English edition, London: Kogan Page 1988, reprinted 1996.

O'Donnell, James, *How Ireland Is Governed*, 6th edition, Dublin: Institute of Public Administration 1979, reprinted 1992.

Peel, Malcolm, *Customer Service*, 1st edition, London: Kogan Page 1987, reprinted with revisions 1993.

Press and Information Office of the Federal Government of Germany, *Facts about Germany*, Bonn 1996.

Quinn, Fergal, *Crowning the Customer*, Dublin: O'Brien Press 1990.

Scott, John F., *English for Business and Secretarial Students*, Dublin: Gill & Macmillan 1992.

Walker, Lin, *Telephone Techniques*, London: Marshall Publishing 1998.

Woolcott, L.A. and Unwin, W.R., *Mastering Business Communication*, London: Macmillan 1983.